ADOBE®
PHOTOSHOP® 7
DIGITAL
DARKROOM

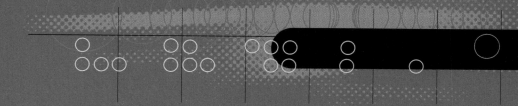

ADOBE® PHOTOSHOP® 7 DIGITAL DARKROOM

Premier
Press™

LISA A. BUCKI

The Premier Press logo, top edge printing, and related trade dress are trademarks of Premier Press, Inc. and may not be used without written permission. All other trademarks are the property of their respective owners.

Publisher: Stacy L. Hiquet

Marketing Manager: Heather Buzzingham

Managing Editor: Sandy Doell

Acquisitions Editor: Kevin Harreld

Book Packager: Justak Literary Services, Inc.

Editorial Assistant: Margaret Bauer

Marketing Coordinator: Kelly Poffenbarger

Technical Reviewer: Michelle Jones

Copy Editor: Marta Justak

Interior Layout: William Hartman

Cover Design: Mike Tanamachi

Indexer: Sharon Shock

Proofreader: Lara SerVaas

Important: Premier Press cannot provide software support. Please contact the appropriate software manufacturer's technical support line or Web site for assistance.

Premier Press and the author have attempted throughout this book to distinguish proprietary trademarks from descriptive terms by following the capitalization style used by the manufacturer.

Information contained in this book has been obtained by Premier Press from sources believed to be reliable. However, because of the possibility of human or mechanical error by our sources, Premier Press, or others, the Publisher does not guarantee the accuracy, adequacy, or completeness of any information and is not responsible for any errors or omissions or the results obtained from use of such information. Readers should be particularly aware of the fact that the Internet is an ever-changing entity. Some facts may have changed since this book went to press.

ISBN: 1-931841-92-6

Library of Congress Catalog Card Number: 2002104492

Printed in the United States of America

02 03 04 05 GG 10 9 8 7 6 5 4 3 2 1

I dedicate this book to family photo bugs everywhere. (You know who you are, because you drive the rest of us nuts while taking our pictures!) May we all appreciate the great service you do by preserving the best of times.

I also dedicate my work here to Steve, Bo, and Rika, my constant supporters and helpmates.

ACKNOWLEDGMENTS

Thanks to everyone at Premier Press for providing this opportunity for me to apply my writing skills on a project that called for mounds of creativity. Challenging projects yield warm and fuzzy feelings of accomplishment that linger all too briefly.

In particular, I extend my thanks to Kevin Harreld, who brought me on board with this project and helped diagnose the figure preparation process, so we could bring you clear and colorful images in this text. The project would not have come together without the creative solutions provided by Stacy Hiquet and Damon Davis. Thanks to both of you for keeping the options open.

The editorial, quality, and production folks really had a trial by fire this time around. They redefined the term "Weekend Warriors" by exceeding the call of duty and working quickly, skillfully, and competently to bring you the top-notch product you hold here. These folks include Project Manager and Editor Marta Justak, Technical Editor Michelle Jones, Compositor Bill Hartman, and Sharon Shock, indexer.

ABOUT THE AUTHOR

An author and consultant, **Lisa A. Bucki** has been involved in computer training and writing for more than 12 years. She also wrote *Managing with Microsoft Project 2002* and *Mac OS X Fast & Easy,* and revised *Photoshop 7 Fast & Easy,* all for Prima Tech. Overall, she has written or contributed to more than 40 books and multimedia products, as well as spearheading or developing more than 100 computer and trade titles during her association with Macmillan. Bucki currently also serves as a consultant and trainer in western North Carolina.

CONTENTS AT A GLANCE

CONTENTS

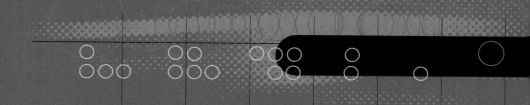

INTRODUCTION

PHOTOSHOP 7 DIGITAL DARKROOM FROM PREMIER PRESS OFFERS INFORMATION FOR THE CASUAL OR AMATEUR PHOTOGRAPHER WITH AN INTERMEDIATE TO ADVANCED LEVEL OF COMPUTER AND GRAPHICS APPLICATION EXPERIENCE. IF YOU'RE LOOKING FOR A GUIDE TO PHOTOSHOP, THIS ISN'T IT. I DON'T SPEND ANY TIME COVERING COLOR THEORY, PRE-PRESS, PRINTING, OR TOOLS LIKE THE HISTORY BRUSH. INSTEAD, I START WITH A CRASH COURSE ABOUT HOW TO TAKE A GOOD PICTURE, AND THEN TRY TO SHOW OFF SOME BASIC AND ADVANCED TASKS YOU CAN PERFORM TO CREATE SPIFFY-LOOKING WEB-READY PHOTOGRAPHIC IMAGES. I'M ASSUMING IF THE IMAGE LOOKS GOOD TO YOU, USING YOUR EYES AS YOUR GUIDE, THEN IT'S OK FOR YOUR FAMILY, FRIENDS, AND WEB SITE.

Although many of the tasks in this book are fairly easy to follow, I don't recommend this book to a new computer user or someone brand new to graphics applications, photography, Photoshop, or Web design. All this information and new technology may be a bit overwhelming to grasp all at once.

This book focuses on digital pictures. Most pictures were taken with a 3.3-megapixel camera, specifically a Casio QV-3000EX.

WHO SHOULD READ THIS BOOK?

Naturally, I'd like to think this book would be helpful to anyone wanting to learn how to work with digital pictures with Photoshop. If you're adventurous and learn quickly by following visual, step-by-step examples, you'll probably appreciate this book. These examples are just one of many possible ways you can use one or several features in Photoshop. If you're looking for technical explanations and discussions on color theory, you'll be disappointed.

This book is for digital camera owners, and those who work with digital pictures and also know how to use a computer. It's also for those who are new to Photoshop 7 and preparing pictures for the Web. If you don't have any experience with photography or computers, I strongly recommend reading other books to learn more about photography, graphics, digital cameras, Photoshop, and the Web, in addition to using this book. (For example, *Photoshop 7 Fast & Easy* from Premier Press provides an easier introduction to Photoshop.) If you are familiar with Windows or Macintosh computers, and have dabbled with digital cameras, Photoshop, and Web graphics in the past, this book is for you!

Adobe publishes Photoshop 7 in both Mac and Windows versions. These most recent versions have been optimized for the new operating system for each platform, specifically Mac OS X and Windows XP. While this book primarily shows illustrations from the Mac version of Photoshop, the features are virtually identical in each version, so users of either platform can benefit from this book.

HOW THIS BOOK IS ORGANIZED

There are four main sections to this book. The first section introduces digital cameras and shows you how to take better pictures and configure Photoshop 7. The second section acquaints you with the Photoshop workspace and covers the basics of working with layers, masks, and channels. The third section offers more advanced coverage about how to experiment with layers, masks, and channels, and shows you how to create animation or automate tasks with digital pictures. The fourth section shows you how to create Web photo albums and optimize images for your Web pages.

The chapters cover basic to advanced topics to show you how to do simple tasks, like straighten a photo, to more sophisticated tasks, like combining information from different pictures. Skip to any chapter if you want to use this book as a reference, or walk through it chapter by chapter to try out different combinations of features in Photoshop.

CONVENTIONS USED IN THIS BOOK

In virtually all instances, this book presents keyboard shortcut combinations for both Mac and Windows. Where a particular key differs, I present the Mac key first, a slash, and then the Windows equivalent. For example, Command/Ctrl+click represents Command+click if you're using a Mac and Ctrl+click if you're using Windows. Control+/right-click means to Control+click on the Mac or right-click in Windows.

 Tips offer hints, explain more about a special feature, or tell you how to use a shortcut to boost your productivity and make work fun.

 Notes provide additional information about a feature, or extend an idea on how to use a feature.

 Cautions warn about pitfalls and glitches in the application or procedures. Many of the cautions are platform specific while others can occur on either platform running Photoshop.

PART 1

D
I
G
I
T
A
L

P
I
C
T
U
R
E
S

WORKING WITH DIGITAL PICTURES

PHOTOSHOP PROVIDES THE MOST DYNAMIC, POWERFUL IMAGE EDITING FEATURES AVAILABLE TODAY. HOLLYWOOD PRODUCTION STUDIOS USE IT TO EDIT HIGH-RESOLUTION DIGITAL IMAGES FOR FEATURE FILMS SUCH AS THE **STAR TREK** SERIES. WEB DEVELOPMENT STUDIOS USE IT TO CREATE GREAT-LOOKING DIGITAL PICTURES FOR WEB SITES. PEOPLE LIKE YOU AND ME USE IT TO ENHANCE OUR OWN PHOTOS TO CREATE GREAT PRINTS AND PHOTO ALBUMS.

BEFORE YOU CAN START EDITING DIGITAL PICTURES WITH PHOTOSHOP, YOU MUST CREATE SOME DIGITAL PICTURES. DIGITAL CAMERAS OFFER AN EASY, INEXPENSIVE WAY TO GENERATE DIGITAL PHOTOS. FILM, PAPER, AND PHOTO SCANNERS CAN ALSO CONVERT TRADITIONAL PHOTOGRAPHS OR 35MM SLIDES AND NEGATIVES INTO DIGITAL IMAGE FILES.

THE FIRST PART OF THIS BOOK CONTAINS A BRIEF OVERVIEW OF HOW TO USE DIGITAL CAMERAS, AND BRIEFLY EXPLAINS HOW TO CONVERT TRADITIONAL PHOTOS INTO DIGITAL FILES. IF YOU ALREADY HAVE DIGITAL PICTURES READY TO USE AND HAVE INSTALLED PHOTOSHOP 7, MOVE AHEAD TO PART 2, "PHOTOSHOP 7 BASICS." IF YOU HAVE INTERNET ACCESS, I HAVE PROVIDED SOME DIGITAL PICTURES ON PREMIER'S DOWNLOAD SITE AT HTTP://WWW.PREMIERPRESSBOOKS.COM/DOWNLOADS.ASP, WHICH YOU ARE FREE TO USE.

CHAPTER 1

TAKING PICTURES

THIS FIRST CHAPTER DELIVERS A SHORT COURSE ON HOW TO GET FAMILIAR WITH THE FEATURES OF A CAMERA AND TAKE PICTURES. TO FIND OUT MORE ABOUT HOW TO SHOP FOR OR USE A CAMERA, VISIT **WWW.PHOTO.NET** OR **WWW.DPREVIEW.COM**, OR PURCHASE A DEDICATED BOOK ABOUT PHOTOGRAPHY. IF YOU'RE LOOKING FOR PHOTOSHOP INFORMATION, YOU WON'T FIND ANY IN THIS CHAPTER. SKIP AHEAD TO CHAPTER 2, "LOADING YOUR DIGITAL IMAGES INTO PHOTOSHOP."

WHETHER YOU'RE USING A CAMERA OR A SCANNER, THE MOST IMPORTANT THING TO REMEMBER WHEN WORKING WITH DIGITAL PICTURES IS THAT THE QUALITY OF A DIGITAL IMAGE IS ONLY AS GOOD AS THE QUALITY OF THE ORIGINAL PICTURE. ALTHOUGH 35MM CAMERAS CAN TAKE GREAT PICTURES, THE QUALITY OF THE SCANNER USED TO DIGITIZE 35MM PHOTOS MAY BE A WEAK LINK. I EMPHAZISE HOW TO USE DIGITAL CAMERAS, INSTEAD OF 35MM ONES, BECAUSE DIGITAL CAMERAS PROVIDE A STRAIGHTFORWARD WAY OF BRINGING A HIGH-QUALITY DIGITAL IMAGE DIRECTLY INTO YOUR COMPUTER.

ABOUT DIGITAL CAMERAS

The first digital cameras appeared on store shelves approximately nine years ago. They cost close to $1,000, and offered a 640×480 fixed resolution, with no capability to focus. Storage media were fairly expensive, with 1–2MB of storage space costing $100 to $200. Today, you can purchase a 4-megapixel camera, which can take a 2,400×1,800 pixel image (or 2,048×1,536 pixels for a 3-megapixel camera, or 1,600×1,200 pixels for a 2-megapixel camera) for between $200 and $1,000. Today's 2- to 5-megapixel digital cameras truly rival the features and image quality originally created by 35mm cameras.

In place of film, lenses, and camera settings on traditional 35mm cameras, digital cameras use a CCD, software, and a storage disk, such as compact flash, smart media, or a miniature hard disk. The CCD (Charged-Couple Device) is the essential chip that makes a digital camera a camera. Most low- to medium-range cameras have a single CCD. CCDs were originally used in video cameras, which initially supported a 640×480 resolution.

High-end cameras can use up to three CCDs to process red, green, and blue light. A camera using three CCDs dedicates one CCD each to process the red, green, and blue channels. The camera combines the images from each of the CCDs into one image, which is stored as a file on the camera's storage card. High-end cameras also usually include larger lenses. High-end cameras can create high-quality digital images because the larger lens brings more light to the CCDs, which in turn can bring more image data to the image file created by the camera.

Next-generation digital cameras may use a new CMOS (Complimentary Metal-Oxide Semiconductor). Still others may use enhanced CCD systems, such as the Super CCD from Fuji Film.

Digital cameras are similar yet different from the traditional 35mm cameras. From a distance, it can be difficult to distinguish a digital camera from a 35mm camera. Both usually have a built-in flash, shutter button, and a lens. In most current models, both can automatically focus and determine whether you need to use a flash. Many medium- to high-end cameras also offer a range of manual settings that enable you to set the aperture, shutter speed, and

exposure settings. It's easy to take a great looking, quick picture with both kinds of cameras, too.

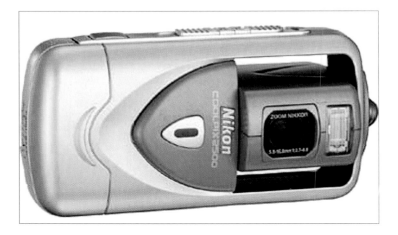

Despite the similarities, digital cameras work much differently than 35mm cameras. One of the main differences is that digital cameras use a storage card instead of film to store images. The two most common types of digital storage media are Smart Media and Compact Flash. A digital camera will either use one card format or the other, not both. Smart Media cards can store from 4MB-128MB of image data, with the amount of storage space varying with the storage capacity of the card. Compact Flash cards range in size, including 32, 128, 256, and 512MB. Sony's Mavica line used to save photos directly to a floppy disk. Now, various Mavica models can save to 156M CD-R and CD-RW media. Some of the first digital cameras, such as Apple's QuickTake cameras, used 1MB and 2MB Smart Media cards and captured 640×480 digital images. The digital picture ranged in size from 60K to 100K.

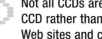 **Not all CCDs are alike. Cost is a better indicator of availability of the CCD rather than the quality of the image it can create. Visit a few Web sites and compare picture quality between cameras you're interested in before purchasing one.**

LOW-COST CAMERAS

Many kinds of CCDs are used in today's digital cameras. Less expensive cameras most likely use CCDs that are limited by the size of the image that can be captured, or by the amount of light it can process. However, most 2- and 3-megapixel cameras in the sub-$1,000 price range—such as the Coolpix 995, Kodak, Canon, Olympus, and Fuji cameras—do a great job taking pictures in regular daylight as well as in low-light conditions. A mid-cost 3-megapixel cameras appears here: Sony's Mavica MVC-CD400.

MULTIMEDIA

Many 3- and 4-megapixel cameras can capture MPEG1 video and audio at 320x240 pixels in addition to capturing still pictures at 2,048x1,536 pixels. What's next? I'm guessing MPEG2 support in the next-generation digital cameras.

HIGH-PERFORMANCE CAMERAS

More pixels means bigger file sizes and more processing time for a camera. However, digital camera performance is increasing as rapidly as computer processor speeds are. And as with computers, if you can't afford a good digital camera today, chances are you'll be able to afford it in six to twelve months. This figure shows the Fuji FinePix F601. The FinePix F601 boasts a 3.1-megapixel Super CCD capable of capturing 2,832x2,128 pixel images. Highest-end professional digital cameras capture images with even more detail, but cost many thousands of dollars. For example, the Kodak DCS Pro Back Plus shoots 4,080x4,080 images and costs $22,995.

COMPARING DIGITAL CAMERAS

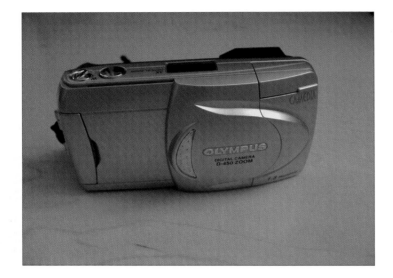

It seems like digital cameras are gaining so many new features each year, it's almost impossible to compare them, much less figure out what a good deal is. Some basic guidelines to use when comparing digital cameras are, in no particular order, features, cost, and quality. I tend to give the quality of the picture the most weight; however, depending on your preferences, you might choose differently. The Olympus digital cameras, like the Casio QV-3000EX shown in this figure for example, are popular because they look and feel very similar to a 35mm camera.

FEATURES

The features a camera supports are often related to the price of the camera itself:

❈ Most low-end cameras in the sub-$250 price range offer fixed or minimal zoom and slow focus, lower-resolution images (640x480 to 1,600×1,200 pixels), limited flash control, and a small amount of storage. You should compare prices and features, as well as image quality between two or more cameras, before actually purchasing one.

❈ Medium-priced cameras ($500–$1,000) offer zoom lenses, improved image quality, more focus settings, more flash settings, and an improved software interface. If you can afford a medium-range digital camera, you'll have plenty of models to choose from.

❈ Higher-end cameras (above $1,000) offer more of all the previous features, as well as larger camera bodies, some of which look almost identical to 35mm cameras. A larger camera body has two advantages. Larger camera bodies usually mean larger lenses. One of the biggest limitations of mid-range digital cameras is that the smaller lens and camera body sizes restrict the camera's ability to capture a broader range of light. Some high-end cameras not only connect directly to a computer to download images to a computer's hard disk, but also work with multiple media, Compact Flash, Smart Media cards, and IBM's Microdrive.

COST

Although many low-end cameras are priced in the $100–$200 range, you can probably find one below $100. However, for a few hundred dollars more, around $400–$600, you can find a decent mid-range camera that can create larger and more realistic pictures. Three- and four-megapixel cameras are starting to appear in the $500–$600 price range. If you can wait for next year's models, you might be able to get twice the camera for your money.

QUALITY

Low-end cameras, in the $100–$200 price range, typically have the poorest quality lenses and CCDs, and usually do not support the addition of filters or other lenses. Some mid-range cameras, however, offer this extensibility. Many mid-range cameras from Kodak, Sony, and Nikon take great pictures. Some models, such as the Nikon Coolpix 775, offer exceptional lenses at reasonable prices. High-end cameras usually support 35mm lenses.

If you've already compared prices between traditional 35mm cameras and digital cameras, you'll immediately notice that digital cameras capable of using 35mm lenses are quite a bit more expensive than traditional 35mm cameras. The quality and size of the lens definitely makes a difference when you're taking pictures. If you already have a 35mm camera, or can't find a digital camera that fits into your budget, you can always scan slides or printed photos into your computer.

USING CAMERA MODES

Most digital cameras have two modes: a picture-taking mode and a picture-viewing mode. This section shows you how to use these camera modes with a few selected digital cameras. In many cases, your digital camera will have similar settings to those covered in this section. However, your camera's operation manual is the best source for finding out how to use your camera.

PICTURE-TAKING MODES

Most digital cameras have at least two modes: automatic shooting mode (often called record mode) and playback mode. Some cameras have a camera connection, or picture download mode. Most cameras usually have an automatic picture-taking mode, whereby the camera sets the shutter speed and focus for you. More expensive cameras also have a manual picture-taking mode, enabling you to focus and set the aperture, exposure, and shutter speed for a picture. Many of these types of cameras also enable you to add various filters and lenses. Some cameras even enable you to capture motion.

RECORD (AUTOMATIC) MODE

Not sure what a digital camera can do? To take a picture, use the default mode (called automatic mode on some cameras), take some pictures, and check out the results in playback mode. Although automatic mode might not create the best pictures for low-end cameras, particularly in low-light shots, you can use automatic mode 90 percent of the time with most cameras and get amazing images.

The following steps illustrate how to take a picture in record (automatic) mode. Depending on the camera you have, you might need to modify the following steps:

1. Put the camera into record mode or automatic shooting mode. Some cameras, like the Olympus D-450, only work in automatic mode. Line up the line on the dial knob with the text and marker on the camera body to select the record or automatic mode. The Casio QV-3000EX appears here. Changing to record mode may power the camera on, or you may have to press a separate power button.
2. Choose a flash setting. The Flash button, which usually has a lightning bolt icon on or next to it, is usually combined with a Flash icon in the status window of the camera.

3. Choose a focus mode. On the QV3000-EX, the focus mode button is the lower-left button shown in the illustration above. The three available settings are manual focus (MF), infinity, and macro (close up) mode.

 Although digital cameras can take great pictures, one of the limitations that you might find, especially if you're using automatic focus, is that the CCD will tend to focus on the subject surrounded by the most light, even if it's farther away.

4. Frame the subject and adjust the focus as needed.
5. Press the shutter button.

 Keep a second storage card and batteries available for storing video. That way you don't have to watch how much space is available on your camera while taking regular pictures.

MANUAL MODE

Automatic mode is great for taking pictures of locations, events, and people in bright light. Low light, or artificial light, will probably require more experimentation to find the best settings for a particular location or event. In this case, you might want to put the camera in manual mode, which enables you to manually set the aperture, shutter speed, or exposure time, in order to capture a more color-rich or motion-sensitive picture. Medium to high-end cameras have manual settings that enable you to set up a digital camera similar to the way you set up a 35mm one. Some cameras also offer a variety of modes so that you can choose whether to give priority to the aperture, for example, or to take night-time or panoramic shots.

If you have an older camera, using manual mode might introduce you to a world of confusing camera settings. Today's 3- and 4-megapixel cameras, however, usually have an M on the mode dial to indicate manual mode. For example, turn the mode dial until the M lines up with the marker on the camera to put the Nikon Coolpix 990 into manual mode. For other cameras, such as the one shown here, you can press a Mode button on the camera and then choose the mode setting you prefer.

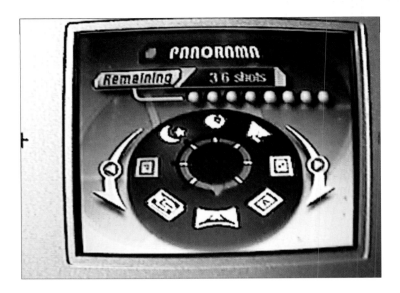

The basic procedure for taking a picture in manual mode varies from camera to camera; check your manual for details. Using a Nikon Coolpix 990, the procedure is as follows:

1. Set the camera to manual mode and then power it on.
2. Press the MODE button. *P* represents Exposure mode and enables you to select combinations of shutter speed and aperture settings. *A* represents Aperture mode, where you set the aperture size, and the camera picks the shutter speed. *S* represents Shutter Priority mode, enabling you to set the speed of the shutter while the camera sets the aperture. (These settings only apply to the Nikon Coolpix 990.)
3. Rotate the dial to choose a setting for the selected mode.
4. Press the shutter button.

 If the camera is in manual mode, you'll probably want to experiment with different shutter speeds, apertures, and exposure settings to see how the camera handles different settings under various lighting conditions.

When you take a picture in manual mode, you have control over the following:

✴ Focus, which determines the clarity of the image.

✴ Aperture, or the amount of light exposed to the CCD. A larger aperture (smaller f-stop numbers) decreases the depth of field and can create a blurry background. Smaller apertures increase depth of field and clarity between foreground and background elements of the picture.

✴ Shutter speed. Faster shutter speeds can freeze motion whereas slower shutter speeds capture blurred motion, but allow more light in.

Depending on your camera, you might also be able to add filters and lenses.

FOCUS

Sometimes a digital camera in automatic mode can't figure out what to focus on, even if it's right in front of the camera. Although digital cameras can have thousands of levels of focus, often the CCD targets the brightest light at the center of the picture to determine what to focus on. In this example, the camera focused on the brighter background rather than the real subject of the photo, the dark basil leaves in the foreground.

Press the shutter button halfway down to preview the focus mode of a camera. Cameras in automatic mode will adjust focus as your subjects move about. If you can't get the camera to correctly focus in automatic mode, set it to manual mode and manually adjust the focus of the camera. Digital cameras rely on light to determine what to focus on. Notice the person in the background is the focus instead of the person in the foreground.

APERTURE

The aperture in a 35mm camera determines how much light strikes the film inside the camera. On a digital camera, the aperture setting adjusts how light interacts with the CCD. View the aperture setting in the camera's software to get a general idea of how the CCD will behave. A wider aperture allows the most light to get in, and, combined with a fast shutter speed, is great for capturing sports action. Also choose a wider aperture setting in low light conditions if no night or low-light mode is available on your camera.

SHUTTER SPEED

The shutter priority settings, in addition to how they capture motion, affect how much light hits the CCD in a digital camera by adjusting the amount of time the shutter remains open. A faster shutter speed means less exposure time to the chip, whereas a slower shutter speed enables the camera to capture more color and light information. In some digital cameras, if the shutter setting is given priority, you set the shutter speed, and the camera will figure out the correlating aperture and exposure settings.

ADDING FILTERS

A few low-end, and some medium-end, digital cameras support adding filters to the lens. On the cameras that support filters, you can neutralize, or filter out, certain light qualities by adding a filter to a camera lens:

✴ Ultraviolet. Filter out bright light with the Ultraviolet filter.

✴ Neutral. This filter is most effective outdoors. It will filter out extreme bright or dark areas, thus equalizing the amount of light that gets

exposed through the lens. Although this is a filter for light, it can help a camera capture a more balanced tonal range of light, reducing the likelihood of capturing overexposed or washed out colors in a photo.

✳ Color. If you're shooting in mid-day sun, adding a red or orange filter to a camera can create a warmer range of color tones.

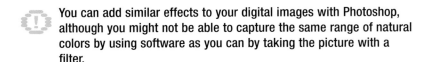

You can add similar effects to your digital images with Photoshop, although you might not be able to capture the same range of natural colors by using software as you can by taking the picture with a filter.

ADDING LENSES

Although most digital cameras can't share 35mm camera lenses, some cameras can share lenses across models, such as the Nikon digital camera series: the 900, 950, and 990. These models can use any of Nikon's Coolpix lenses, including macro, telephoto, wide-angle, and fish-eye lenses. However, you cannot attach any of Nikon's 35mm lenses to any of Nikon's Coolpix digital cameras. Although most people will probably own only one digital camera, if you want to shoot with multiple cameras or upgrade to a newer Coolpix model, you don't need to buy new lenses. This section highlights the macro and fish-eye lenses.

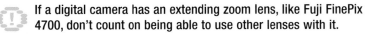

If a digital camera has an extending zoom lens, like Fuji FinePix 4700, don't count on being able to use other lenses with it.

MACRO

This lens enables you to get up close and personal with your subject. Unlike other lenses, which require that you be at least 4cm (centimeters) from your subject, this one allows you to get as close as 4mm (millimeters). If you can attach a macro lens to your camera, you can take extreme close-up shots.

Zoom in toward your subject when taking a picture with a macro lens. Some cameras, like the Nikon Coolpix 990, have specific manual menu settings for use with macro and fish-eye lenses.

Avoid using the built-in flash with a macro shot. The flash will probably prevent the camera from capturing any detail from the close-up image.

FISH-EYE

A fish-eye lens is a super wide-angle lens. The lens extends out beyond the scope of a normal lens, up to 180 degrees, and has a more bulbous appearance than a normal camera lens. Around the edges of the image, straight lines are rendered as curves. Some digital cameras, like the Nikon Coolpix 990, have a built-in zoom. However, when taking a picture with a fish-eye lens, you want to zoom out, not in, to take full advantage of it.

A fish-eye lens creates an extreme, wide-angle, distorted image by magnifying the center of the picture and shrinking the edges of the picture. The captured image is a little wider than an image taken with a normal lens. You can use Photoshop to merge a picture taken with a fish-eye lens with pictures taken with a regular lens to create a panoramic view of a skyline or horizon.

If you have access to virtual-reality software, which is included with Nikon's Coolpix 990 camera, you can use a fish-eye lens to take pictures and create a virtual world from those pictures. See your manual for details.

Add a fish-eye lens effect to a picture using the circular selection and the Spherize filter features.

MOTION-CAPTURE MODE

Many 3- and 4-megapixel cameras can capture MPEG1-quality video and audio. Although the size of the video is small in comparison to still pictures, sometimes it's more meaningful to capture audio and motion. You can import QuickTime movies into Image Ready and work with an individual frame or with the full video.

 A high-resolution alternative to MPEG1 is the continuous shot feature in the Nikon Coolpix 990. It can take continuous pictures—enough to fill up your storage disk—in manual mode.

The basic procedure for capturing video (assuming your camera allows it) is as follows (the precise instructions for your camera might differ; check your manual for details):

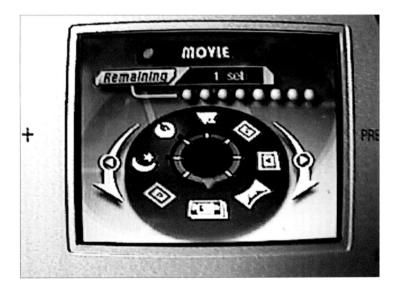

1. Set the camera to record moving images and then power it on, if needed.

2. Hold down the shutter button and point the camera at the action you want to capture. Use your camera's LCD screen to view the action. The LCD screen is the real-time viewfinder located on the back side of the camera. Move the camera, or follow your subject as it moves, to create your movie.
3. Release the shutter button to stop capturing motion, or let the camera run out of storage space.

 Although MPEG1 video is captured at 320×240 pixels compared to 2,048×1,536 pixels for a still image, it can fill up the storage card pretty quickly. Carry extra storage cards, or keep a laptop and PC card adapter nearby, so you don't find yourself having to erase something because you ran out of space.

PLAYBACK MODE

After you've taken a few digital pictures, you'll want to view them. Here's how (note that the precise instructions for viewing images on your camera might vary from those listed here; check your camera's manual for details):

1. Set the camera to Play mode.

2. Press the up or down arrow buttons to view various images stored in your camera using your camera's LCD screen.

 If the camera has a cable to connect it to a television, you can view the pictures on a TV and use the camera to select images.

3. Press the grid button to view multiple images at once.

 Most digital cameras have a slide-show feature. Select the pictures you want to use for the slide show, put the camera into slide-show mode, connect the camera to a TV or projector system, and voilá! You have a slide show controlled by your digital camera.

IMAGE FILE FORMATS

A digital camera, much like a scanner, converts analog light information into digital ones and zeros, which represent the location and color of each pixel in an image. All this image information is stored in a single file. The information in this file can be stored raw, or uncompressed, thus preserving all the original image data.

The image can also be made smaller by compression. Compression involves storing iterative information in a file in one place, instead of several places in the file. The goal of compression is to reduce the size of the file without losing any of the original information. Some compression methods, such as a high-end JPEG file format, preserve most of the quality of the original image. However, other compression formats, such as low-end JPEG file format, often lose image quality during the compression process.

The term file format describes a type of file, such as a text or graphic file. The most commonly used Web graphic file formats are JPEG, GIF, and PNG.

Most digital cameras use the JPEG file format as the default for storing picture files on the camera's storage card. Some cameras, such as the Nikon Coolpix 990, allow you to capture raw or uncompressed images, which are then stored as TIFF files. Many of the latest 3- and 4-megapixel cameras also support MPEG1 audio and video files.

THE JPEG FILE FORMAT

As mentioned previously, JPEG, short for Joint Photographic Experts Group, is the standard file format used with digital cameras today. Although not all cameras take advantage of this option, JPEG offers various rates of compression. Compression rates are generally presented as plain-English options, such as "economy," "normal" and "fine" or "good" and "better."

The compression rate affects how large the image file will be. For example, with my 3.3-megapixel camera (1,024x768 pixels), a normal file is about 300KB. If you plan to take pictures for a Web site, this setting will work great for you. This picture, taken in Normal mode with a Casio QV-3000EX, captures a clear, crisp image.

A Fine picture, on the other hand, may be 500KB–1.2MB. If you plan to print your images, this is the setting for you. If you have a limited amount of storage space, you'll probably want to use the smallest file size possible ("economy," if available, or "normal" or "good," rather than "fine" or "better"). However, if you invest in a large storage card, use the largest compressed file size possible to yield more detailed images. This picture, shot in Fine mode with the same camera, shows a little more detail than the previous photo.

THE TIFF FILE FORMAT

If you prefer to work with uncompressed image files, set your camera to capture uncompressed TIFF images (not all cameras allow this; check your manual for details). Be aware, though, that doing so will add lots of processing time to your picture taking. A 2-megapixel image, 1,600×1,200 pixels, can take up 8MB of storage space. Because this uncompressed file is rather huge (compared to JPEG files), it will take the camera a minute or two to write this image data to the storage card. In many cases you might not notice a significant increase in image quality.

 If your camera has a "fine" or "better" setting for JPEG images, take a few pictures with this setting and compare it to the TIFF versions. Unless you absolutely need an uncompressed image, the file JPEG image might be the better file format, enabling you to save more images in less time.

TAKING A GREAT PICTURE

Many books and Web pages discuss the best way to light, compose, and shoot a picture. The information presented in this chapter includes what I consider to be some basic picture-taking concepts, which you can take to heart or ignore. After all, it's not like you're wasting film.

LIGHTING THE SUBJECT

Light plays a big role in any picture. Light, and its counterpart, shade, can enhance or hide image clarity, color, and the overall composition of a picture. Here's a brief summary of lighting issues to consider before taking a picture:

* When taking pictures outdoors or indoors in natural light, try to shoot with the sun behind you or to the side of you at an angle to minimize washing out colors or dramatic shadows.
* If the sun is behind the subject, try to counter its brightness by using the built-in flash on the camera.
* Try to keep the light source at an angle behind you in order to provide an even light over the subject. The most difficult pictures to take are low-light ones or pictures taken with artificial light, such as a flash.
* If you take a picture with a flash, you are probably all too familiar with the red-eye effect. Red eye occurs when a picture is taken in low light, and the flash reflects off the pupil of the eye before the eye can adjust to the bright light. Most pictures with color and light-related inaccuracies can be corrected with Photoshop.

I must admit I don't have a professional photography studio. I prefer to take pictures of people and places in their natural state. But if you want to invest in additional flash bulbs and tripods, go for it.

The following steps illustrate when to consider lighting issues while taking a picture with the camera in automatic mode.

1. Set the camera to automatic mode and power it on.
2. Press the flash button and choose a flash setting.
3. Note the location of the light source in the picture. You might want to change the location of the camera, or move the subject to change the way the subject is lit. If your camera has a built-in flash, you can put the camera in force flash mode, using the built-in flash as a filler flash to handle shots in which the light source is behind your subject.

4. Press the shutter button. Lighting a subject from a side angle can create more dramatic effects compared to the same subject lit from above. In this example, side lighting creates dramatic shadows.

 For best results, hold the camera steady as you press the shutter button.

NATURAL LIGHTING

Taking pictures in the sunlight can be either extremely easy or somewhat difficult, depending on the time of day. For example, if you take a picture at noon, when the sun is directly overhead, you might need to move your subject into the shade to prevent the sun from washing out the image. However, if you take a picture at sunrise or sunset, you can capture a wider range of colors with a warmer light.

Although I don't usually put much thought into using a flash when I take pictures in daylight, here are a few things to consider when taking pictures in natural light. If you're taking a picture in the shade, you may want to force your camera to use a flash (also known as a fill flash) to make the subject of your photo stand out from the background. Light from a sunrise casts a bluish hue, compared to light from a sunset, which can have a reddish or orange tint.

TUNGSTEN LIGHTING

Tungsten, or halogen-generated light, can cast a yellow or orange hue on your subject. You can easily correct this type of light using Photoshop 7. For more information about correcting colors and adjusting light, see Chapter 5, "Correcting Images."

FLUORESCENT LIGHTING

Fluorescent light casts a greenish hue on your subject. Again, you can correct for this using Photoshop. For more information about correcting colors and adjusting light, see Chapter 5.

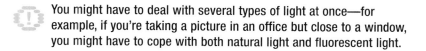

You might have to deal with several types of light at once—for example, if you're taking a picture in an office but close to a window, you might have to cope with both natural light and fluorescent light.

FRAMING THE SUBJECT

Have you ever taken a picture and mistakenly cut off the top of someone's head? In addition to keeping the subject in the camera's viewfinder, try to frame some of the background picture elements. Framing is the process of arranging the elements in a picture so that the subject is complementary to the other elements in the picture. Framing can be as simple as turning the camera sideways to change the angle or perspective of a picture or including a few trees to help frame some clouds. In the example here, the angles of the stone path and old timber nicely frame Bo and add interest to the photo; part of Bo's body is left out of the frame to focus on his intense expression. The following steps illustrate when and how to consider framing your picture during the picture-taking process.

1. Set the camera to automatic mode and then power it on. Set the camera to save the image at the highest-resolution available.

2. Use the built-in display to frame the subject. Alternatively, you can use the viewfinder to center the subject, and view the picture limits.
3. Hold the shutter button halfway down if you want to adjust the focus as you frame your picture.
4. When you're ready to take a picture, press the shutter button.

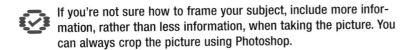 If you're not sure how to frame your subject, include more information, rather than less information, when taking the picture. You can always crop the picture using Photoshop.

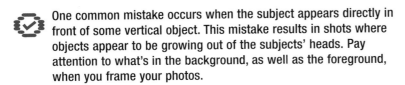 One common mistake occurs when the subject appears directly in front of some vertical object. This mistake results in shots where objects appear to be growing out of the subjects' heads. Pay attention to what's in the background, as well as the foreground, when you frame your photos.

COMPOSING A PICTURE

Composition takes framing a step further down the path of creative picture taking. Composing a picture is similar to composing a song, except instead of writing a song with notes, you compose a story with images. When I compose photographs, I try to tell a story. If there are no people in the picture, I try to balance light and shade, or highlight contrasting colors.

If you're not quite sure what I mean by "composition," try taking a look at some of photos on photography Web sites, such as **www.photo.net**. Pick one or two photos you like, and then try to decide why you like them. Consider these things when you compose your own photos.

The following sections highlight a few tips to consider when composing a picture.

KEEP THE SUBJECT OFF-CENTER

Try to keep the subject or focal point of the picture slightly off-center. Look for another picture element to include in the photo when you take the picture. Arranging the subject slightly off-center (the rising sun is off-center in this example) makes a picture more interesting and less two-dimensional.

THE RULE OF THIRDS

Putting a picture together can mean trying to figure out how to break up space. One way of looking through the viewfinder is to break up the space that you see into thirds. If you can see distinct subjects in each third of the picture, you're following the rule of thirds.

COMPOSING WITH COLOR

Another way to compose a picture is to place certain colors next to each other, as with the dramatic red color of the fall leaf contrasting with the drab pavement. The following steps illustrate the process of evaluating colors during the picture-taking process.

1. Set the camera to automatic mode.
2. Use the built-in display to frame the colors in the picture.
3. Press the zoom in and zoom out buttons to include or exclude other colors, or view alternative compositions.
4. Press the shutter button.

 You can also experiment with adding colors to pictures using Photoshop 7. See Chapter 7, "Creating Objects and Gradients," to find out more about adding color to pictures with Photoshop.

TAKING PICTURES OF PEOPLE

Whether you're in a studio or out on the street, the one thing to keep in mind when taking pictures of people is to keep the light behind you or to your side, and have the person face the camera. Having the light source stream in from the side of the subject can add interesting shadow effects and bring depth and texture to the picture. Try to keep the person or people in your picture comfortable and relaxed, focusing more on their faces than their clothing. Include more than one person in a picture, if possible, and try to capture the moment. The following steps illustrate a simple process for taking pictures of people. A more elaborate process might involve setting up lighting in a studio.

1. Set the camera to automatic mode and then power it on.
2. Stand to the left or right of the light source.
3. Frame the subject or subjects with the built-in display or viewfinder.
4. Press the shutter button.

 When taking pictures of people with a flash, try not to stand too close or too far away from the subject.

CAPTURING MOTION

Digital cameras aren't always smart about how to focus on moving subjects. You will probably need to take continuous pictures to get the best shot of an athlete or performer. If the subject is moving quickly, you might need to set your camera to manual mode and increase the shutter speed to reduce blurring. The following steps explain how to take continuous pictures with a Nikon Coolpix 990. (Other cameras might vary. For example, the Sony DSC-S70 has a Movie setting on its mode dial.)

1. Set the camera to manual mode and then press the Menu button. Press the arrow buttons to choose Continuous. Continuous mode enables a Nikon Coolpix 990 to capture up to 16 consecutive pictures.
2. Frame the subject in the viewfinder or built-in display.
3. Rotate the camera if the subject fits better in a portrait view. Compare the following shots, taken with the continuous mode on a Casio QV-3000EX.
4. Press the shutter button.

 Keep several storage cards and batteries on hand if you plan to shoot continuous pictures. Fluid motion can range from 24 to 30 frames per second, and 3-megapixel images taken in Fine mode can require over 1MB of space per picture.

CHAPTER 2

LOADING YOUR DIGITAL IMAGES INTO PHOTOSHOP

EACH DIGITAL PICTURE EXISTS AS A SINGLE FILE, MADE UP OF A MOSAIC OF PIXELS STORED AS BINARY CODE. YOU USE HARDWARE, SUCH AS A DIGITAL CAMERA OR SCANNER, TO CREATE A DIGITAL PICTURE. THE PREVIOUS CHAPTER, "TAKING PICTURES," BRIEFLY EXPLAINED HOW TO CAPTURE A PICTURE WITH A DIGITAL CAMERA. THIS CHAPTER EXPLAINS HOW TO GET THAT PICTURE INTO A COMPUTER. IF YOU HAVE SLIDES, 35MM NEGATIVES, OR PRINTS, SEE THE SECTION ON HOW TO USE A SCANNER OR A WEB-BASED PHOTO SERVICE TO CONVERT TRADITIONAL PHOTOS INTO DIGITAL PICTURES.

MANY DIGITAL CAMERA AND SCANNER MANUFACTURERS INCLUDE OR INSTALL PHOTOSHOP PLUG-INS THAT ENABLE YOU TO LOAD YOUR DIGITAL IMAGES DIRECTLY INTO PHOTOSHOP. BECAUSE YOU'RE LOADING DIGITAL IMAGES, WHICH TEND TO BE LARGE IN SIZE, YOU'LL SEE BETTER RESULTS WITH A FASTER COMPUTER OFFERING AT LEAST A GIGABYTE OF FREE HARD DISK SPACE. THE REST OF THIS CHAPTER SHOWS YOU HOW TO TRANSFER DIGITAL PICTURES TO YOUR COMPUTER, AS WELL AS HOW TO FIND IMAGES YOU'VE STORED AND HOW TO USE WATERMARKING TO IDENTIFY YOUR CREATIONS.

OBTAINING DIGITAL IMAGES

With the right equipment, you can import all kinds of photographs—be it on a traditional film negative, on photographic paper, on a slide, or from a digital camera—to a computer. This section shows you how to download images from a digital camera, and it reviews the general process of scanning and converting photos into digital images.

DOWNLOADING IMAGES FROM A DIGITAL CAMERA

Almost all cameras include software that enables you to download files from the camera to your computer. Other digital cameras also include bundled software packages that allow you to edit and organize your photos. At a minimum, you must install the software that enables you to download your files; the other software will be optional if you plan to use Photoshop as your primary image-editing program. This section covers the basic steps you can follow to connect your camera to a computer and download images. Refer to your camera's manual for details.

Depending on what type of camera you have, you can either download pictures by connecting the camera to your computer via a cable or by using a storage card adapter. Both are described in the following sections.

CONNECTING WITH CABLES

The first digital cameras supported a serial cable connection to enable cameras to download their files to a computer. The latest 3- and 4-megapixel cameras, however, support the faster USB cable and connector (some cameras also offer serial adapters, as well).

To download images from your camera to a Macintosh or Windows-based system using a USB cable, do the following (note that the specific procedure for your camera might differ a bit; consult your manual for details):

1. Connect the larger end of the USB cable to your computer.
2. Connect the smaller end of the cable to the digital camera.
3. Put the camera into the Play mode.

OTHER CAMERA IMPORTS

Some digital cameras install Photoshop 7 plug-ins that enable you to download images directly from the camera into Photoshop 7. Choose Import from Photoshop 7's File menu to access the camera's Photoshop plug-in (this assumes that the camera is connected to your computer). Windows XP offers built-in import capabilities via Windows Image Acquisition (WIA). If the WIA recognizes your camera or scanner, the camera or scanner name appears on the Import submenu of the File menu in Photoshop.

4. Start the download application on your computer. Choose a menu command in the camera's software application to start downloading the images from the camera to your computer (refer to your camera's manual for details).

 Some cameras allow you to view images only on your computer, and require an additional step to actually copy a file to your hard drive. In other cases, you may not need to use download software; the camera will mount as a disk on the desktop (similar to the way storage card adapters mount, described next), and you can simply copy the images to the desired folder on your system.

USING STORAGE CARD ADAPTERS

A faster way of getting those pictures off the storage card in your camera is to purchase a media card reader peripheral for a desktop computer. There are several USB storage card readers for both Compact Flash and Smart Media storage cards. Most readers work with either a Macintosh or a PC computer. If you plan to upload digital photos frequently, readers present a convenient, cheap ($20-$40 for a basic reader), and attractive alternative to connecting your camera repeatedly.

When you insert a storage card into a reader (or insert a PC card adapter into a laptop), the pictures from your camera mount as a disk on the desktop, as shown next. Double-click on the disk icon to open a folder for the camera storage card; then navigate to the folder that holds the images to copy, if applicable. (My camera creates a separate folder to hold the shots for each date on its Compact Flash card.) You can copy selected images to your hard disk, empty the storage card, and then eject the storage card by dragging its icon to the Trash Can or Recycle Bin icon.

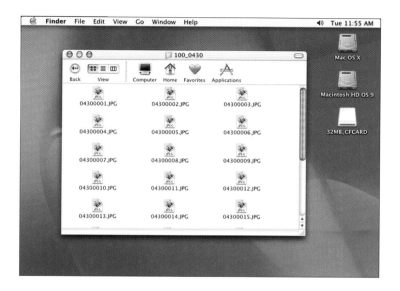

If you have a laptop computer, you can purchase a PC card adapter for the storage card (these start at $10 or so) and access your pictures directly from the card. Simply insert the card into the PC adapter, insert the PC card into a laptop, double-click the icon for the mounted storage media, and copy the pictures to your hard drive. When the image files are on your computer, you can remove the pictures from the storage card, eject the card from the laptop, re-insert the storage card into your camera, and you're ready to take more pictures.

Sony's latest digital cameras store pictures on a Memory Stick. Some of Sony's laptop computers have a Memory Stick port built into them, enabling you to simply insert the Memory Stick and access your pictures. If your laptop lacks this port, you can purchase a floppy disk or PC-card adapter for the Memory Stick.

NEW DOWNLOAD TOOLS IN MAC OS X AND WINDOWS XP

Both of the latest operating systems, Mac OS X and Windows XP, include utilities for downloading digital camera images. (Older models may not be supported, in which case you'll need to rely on the software that came with your camera.)

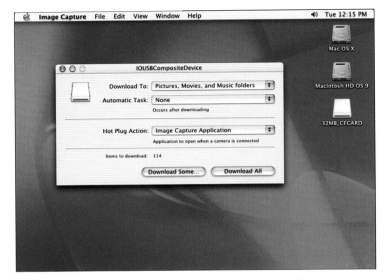

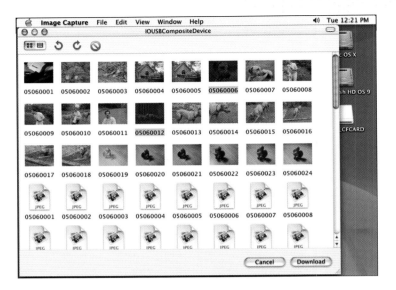

When you attach your camera to your Mac OS X system and select the Play mode, the Image Capture feature loads, as shown above. You can choose the folder to hold the downloaded images using the Download To pop-up menu. If you then click Download All, Image Capture downloads all the images available on the camera's storage media. If you click Download Some, a window appears so that you can choose images to download. Use Command+click to choose the images to download (see below); then click the Download button. After the download finishes, open the Image Capture menu and click Quick Image Capture. Then drag the icon for the mounted storage media to the Trash and disconnect and turn off the camera.

In Windows XP, also start by connecting the camera to the USB port and selecting the camera's Play mode. The Scanner and Camera Wizard starts to load drivers for your camera, if applicable. When you subsequently connect the camera, a window opens to prompt you to choose what action to take with the newly connected media, as shown below. You can choose to copy the pictures to your computer, view an onscreen slide show of your pictures, or print them. Click the desired option and then click OK. When you finish the selected activity, you can power the camera off and then disconnect it.

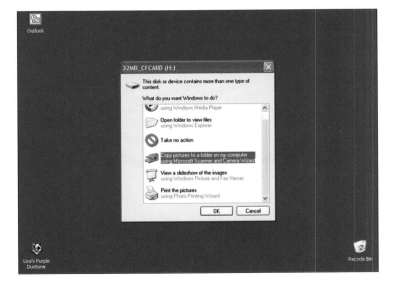

CONVERTING 35MM SLIDES AND NEGATIVES TO DIGITAL IMAGES

If you have 35mm slides or negatives, you can pay your local photo shop to scan them onto a CD-ROM disc using a film scanner, or you can create a Photo CD. If you use this type of service, work with the highest resolution image available on the CD-ROM or Photo CD.

There are also several Web site services such as **www.kodak.com** and **www.shutterfly.com** that will also transfer slides, negatives, and prints for a fee. After your photos are on a CD, you can load them onto your computer and edit them using Photoshop. Other services will convert images and post the digital ones on their Web site where you can download them directly to your computer over the Internet.

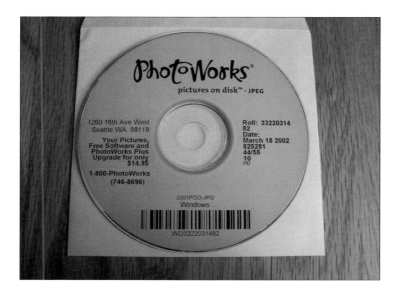

If you're interested in buying a film scanner, the prices will likely change your mind; they can range in price from several hundred to several thousand dollars. Unless you have a large number of pictures, it's probably more economical to send those 35mm slides or negatives to the shop.

 If you have a 35mm camera, you can send your rolls of 35mm film to a Web business to have the pictures developed and printed, and also scanned and posted to Web pages. Some Web sites offer to develop and print a certain number of pictures for free. Visit **www.snapfish.com**, **www.photoworks.com**, **www.ofoto.com**, **www.myfamily.com**, **www.shutterfly.com**, or **www.kodak.com** to find out more about each site's special offers and Web photo services.

CONVERTING PRINT IMAGES TO DIGITAL IMAGES

Chances are, you have several photo albums of pictures taken with everything from instamatic throwaway cameras to high-end cameras wielded by professionals. Fortunately, these pictures are not lost to you now that you've entered the digital world; you can use a scanner to convert these pictures to digital images and place them on your computer.

These days, you can buy several types of flat-bed and sheet-fed scanners and pay reasonable prices ($100 to $300). Film and photo scanners cost a little more (closer to

the $500 price range). Although the traditional flatbed scanner offers the most consistent conversion of color and image into a digital format, you can purchase more inexpensive scanners, such as hand- and paper-fed scanners.

Before scanning an image, consider using a scanner that can capture the highest resolution image. For example, choose a 36-bit scanner over a 24-bit scanner. A 24-bit scanner can capture up to 16.7 million colors for any given pixel, which is the same resolution of a Photoshop RGB image file. If a scanner captures an image at 36 bits, each pixel contains a wider range of color information. A larger, more detailed, image will be captured by a 36-bit scanner, even though your monitor won't be able to display more than 24 bits of color information.

 There really isn't a way to compare a 3- or 4-megapixel camera's image file resolution (approximately 2,048×1,536 to 2,400×1,800 pixels) to a scanner's 24- or 36-bit capture resolution. One of the dynamic elements of a scanner (not found on a digital camera) is that you can configure how many dots per inch (dpi) are captured during the scanning process. Increasing the resolution results in a final picture that looks more rich and realistic. A good general rule to use when taking a picture or scanning an image is to capture the image at the highest possible resolution.

A scanner performs two tasks, similar to what a digital camera does. First, the scanner captures the image placed on the scanner bed. Then it converts the image into a digital file that you can view or save to your hard drive. Low-cost scanners are similar to a copy machine, using one pass of a light source to capture and convert the photo image into a file. Higher-end scanners will have higher-quality CCDs and can support up to three passes of the light source to capture red, green, and blue channel information to produce a higher-quality image.

In order for a scanner to work, you must first install its driver software so the computer can control the scanner hardware. Most scanners are bundled with an application, such as a light version of Photoshop, that enables you to control the scanner, as well as view, edit, and save the scanned image. After the software is installed, you might need to calibrate the scanner to make sure the light source is properly oriented and then configure the color management software to work with the scanner settings.

When you scan an image into your computer, try to set the resolution (dots per inch, or dpi) to at least 600 dpi. The dots-per-inch setting determines how many of the pixels the scanner software will use to create the resulting image. Higher dpi settings tend to capture more image information. Lower dpi settings capture less information.

The scanner software might save the scanned image in a file format other than JPEG, GIF, or TIFF. If Photoshop 7 cannot open the file, try opening it with Adobe ImageReady and then converting it to a Photoshop-compatible file format.

OTHER SCANNER IMPORTS

WIA technology in Windows XP enables you to scan images directly into Photoshop 7. Choose Import from Photoshop 7's File menu to access the WIA choice. The market currently lags behind in offering native driver software for USB scanners under Mac OS X. If you're using Mac OS X, you'll probably have to install and use your software with the Classic Environment. Even so, some scanner software enables you to scan images into Photoshop 7; Photoshop merely loads in the Classic Environment itself for the process to work.

BROWSING IMAGES WITH THE NEW FILE BROWSER

Photoshop 7 includes a new feature called File Browser. File Browser displays a preview thumbnail of each image in the currently selected folder. If you click on an image, you also can see metadata information (such as image size, color mode, and the File Info for a file) in order to verify that you're opening the correct file. The following steps show you how to find and open a file with File Browser.

1. Open the File menu and choose Browse.
2. In the File Browser window that opens, click on the arrows (plus icons in Windows) in the folder tree in the upper-left pane to navigate to the desired folder. Clicking an arrow (plus icon) will display the folders within a particular disk or folder on your system or a network drive.

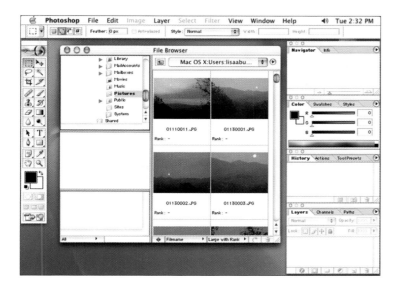

3. Select the desired folder when you see it in the folder tree. The images in that folder will appear in the right pane of the File Browser window, as shown above.

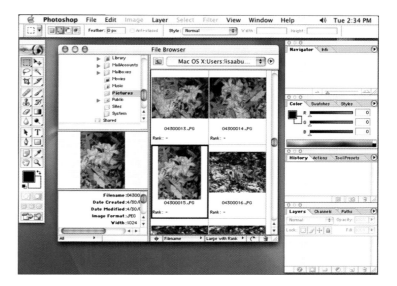

4. To preview an image, click on its thumbnail. Its metadata will appear in the lower-left pane of the File Browser. An additional preview thumbnail appears for you to review as well.
5. To open an image directly in Photoshop, double-click on the image thumbnail in the right pane of the File Browser.
6. Open the Window menu and choose File Browser to close the File Browser window. Or, you can click the window Close button, found on the upper-left corner of the File Browser window in the Mac version of Photoshop, and the upper-right corner of the File Browser window in the Windows version of Photoshop.

WATERMARKING YOUR IMAGES

Photoshop works with digital rights management company Digimarc to enable you to embed a digital watermark in your Photoshop images and read the digital watermark information in other images. Then, others who want to use your images can find your contact information via Digimarc to license the images from you.

To be able to add a digital watermark, you must register online with Digimarc. You can watermark up to 99 images for free. Beyond that, Digimarc charges a subscription fee based on the number of images you plan to watermark per year. You can begin registration within Photoshop, as noted in the following steps.

You must have an image file open, as well as a layer that's not locked, before you start the registration process. Ideally, open an image to which you want to add a digital watermark.

1. Open the Filter menu, select Digimarc, and then choose Embed Watermark. The Embed Watermark dialog box appears.

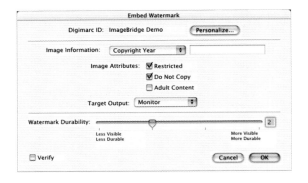

2. Click on Personalize. The Personalize Digimarc ID dialog box will open.
3. Click on Info. Your Web browser will open, and you'll be prompted you to connect to the Internet if you don't have an Internet connection that's always on. Follow the prompts that appear to connect to the Internet. After your system connects, your Web browser will display the initial Digimarc registration page with pricing information.
4. Click on the Sign Up Today link or button. The Digimarc ImageBridge™ Watermarking Subscription Quote Step 1 of 4 page will appear.

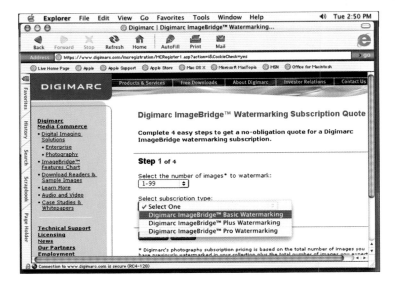

If a Security Notice (Alert) message box appears, click on OK to continue.

5. Choose 1-99 from the top pop-up menu.
6. Choose Digimarc ImageBridge™ Basic Watermarking from the bottom pop-up menu.
7. Follow the prompts to continue the registration process. You'll need to read and accept the Digimarc ImageBridge™ Watermarking Subscription Terms & Conditions page, as well as the license agreement information. A Digimarc ID Signup page then prompts you to enter information to complete the registration.
8. When you finish entering registration information, click on the Submit button, and click on Yes, if you see a Security Notice (Alert) message box. After Digimarc processes your request, the Web page indicating that your ID has been assigned appears.
9. Click on the Print button on the toolbar to print your Digimarc PIN and ID information.
10. Close your Web browser (Explorer, Quit Explorer on the Mac or File, Close in Windows) and disconnect from the Internet.

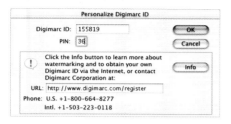

11. Type your Digimarc ID and PIN in the appropriate text boxes in the Personalize Digimarc ID dialog box and then click on OK. The numbers will appear in the boxes. The Personalize Digimarc ID dialog box will close, and the PIN and ID will be stored in the Embed Watermark dialog box.

 For some images, you may see a prompt to flatten the image (combine its layers) or rasterize a shape or text layer (convert the layer's content to a bitmap or raster format rather than a shape or vector format). In such cases, you can click on OK to proceed with flattening/rasterizing and adding the watermark. However, if you haven't finished editing the image, you may want to click on Cancel instead. You can then finish the edits, make a copy of the image file (so you have a version of the file that you can edit later), and embed the watermark in the original.

12. Enter or change any additional watermark settings as needed; then click on OK. The Embed Watermark dialog box will close, and the digital watermark will be applied to the current image.

Embedding a digital watermark adds your Digimarc ID to it and also identifies the image as copyrighted. Digital watermarking doesn't work well on images created primarily with solid colors; in addition, the image must be adequate in size (generally 100×100 pixels for images to be used digitally and 750×750 pixels for images to be printed) to hold the watermark information. Also note that you should embed the watermark before you convert the image to a file format that will compress the image information, such as the JPEG or GIF format. Follow the process detailed next when you need to add a watermark.

The process for embedding the digital image begins as the registration process did. Open the image to which you want to add a watermark in Photoshop. Open the Filter menu, select Digimarc, and then choose Embed Watermark. Flatten the image, if prompted, and then the Embed Watermark dialog box will open.

Specify additional copyright information, as follows:

* Copyright Year—Enter the year Photoshop should mark the image as copyrighted.
* Image Attributes—Check options to identify the image as appropriate for particular types of usage.
* Target Output—Choose an output type from the pop-up menu. Photoshop will adjust the Watermark Durability setting to reflect the selected type of output. (You can further change those settings, if needed.)

If your image is set with 200 dpi or more and you choose Web from the Target Output drop-down list, the DPI Inconsistency dialog box appears to remind you to convert (resample) the image to less than 200 dpi. Click on OK to close the reminder dialog box. You will also see the DPI Inconsistency dialog box if the image is set to less than 300 dpi and you choose Print from the Target Output drop-down list; in this instance, it recommends that you resample the image to 300 dpi or more. Also note that once you add the watermark using one type of target output, you can't repeat the process for another type of output. So, choose the proper Target Output type the first time.

Click on OK. Photoshop will apply the watermark and mark the image as copyrighted. The copyright symbol will appear beside the file name in the file window title bar.

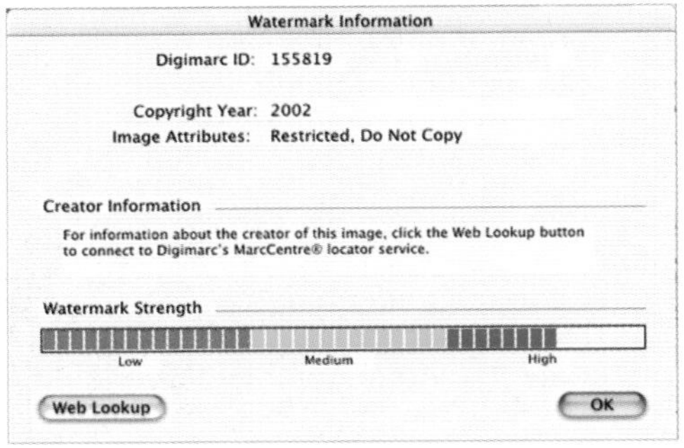

Watermark Information

Digimarc ID: 155819

Copyright Year: 2002
Image Attributes: Restricted, Do Not Copy

Creator Information

For information about the creator of this image, click the Web Lookup button to connect to Digimarc's MarcCentre® locator service.

Watermark Strength

Low   Medium   High

Web Lookup   OK

When you open an image that you think has a digital watermark in Photoshop, you can check for the watermark and look up the identity of the image's creator. Open the Filter menu, select Digimarc, and then choose Read Watermark. The Watermark Information dialog box will open. It will identify the creator ID (Digimarc ID) for the person or organization that created the image, the copyright year, and the usage restrictions that were placed on the image. Click on Web Lookup. Your Web browser will open, and your system will connect to the Internet, if required. The Digimarc Web site then displays the Digimarc information for the image's creator. You can print the information, if needed, and then close your Web browser and disconnect from the Internet. Finally, click on OK in the Watermark Information dialog box to close it.

PICTURE INFO AND PREFERENCES

CHAPTER 3

VIEWING PICTURE INFORMATION AND SETTING PREFERENCES

WHEN YOU TAKE A ZILLION PICTURES WITH A DIGITAL CAMERA, IT MIGHT BECOME DIFFICULT TO REMEMBER WHICH SETTINGS YOU CHOSE FOR A PARTICULAR PICTURE, OR EVEN THE GENERAL PHYSICAL CHARACTERISTICS OF A PICTURE, SUCH AS HOW BIG IT IS, OR WHY AND WHEN IT WAS TAKEN. SOME 3- AND 4-MEGAPIXEL CAMERAS CREATE A FILE ON THE STORAGE CARD CONTAINING THE APERTURE, SHUTTER SPEED, EXPOSURE, FILE FORMAT, AND OTHER INFORMATION FOR EACH PICTURE TAKEN. USING PHOTOSHOP, YOU CAN ADD YOUR OWN CUSTOM INFORMATION TO AN IMAGE FILE, AND ALSO FIND OUT OTHER INFORMATION ABOUT A PICTURE AFTER YOU'VE OPENED IT. CLICK ON THE FILE MENU AND CHOOSE OPEN; THEN DOUBLE-CLICK ON AN IMAGE FILE TO OPEN IT.

VIEWING AND CHANGING A FILE'S SIZE AND RESOLUTION

If you plan to post your pictures to a Web site or print them, you'll probably need to know the dimensions of the original file. In either case, you'll probably be resizing a picture so that it can load quickly to a Web browser or a printer. When you open a file in Photoshop, you might only see a reduced or partial image in the workspace. Choose Navigator from the Window menu to figure out how much of the image is visible in the workspace.

In addition to (or instead of) changing the file's size, you can change its resolution. For example, you could increase an image from 72 pixels per inch to 300 pixels per inch.

To find out your image's dimensions in pixels, first open that image in Photoshop; then do the following:

1. Choose Image Size from the Image menu.

2. View the Width and Height of the entire image in the Image Size window. The width and height data can be represented in pixels or as a percentage of the original size of the image.

3. Type a different value into either the Pixel Dimensions Width or Height text fields if you want to change the size of the image in the image window. If the Constrain Proportions check box is selected, Photoshop automatically determines the secondary dimension of the entire image.

4. Click on the Resample Image pop-up menu to choose a resampling or interpolation method for the image. When this option is selected, Photoshop uses an algorithm to determine which pixels to remove or add to an image to resize the image to the selected dimensions.

5. If needed, enter a new value in the Resolution text box. (Note that the Resample Image check box must be checked if you want to change both the image's size and resolution.)

6. Click OK to save any changes you've made or click Cancel to ignore any changes made to the Image Size window.

Take the highest quality image possible with your digital camera. Whether you plan to create a thumbnail or the full 2,048×1,536-pixel image, it's always best to start with as much picture information as you can. After all, you can always take pixels away from a picture, but adding pixels to a low-resolution image doesn't always have the best results.

Choose Document Sizes from the pop-up menu that appears when you click the arrow to the left of the scroll area at the bottom of the image window. The actual and current uncompressed image sizes appear at the bottom-left corner of the document window. Even though a JPEG file occupies 1MB of hard disk space, the same file can grow up to 12MB when opened in Photoshop. Photoshop stores this image data in its scratch disk space. See the section at the end of this chapter called "Configuring Plug-Ins and Scratch Disk Preferences" to find out how to select up to four scratch disks.

View the dimensions of the image window by Command/Ctrl+ clicking just left of the pop-up menu at the bottom of the image window. Title Width, Title Height, Image Width, and Image Height data will appear in a pop-up menu.

VIEWING A FILE'S TYPE AND COLOR MODE

Most digital cameras create JPEG images as the default image file format. However, other file formats, such as TIFF, are also possible. No matter what format you use, however, Photoshop converts the image data and displays it in RGB (red, green, and blue) mode when you open an image file. Although the image data is represented in reds, greens, and blues, the original file remains unchanged on your hard drive. Photoshop uses a color mode to determine the color model for how an image is displayed and printed. Most of the examples in this book use RGB (red, green, blue) mode. Some use grayscale mode. Color modes determine the number of colors that can be displayed in an image, and also affect the number of channels and the file size of an image.

To determine the file's format and color mode, do the following:

1. With the file whose type you want to determine open in the Photoshop workspace, choose File, Save As.

2. The file's current format is selected in the Format pop-up menu in the Save As dialog box.
3. Click on Cancel to exit the Save As dialog box without saving any changes.

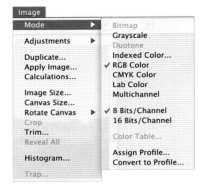

4. To view the color mode of the image window, choose Mode from the Image menu. A check mark appears beside the selected mode.

5. Press Esc to close the Image menu.

 Most digital cameras append three letters to the end of an image file to indicate the type of file it is. For example, if a file name ends in JPG, it's probably a JPEG image file.

VIEWING COLOR SETTINGS FOR A FILE

Most of the color-management controls in Photoshop are located in the Color Settings dialog box. Photoshop comes with seven preconfigured color settings. Each setting consists of a group of predefined color configurations designed to produce consistent color for publishing to the Web and other forms of publishing such as prepress output. You can choose a predefined setting or create your own custom combinations of settings. However, you must choose your color-management settings before opening or creating a file.

The Color Settings window consists of two main sections: workspaces and color-management policies. A workspace represents the default color profile for a newly created document, using the related color model. If Apple RGB is selected as the current RGB workspace, each new RGB document created will use colors as defined by the Apple

RGB gamut. The default color workspace setting for RGB files is RGB IEC61966-2.1. If you plan to share image files across computer platforms, use this color setting.

A color-management policy is a predefined color-management configuration that can be set in the Color Settings window. A warning will appear to let you override a default policy behavior on a case-by-case basis if you choose to use this feature for RGB, CMYK, or grayscale color management.

To view Photoshop's (or change) color settings, do the following:

1. Open the Photoshop (Mac) or Edit (Windows) menu and choose Color Settings.

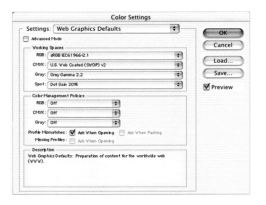

2. Click on the Settings pop-up menu to view the preconfigured settings installed with Photoshop.

3. Review the settings chosen for Working Spaces and Color Management Policies.

4. Click on any pop-up menu to view additional options for each setting. Change any options as needed.

5. Click on OK to close the dialog box.

 Press Command/Ctrl+Shift+K to open the Color Settings window.

SETTING YOUR PREFERENCES

Many of Photoshop's default settings, such as where the floating windows are located in the workspace when you start the application and how files are named when being saved, can be changed in the Preferences window. On a Windows PC, preferences are stored in the Registry. On a Mac, they are stored in an Adobe Photoshop 7 Settings folder in the Preferences folder of the System folder. Preference settings are saved only when you exit or quit the application.

CHOOSING GENERAL PREFERENCES

Photoshop's General Preferences enables you to configure those features that affect any image window. For example, if you resize an image, the Resample Image pop-up menu contains a default value. You can change the default value for sampling or interpolating an image—as well as many other default settings—by using the General settings in the Preferences dialog box.

The following is a brief summary of the General Preferences settings for Photoshop:

❋ Color Picker—Enables you to choose the kind of color picker window that appears whenever you want to select a foreground or background color for a drawing tool, stroke, fill layer, or gradient.

❋ Interpolation—Determines which algorithm Photoshop uses to resize an image. The algorithm resamples the pixels in an image to determine how to restructure the resulting larger or smaller image. Bicubic interpolation, which is the default setting, provides the best quality image.

❋ Redo Key and History States—Control how many times you can undo any number of previously executed commands or tasks in the image window.

❋ Print Keys—Controls which key combinations you must press to preview and print an image or print it directly.

❋ Export Clipboard—If you select an image in the window and choose the Copy command from the Edit menu, the image in the Clipboard is available to any other applications from the Paste command. This feature prevents the image in the Clipboard from being deleted when you switch to another application.

❋ Show Tools Tips—If you let your cursor hover over a tool in the toolbox, this feature enables Photoshop to display a small window containing the name of that tool and the letter you can use as its shortcut.

❋ Keyboard Zoom Resizes Windows—If you use the Command/Ctrl+Plus or Command/Ctrl+Minus keys to zoom into or out of a picture, checking this check box will automatically resize the window to match the changing image size.

❋ Auto-update open documents—If you have the same image document (such as a Photoshop document) open in ImageReady and Photoshop, selecting this check box will update the image in Photoshop each time a change is made in the non-Photoshop application. Depending on the size of the image you are working on, this auto-updating feature can slow down Photoshop, as well as your computer system.

❋ Show Asian Text Options—If you have Japanese, Chinese, Korean, or other Asian-language fonts, check this feature to view additional text-related settings.

❋ Use System Shortcut Keys—Controls whether Photoshop uses OS X or Photoshop shortcut keys for the View, Extras and Image, Adjust, Curves commands. When checked, Photoshop uses the OS X shortcut keys.

❋ Beep When Done—If checked, the computer's alert sound is played whenever a progress bar indicator-related task is completed.

❋ Dynamic Color Sliders—Enables you to dynamically change the foreground or background colors from the Color palette window. Drag each color slider to define the color you want to use with a drawing tool, stroke, or fill layer.

❋ Save Palette Locations—Preserves the last locations of the palette windows when you exit or quit Photoshop.

❋ Show Font Names in English—Displays non-English font names, such as some Asian fonts, in English.

❋ Use Shift Key for Tool Switch—Enables you to press the Shift key, combined with a letter key on the keyboard, to cycle through a tool in the toolbox.

✳ Reset All Warning Dialogs—Reverts dialog warnings to their default configuration. Some warning dialogs can be configured to never appear if a check box is selected the first time you see it. Pressing this button allows all those warning dialogs to appear.

✳ Reset All Warning Dialogs—Turns all warning dialog boxes back on, as if it's the first time you're using Photoshop.

To access these preferences, do the following:

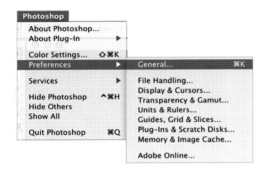

1. Open the Photoshop (Mac) or Edit (Windows) menu, choose Preferences, and select General.

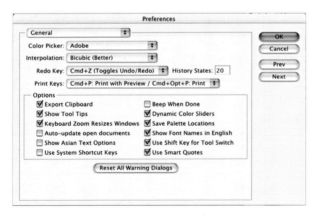

2. Examine the default settings, changing any you desire by selecting them from the pop-up windows or checking the check boxes. (I usually

do not change any of the default settings.) Most of the general preferences affect the user interface, such as whether Tool Tips appear in the toolbox and where or how windows appear in the workspace.

 Bicubic interpolation provides the best image quality if an image is resized. This is probably one setting you won't want to change.

 If you've changed the location or order of any of the floating windows (also called floating palettes), select Reset Palette Locations from the Window menu to restore the floating windows to their default locations on the right side of the workspace.

3. To change the number of times you can undo tasks, type a lower or higher number into the History States text box.

4. Click on OK to accept your changes and close the Preferences dialog box.

CHANGING PREFERENCES FOR HANDLING FILES

Many of the things that Photoshop does when you start the application, open an image, or save a file can be adjusted by accessing Photoshop's File Handling preferences settings. Most of the default settings should work great for most people, but if changing a little feature here or there can make you more productive, keep reading.

Photoshop is initially set up to automatically save a preview image of a file when you choose the Save command. It also automatically changes the file name extension of any file you save. You can adjust these settings in the Preferences dialog box. Here's how:

1. Choose Preferences from the Photoshop (Mac) or Edit (Windows) menu and then select File Handling. Alternatively, you can press Command/Ctrl + K to open the Preferences window. Then press Command/Ctrl + 2 to view the File Handling preferences.

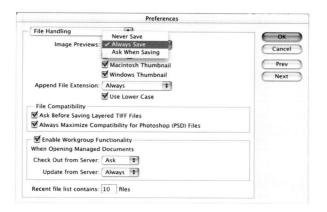

2. Click on the Image Previews pop-up menu to choose whether you want to save a thumbnail image of the picture whenever you execute the Save command.

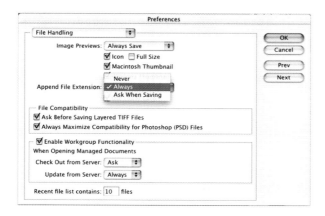

3. Click on the Append File Extension pop-up menu to view the options for this preference.

4. To activate any of the various features in the box, check their corresponding check box.

5. Type a number in the Recent File List Contains text box to set the number of previously opened files that appear when you choose the Open Recent menu command from the File menu.

6. Click on OK to accept your changes and close the Preferences dialog box.

SELECTING DISPLAY AND CURSOR PREFERENCES

Photoshop stores an image's color information in 8-bit grayscale channels if an image is set to RGB, CMYK, Lab, or multi-channel color modes. Alpha channels are used for creating and storing masks. Each alpha channel is an 8-bit grayscale image. Choose the Display and Cursor preferences command to adjust how alpha channels are displayed in the Channels window. You can also change the cursors for the toolbox tools by using the Display & Cursors settings in the Preferences dialog box.

1. Open the Preferences (Mac) or Edit (Windows) menu, choose Preferences, and select Display & Cursors.

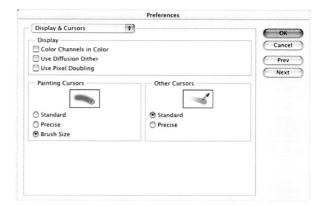

2. You have a few display settings available to you:
* Color Channels in Color—Each color channel in the Channels palette appears in red, green, or blue (if an image is in RGB mode) instead of as a grayscale image if this option is enabled.
* Use Diffusion Dither—Enable this option to soften hard edges of color in the image window.
* Use Pixel Doubling—If this check box is checked, it provides faster previews with the Move tool. Pixels in the image are temporarily doubled, halving the resolution of the image.

 For more information about channels, see Chapter 9, "Customizing Images with Masks," or Chapter 10, "Making Images Stand Out with Channels."

Don't confuse display preferences with color-management features. Display preferences only change the way the image appears in the document or palette windows. These options have no effect on the pixels in the image file. Choose Color Settings from the Photoshop (Mac) or Edit (Windows) menu to view the color-management settings for Photoshop.

3. Click on the Standard, Precise, or Brush Size radio button as needed in the Painting Cursors area. The cursor you select appears in the Painting Cursors preview box.
4. Select on either the Standard or Precise radio button in the Other Cursors area. The cursor you select appears in the Other Cursors preview box.
5. Click on OK to accept your changes and close the Preferences dialog box.

ADJUSTING TRANSPARENCY AND GAMUT PREFERENCES

When you display the Transparency & Gamut settings in the Preferences dialog box, you can adjust Photoshop's transparency grid. The transparency grid represents the transparent areas of a layer in the image. Wherever you see the transparency grid in an image, Photoshop is telling you there's no image data in that part of the image. See Chapter 11, "Experimenting with Layers," to find out more about layers and transparency.

Additionally, in the Gamut Warning area, you can specify what color appears when an image contains a color that is not printable. A gamut, or color space, defines the range of printable colors for any particular image. The range of colors you can see is much larger than the RGB gamut, or any other color model. To avoid creating images that are not printable, configure Photoshop to display a gamut warning to help you identify the colors that are not defined by the gamut.

The transparency grid appears in the document window if all or part of an image is defined to be transparent. The default grid consists of white and gray squares. To configure these settings, do the following:

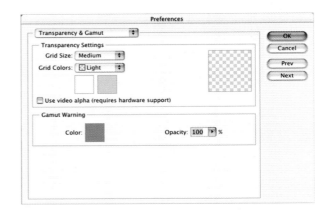

1. Open the Photoshop (Mac) or Edit (Windows) menu, choose Preferences, and select Transparency & Gamut.
2. View the Grid Size options for the transparency grid in the pop-up menu. Medium is the default setting; choose Large or Small to increase or decrease the size of the squares in the grid. Preview the grid in the thumbnail located to the right of the pop-up menu. Choose None to make transparent areas appear white in the document window.
3. Click on the Grid Colors pop-up menu to choose a different combination of grid colors for the transparency grid. Alternatively, click on either one of the color picker squares to select the color of your choice from the color picker window. Click on OK to save the newly selected color.
4. Click on the color square in the Gamut Warning area to pick a gamut warning color. A Color Picker window appears. Click on a color to select it. Click on OK to save the color change. The gamut warning color will replace any out-of-gamut colors when the image is previewed. Check the Color Settings window to make sure the color-management settings match the gamut warning settings.
5. Type a number into the Opacity text field. A lower value reveals more of the underlying image below the gamut warning color.
6. Click on OK to save your changes and exit the Preferences dialog box.

 Press Command/Ctrl+K to open the Preferences window. Press Command/Ctrl + numbers one through eight to access each of the Preferences panels.

SETTING UNITS AND RULERS PREFERENCES

The Units & Rulers settings in the Preferences dialog box enable you to specify default ruler settings. Rulers appear in every document window; you use them to align the artwork you create or edit in Photoshop. Additionally, this window enables you to set preferences for column size and point/pica size. These settings affect the way Photoshop works with actions so that it relies more on proportional size and location information than on specific pixels or other measurement information. See the section on the Actions palette in Chapter 4, "Using Photoshop 7 Tools."

1. Open the Photoshop (Mac) or Edit (Windows) menu, choose Preferences, and select Units & Rulers.
2. Click on the Rulers pop-up menu to view a list of available units for the window ruler. Select the one you want to use. (To view your ruler changes later, open an image document and then choose Show Rulers from the View menu.)
3. Click on the Width or Gutter pop-up menus to set the column width unit to inches, points, picas, or centimeters. Type a number in the Width or Gutter text boxes to change the default widths for these settings.

 To create a document containing columns, choose New from the File menu. Then click on the Width pop-up menu and choose Columns.

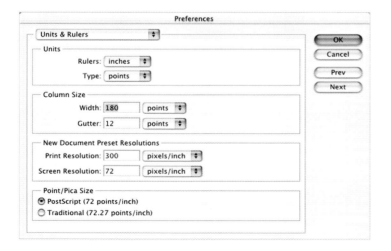

4. Click on the Print Resolution or Screen Resolution pop-up menus to set the default resolution unit pixels/inch or pixels/cm. Type a number in the Print Resolution or Screen Resolution text boxes to change the default resolution settings.
5. Choose PostScript to set the Point/Pica size for the document to 72 points per inch if you are printing to a PostScript device. You probably don't need to select this option, but if you do choose Traditional, the Point/Pica Size is set to 72.27 points per inch.
6. Click on OK to save your changes and exit the Preferences dialog box.

CUSTOMIZING GUIDES, GRIDS, AND SLICES

Guides and grids are visual tools that can be applied to the image window. You can move, remove, or lock a guide or grid to help design your image document. Slices help you define functional areas in images that you're preparing for the Web. Guides, grids, and slices cannot be printed. Use the Guides, Grid & Slices settings in the Preferences dialog box to add or change the color of guide, grid, and slice lines. For example, you might want to create a guide with different colors than the image you are creating or editing.

 To view the grid, open the View menu, point to Show, and then click Grid. The grid lines are drawn over the image window. Choose New Guide from the View menu to create a guideline. Then click on the View menu, point to Show, and click Guide to view the guide in the window.

1. Open the Photoshop (Mac) or Edit (Windows) menu, choose Preferences, and select Guides, Grid & Slices.
2. Click on the Color pop-up menu in either the Guides or Grid area (or the Line Color pop-up menu in the Slices area) to view your color options; select a color to change it. Choose Custom to pick any color you like from the Color Picker window. Click on OK to save the newly selected color and return to the Preferences window.

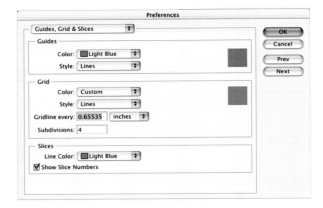

3. Change the style of guides or grids from the corresponding pop-up menus. Guides can appear as lines or dashed lines. Grids can be displayed as lines, dashed lines, or dots.
4. Set the distance between gridlines by typing a number in the Gridline Every text box. Specify the unit of measurement in the accompanying pop-up menu.
5. Adjust the number of subdivisions for the grid by typing a larger or smaller number in the Subdivisions text box.
6. If you want to disable the display of slice numbers in slices, clear the Show Slice Numbers check box.
7. Click on OK to save your changes and exit the Preferences dialog box.

CONFIGURING PLUG-INS AND SCRATCH DISK PREFERENCES

It might be hard to believe that with 50 or more megabytes of memory allocated to Photoshop, it also needs hard disk space to run its special brand of virtual memory so that you can open, edit, and save an image document. Most image data from any open image file is stored on the hard disk in Photoshop's scratch disk. As you open, edit, save, and close image files in Photoshop, the scratch disk loads, moves, and deletes data from one to four scratch disks. You can also configure Photoshop to recognize plug-in files that are not located in Photoshop's Plug-ins folder.

Photoshop's scratch disk settings work with Windows or Mac OS (prior to OS X) virtual memory settings. Adobe

recommends setting the Mac OS virtual memory setting to 1MB more than the amount of physical memory installed in your computer. I turn virtual memory off on my Mac, but leave it on with my Windows PC when I use Photoshop.

To alter the scratch-disk settings, as well as enable additional plug-ins for your system, use the Plug-Ins & Scratch Disks Preferences window and review the following list of items:

1. Open the Photoshop (Mac) or Edit (Windows) menu, choose Preferences, and select Plug-Ins & Scratch Disks.

2. Click on a pop-up menu to assign a hard disk as a scratch disk. Choose the hard disk with the greatest amount of free space as the first scratch disk. The amount of scratch disk space affects the number and size of files you can work on in Photoshop.
3. Check the Additional Plug-Ins Folder check box to enable additional plug-ins folders. These plug-ins appear in the Filter menu. There are many software publishers of Photoshop plug-in packages. Some of these publishers include Alien Skin, Altamira Group, Andromeda Software, Auto F/X, Chromagraphics, Xaos Tools, MagicMask, Scantastic, and 3D Dizzy. Some of the more popular plug-in packages are Total Xaos, Eye Candy, and Xenofex. To find out more about Photoshop plug-ins, visit **www.adobe.com/store/plugins/ photoshop/main.html**.

4. In the Choose an Additional Plug-Ins Folder dialog box that opens, navigate to and select the folder where you will install your Photoshop plug-ins.
5. Click on OK to save your changes and exit the Preferences dialog box.

 On a Windows PC, Photoshop uses a hard disk volume as its primary paging disk, in addition to a primary scratch disk. However, the paging disk is usually the startup disk. Choose a volume that is not the startup disk as the primary scratch disk in the Preferences window. If the same volume is used for both features, Photoshop's performance may be noticeably slower.

CHANGING IMAGE CACHE PREFERENCES

Image caches are used to speed up your access to all the application code and image data spread across your hard disk and the 50 or more megabytes of memory allocated to Photoshop. A cache is a small amount of disk space set aside to store images that have been loaded into memory previously. Photoshop uses the cache settings to determine how much memory and disk space to allocate when you open a file. The higher the number, the more memory and disk space is set aside for each file. When you reload a cached image, Photoshop uses the image data stored in memory and on your hard drive to make the contents of the window redraw more quickly to your screen. To alter your cache settings, do the following:

1. Open the Photoshop (Mac) or Edit (Windows) menu, choose Preferences, and select Memory & Image Cache.
2. Type a number into the Cache Levels text box to set the number of cache levels for Photoshop. Enter 4 or 5 if you plan to work with image files that are up to 50MB.

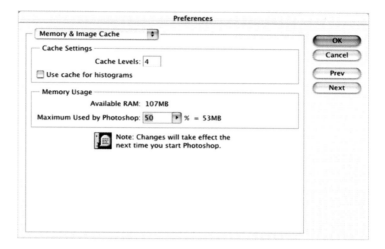

3. By default, the Use Cache for Histograms option is checked. Photoshop uses histograms to provide a snapshot of the tonal range of a picture and to illustrate how pixels are distributed across an image, graphing the number of pixels at each level of color intensity. A higher black bar in a histogram indicates that there are more pixels in that particular color intensity level. Open an image and choose Histogram from the Image menu. When the Use Cache for Histograms option is checked, Photoshop displays a histogram based on a representative sampling of pixels in an image, instead of sampling all the pixels in an image.
4. Adjust the Maximum Used by Photoshop setting in the Memory Usage area to increase the amount of RAM allocated to Photoshop the next time you start the program. You can click on the arrow beside the Maximum Used by Photoshop text box, drag the slider, and click the arrow again to specify the desired amount of memory. Or you can drag over the entry in the Maximum Used by Photoshop text box and type a new entry.
5. Click on OK to save your changes and to close the Preferences dialog box.

PART 2

PHOTOSHOP 7 BASICS

THE PHOTOSHOP WORKSPACE CONSISTS OF A MENU BAR, TOOLBOX, FLOATING PALETTE WINDOWS, IMAGE WINDOW, AND THE OPTIONS TOOLBAR. EACH WINDOW IN THE WORKSPACE CAN BE CLOSED OR HIDDEN BY CHOOSING THE CORRES- PONDING COMMAND FROM THE WINDOW MENU OR BY CLICKING THE CLOSE BOX OF A WINDOW. DRAG THE TITLE BAR OF A WINDOW OR TOOLBAR TO MOVE IT TO A NEW LOCATION IN THE WORKSPACE. PRESS THE F KEY TWICE TO HIDE THE DESKTOP AND MENU BAR. CLICK ON THE WINDOW MENU, SELECT WORKSPACE, AND CHOOSE RESET PALETTE LOCATIONS TO RETURN THE PALETTES TO THEIR DEFAULT LOCATIONS IN THE WORKSPACE. THE PHOTOSHOP WORKSPACE CAN BE INTIMIDATING; HOWEVER, AS YOU LEARN TO INTERACT WITH THE WORKSPACE AND YOUR IMAGES, YOU'LL EVENTUALLY CUSTOMIZE A MORE EFFICIENT, COMFORTABLE WORKSPACE. THIS PART OF THE BOOK FAMILIARIZES YOU WITH THE PHOTOSHOP WORKSPACE AND SHOWS YOU HOW TO DO SOME BASIC TASKS, SUCH AS CORRECTING AN IMAGE, APPLYING AN EFFECT, OR CREATING A MASK.

CHAPTER 4

USING PHOTOSHOP 7 TOOLS

THIS CHAPTER GIVES YOU A QUICK TOUR OF THE TOOLS AND
WINDOWS IN PHOTOSHOP 7 THAT YOU WILL MOST LIKELY USE
TO OPEN, EDIT, AND CREATE WEB- AND PRINT-READY DIGITAL
PICTURES. SEVERAL WINDOWS APPEAR IN THE WORKSPACE
WHEN YOU FIRST OPEN PHOTOSHOP. THE TOOLBOX OPENS ON
THE LEFT AND FOUR FLOATING PALETTE WINDOWS (THREE IN
THE WINDOWS VERSION OF PHOTOSHOP) OPEN ON THE RIGHT
SIDE OF THE WORKSPACE. IF YOU CLICK ON A TOOL, OPTIONS
FOR THAT TOOL APPEAR IN THE OPTIONS BAR AT THE TOP OF
THE WORKSPACE.

ANATOMY OF THE TOOLBOX

Photoshop 7 is packed with 55 selection and drawing tools—22 of which initially appear in the toolbox window. Each tool has a corresponding letter that you can press to make the tool the active tool in the image window. Although you can use all these tools to work with digital pictures, this book focuses on those you'll use most frequently to create and edit digital pictures with Photoshop 7 and ImageReady. The toolbox resides on the left side of the Photoshop workspace. When you select a tool, the bar below the menu bar, which Adobe calls the options bar, changes to offer the options pertaining to the selected tool or palette.

Rectangular Marquee Tool [M]/Elliptical Marquee Tool [M]/Single Row Marquee Tool/Single Column Marquee Tool

Lasso Tool/Polygonal Lasso Tool/Magnetic Lasso Tool [M]

Crop Tool [C]

Healing Brush Tool/Patch Tool [J]

Clone Stamp Tool/Pattern Stamp Tool [S]

Eraser Tool/Background Eraser Tool/Magic Eraser Tool [E]

Blur Tool/Sharpen Tool/Smudge Tool [R]

Path Selection Tool/Direct Selection Tool [A]

Pen Tool [P]/Freeform Pen Tool [P]/Add Anchor Point Tool/Delete Anchor Point Tool/Convert Point Tool

Notes Tool/Audio Annotation Tool [N]

Hand Tool [H]

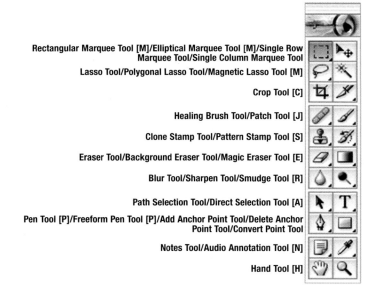

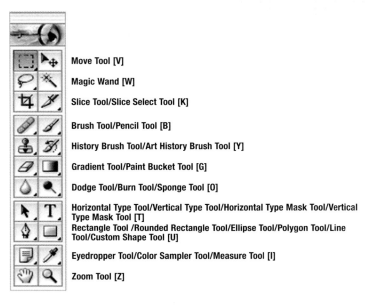

Move Tool [V]

Magic Wand [W]

Slice Tool/Slice Select Tool [K]

Brush Tool/Pencil Tool [B]

History Brush Tool/Art History Brush Tool [Y]

Gradient Tool/Paint Bucket Tool [G]

Dodge Tool/Burn Tool/Sponge Tool [O]

Horizontal Type Tool/Vertical Type Tool/Horizontal Type Mask Tool/Vertical Type Mask Tool [T]

Rectangle Tool /Rounded Rectangle Tool/Ellipse Tool/Polygon Tool/Line Tool/Custom Shape Tool [U]

Eyedropper Tool/Color Sampler Tool/Measure Tool [I]

Zoom Tool [Z]

SELECTION TOOLS

You use the selection tools to select a specific area, a range of colors, or an image that has been pasted into a Photoshop window. You'll find more than a dozen selection tools in the toolbox. Several are visible, and the rest are hidden. Control-click (right-click in Windows) on a tool with an arrow in the lower-right corner to view a shortcut menu of related tools; then click on the tool to use.

You'll find the following tools indispensable as you use Photoshop 7:

 ✳ **Move tool.** Use this to select and move any object or image in the window.

 ✳ **Marquee tools.** Use these to select a rectangular, ellipse, single row, or single column of information in the window.

 ✳ **Magic Wand tool.** Enables you to click on a color to select a common range of colors in an image. For example, select a particular shade of blue in a blue sky by using the Magic Wand instead of trying to use one of the other selection tools, like the rectangle or lasso.

* **Crop tool.** Trim the edges off a picture with this tool. Alternatively, use the Image Size window (open the Image menu and choose Image Size) to resize the entire image.
* **Slice tools.** Use these tools to cut or break up a large image into multiple, smaller files called slices. Slicing an image enables it to load more quickly when viewed by a Web browser.
* **Hand tool.** Move the content in the window with the Hand tool.
* **Zoom tool.** Zoom into or away from the window with the Zoom tool.

Most 1-, 2-, and 3-megapixel cameras create large images. Photoshop automatically opens these files at a smaller scale, such as at 50%, so you can view the entire image without having to scroll around the window.

IMAGE-EDITING TOOLS

Whether you are touching up a photo or creating a photo-realistic image, Photoshop provides a full range of image-editing tools for editing both bitmap and vector graphics. Photos are bitmap or pixel-based graphics. Bitmap graphics don't scale well. For example, if you try to resize an 8×10 pixel image to 400×400 pixels, chances are you probably won't recognize the original, small image. Vector graphics, on the other hand, are calculated by using software algorithms, designed to retain image quality as the image grows or shrinks in size. Use the shape tools to create vector graphics, such as buttons and line art to use with your photos and Web pages.

* **Eyedropper tools.** Choose from a Color Sampler, Measure, or the traditional Eyedropper tool to select colors for image editing. Select the Eyedropper tool. Then click on a color in the window. The Eyedropper replaces the foreground color in the color well. Holding down the Option key while selecting a color replaces the background color in the color well.

* **Healing Brush and Patch tools.** Use these two new tools to repair scratches, stains, and spots that appeared in the original photo, as well as artifacts created by digital capture and processing techniques. You select an area in the image to use to serve as the patch or repair "pattern" to apply and then click to apply the change to the damaged location in the image.

* **Stamp tools.** Clone part of an image with the Clone Stamp tool, or use the Pattern Stamp tool to add a pattern to an image.
* **Mask tools.** Use a selection tool to select part of an image. Apply the Quick Mask tool to the image. The selected area remains editable, while the unselected area cannot be edited. Mask tools let you customize specific areas of an image without the risk of accidentally changing the rest of the image.

* **Drawing and Text tools.** Choose drawing tools, such as a brush, pencil, or pen, to create a bitmap or vector graphic in any image window.

* **Color Selection tools.** Change or switch the foreground and background colors from the toolbox using these tools.

SAMPLING BRUSHES AND PALETTES

Photoshop 7 enables you to create your own custom brushes, giving you maximum creative power for editing and developing image files. The fastest way to create a new brush is to base it on a shape available in your image. To sample a brush, you have to select a portion of the image on a layer by using one of the selection tools.

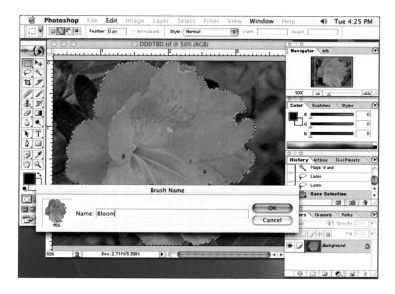

Select the image content to save as a new brush shape. Open the Edit menu and choose Define Brush. The Brush Name dialog box will open. Type a brush name in the Name text box and then click on OK. The new brush will be included in the Brush drop-down list on the options bar choices for painting tools.

Photoshop 7 offers a new Brushes palette that you can use to work with available brushes, including custom brushes that you've created. You can use one of two methods to open (or hide) the Brushes palette.

1. Open the Window menu and choose Brushes. The Brushes palette will open in its own window (or close).
   OR
2. Click on the Toggle the Brushes Palette button at the right end of the options bar when a painting tool has been selected. The Brushes palette will open in its own window (or close).

Using a custom brush shape works just like using any other brush shape provided with Photoshop. This next set of steps shows how to select a custom brush to get you excited about the possibilities in your own work.

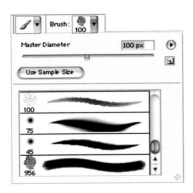

1. Click on the Paintbrush tool in the toolbox. It will become the active tool.
2. Open the Brush pop-up menu on the options bar and click on the custom brush to use. Also, drag the Master Diameter slider to adjust the brush size; then close the pop-up menu. The custom brush you selected will become the active brush shape.

 Custom brushes typically appear at the bottom of the list of brush choices.

3. Select the foreground color using the method of your choice. The color you select will become active for the Paintbrush.

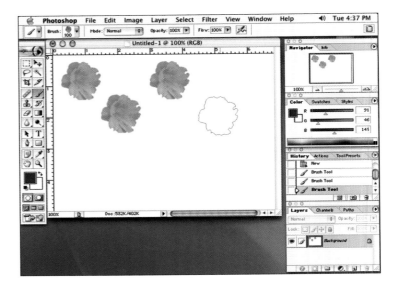

4. Click on the picture in the work area. Each time you click, a paint stroke in the shape of the brush will appear.

NAVIGATING THE PALETTE WINDOWS

By default, Photoshop opens four floating palette windows (three in the Windows version) to the right of the image window. Each window can contain one or all possible palettes. Each palette contains unique information about the image in the window. Some palettes enable you to modify the image, too.

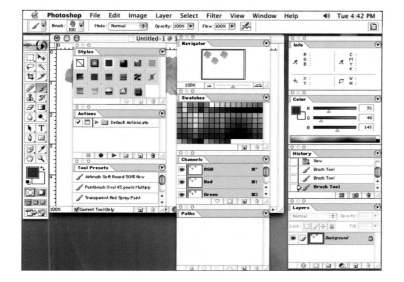

You can open and hide each palette window using the Window menu; you also can close or hide a palette by clicking on its window Close box. You can drag each tab in a palette window to its own separate window. If you dragged each of the palette tabs into its window, you'd find 11 floating palettes. As shown in the accompanying figure, these palettes include the following:

❋ The Navigator palette enables you to adjust the magnification level or scroll an image instead of manually resizing the image window.

❋ The Info palette displays the RGB and CMYK color values wherever you place the mouse pointer in the image window. It also shows current x and y coordinates of the mouse pointer.

❋ The Color palette displays the current foreground and background colors. Type in a new value for each color or drag the sliders to change a color. Alternatively, click the color ramp at the bottom of the window to pick a new foreground color. Option/Alt+Click to choose a background color.

❋ The Swatches palette enables you to choose a new foreground or background color, or save or load a set of colors to the Swatches window. Click to choose a foreground color and Command/Ctrl+click to choose a background color.

❋ The Styles palette displays layer styles—predefined or custom groupings of layer effects. Click on a style to apply it to a layer in the image window.

❋ The History palette shows each edited state of the image for the current work session. Click on a state to revert a document to a previous edit. The History palette is cleared when you quit or exit Photoshop.

❋ The Actions palette enables you to record, play, or edit tasks and save or load action files. For example, if you create the action that applies a filter effect to an image, you can apply that action to other images using the Batch command in the File, Automate submenu.

❋ The Layers palette shows a list of all layers and layer sets of an image. Layers appear in the order they are organized in the image window. For example, the background layer is always at the bottom of the list. You can create, hide, display, copy, merge, view, and delete layers from this palette.

❋ The Channels palette displays a list of color channels for each layer of an image. Create, hide, display, copy, and delete channels, including alpha channels, in this palette.

❋ The Paths palette shows a list of the saved vector graphics in an image. Create or delete a path, or choose selected, fill, stroke paths from this palette.

❋ The Paragraph palette displays the current alignment, justification, and hyphenation settings for any text selected in the image window. Adjust these settings of the selected text here.

 You also can create double-pane windows by clicking and dragging a palette to the top or bottom edge of another palette. Release the mouse and watch the palette grow to fit two viewable palettes in the one window.

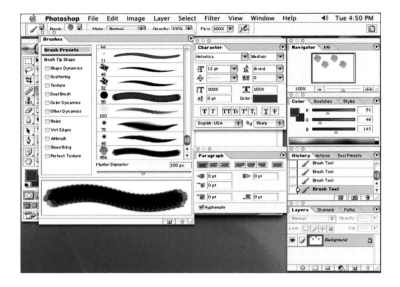

You also can use the Window menu to display three additional palettes offering options for tools, as follows:

✳ The Brush palette enables you to choose a brush style and work with brush presets—collections of additional settings to apply to the brush.

✳ The Character palette shows the current font, font size, and style if you've typed some text into the image window. Select text in the image window and use the Character palette to edit these font settings. You can adjust kerning, vertical and horizontal scale, baseline shift, and the color of the font here.

✳ The Paragraph palette shows the alignment settings available for added text, including indention settings.

VIEWING A PICTURE WITH THE NAVIGATOR PALETTE

You can find out exactly what part of the window you're eyeballing by using the Navigator palette. A colored rectangle highlights the palette viewed area, and the scale of the image appears in the lower-left corner of the palette. You can pan and zoom the image by dragging the triangle-shaped slider control located at the bottom of the palette window. The following figure shows changes in the Navigator palette and image window after using the slider control to zoom into an image.

 Change the color of the rectangle by choosing Palette Options from the pop-up menu in the Navigator palette. This menu is selected by clicking the small triangle in the upper-right corner of the Navigator panel.

VIEWING COLOR SETTINGS WITH THE INFO PALETTE

If you need to know the exact combination of colors in your image, or if you're simply curious about color values, they're easy to find in the Info palette. Place the mouse pointer anywhere in the image, and the Info palette will show a breakdown of the current color information. Color values and cursor coordinates are updated instantly.

1. Open an image.
2. Move the mouse pointer over a colored area in the image.
3. Red, green, and blue values are shown on the left side of the Info palette as you move the cursor around in the image window. Cyan (C), magenta (M), yellow (Y), and black (K) values appear on the right.

4. The x and y coordinates of the mouse pointer appear in the lower-left corner of the Info palette.

 An exclamation point will appear beside a color value that is out-of-gamut or beyond the scope of the predefined colors for a document's color space.

HANDLING COLOR WITH THE COLOR, SWATCHES, AND STYLES PALETTE

You can use the Color palette to select the foreground and background color. To choose a new foreground color, click on one you like in the color ramp located at the bottom of the palette. (Option/Alt+click to specify a background color.) Drag the slider control to view the tonal range of the selected color. Add or experiment with colors using the Swatches palette, which enables you to save or load swatches from other image-editing sessions.

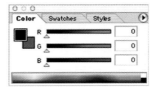

The Styles palette enables you to save, edit, and load layer styles. Each style is a set of one or more layer effects that can be applied to any layer in a Photoshop or ImageReady document.

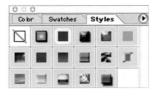

When editing pictures, you'll probably rely more on the colors used within a particular document instead of creating new colors from the Color palette.

The easiest way to switch to a foreground color in an image is to use the Eyedropper tool to click on the color you want to use, as described next:

1. Open an image file. Click on the Eyedropper tool in the toolbox.

2. Click on a color in the Color palette or on the image.
3. Select the Paint Bucket tool from the toolbox.

4. Click on the area in the window where you want to apply the color with the Paint Bucket tool. The new color replaces the range of colors where you clicked. In this example, I've used a selection tool to select one of the red circles in the flower, turning it blue using the Paint Bucket tool.

EDITING TEXT WITH THE CHARACTER PALETTE

You can add a date and timestamp, or add a narrative to digital pictures using the Text tool in the toolbox. Photoshop adds text directly to the image as a separate layer. You can also view text settings and modify text with the Character palette. As long as text remains in its own, original layer, you can edit it. If you choose Flatten Image from the Image menu, or merge the text layer with other layers, you will no longer be able to modify that text. To add text, do the following:

1. Open an image into the Photoshop workspace.
2. Click on the Text tool in the toolbox. Place the insertion point where you want the text to appear in the image.
3. Type some text into the image; then click on the Commit button (at the far right end of the options bar) to finish the entry.
4. Click on the Layers palette. The text appears as a separate layer there.
5. Click the text layer to make the text layer active. You can then use tools to edit the text.

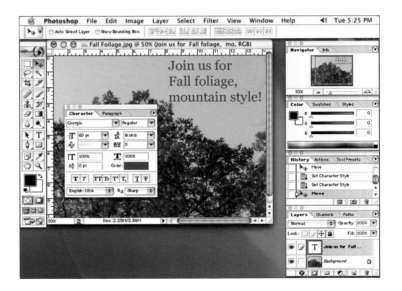

6. Select Character from the Window menu. Choose different settings in the Character palette to change the font, font size, and other text characteristics.

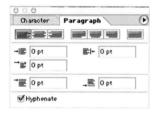 Fonts that appear in Adobe Photoshop are installed with your operating system. To access additional fonts in Photoshop, you must install additional fonts in Mac OS X or Windows XP.

ORGANIZING TEXT WITH THE PARAGRAPH PALETTE

Using the Paragraph palette, you can change text alignment—options are left-alignment, center-alignment, and right-alignment. You can also enable hyphenation and set additional format options such as indenting the first line, indenting the left or right margins, or adding a space before or after a paragraph. This palette doesn't appear among the ones on the right-hand side of the page; you'll learn how to access it next. To organize your text, do the following:

1. Click the layer containing the text you want to alter.

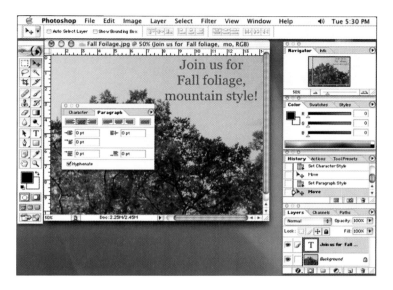

2. Open the Window menu and choose Show Paragraph.
3. Select left-, center-, or right-alignment for the selected text.
4. Click on the Move tool on the toolbox.
5. Drag the text on the selected text layer to fine-tune the text location.

REPLAYING EVENTS WITH THE HISTORY PALETTE

There are so many tools, effects, and filters in Photoshop 7 that often the best way to create an image is to experiment. Sometimes, however, experiments go awry. If this happens to you, you can use the History palette in Photoshop 7 to go back to a previous state of the document. To do so, simply click on an item in the History palette's History list to view a previous incarnation of the window.

AUTOMATING TASKS WITH
THE ACTIONS PALETTE

You can add filters, effects, and Web behaviors to the current image using the Actions palette. Each action automates one or more Photoshop 7 tasks. (This is akin to macros in other applications.) Create your own actions by recording them using the built-in controls in the Actions palette. To use this palette, first open an image and then do the following:

1. Open the Actions palette (click on the Actions tab or choose Window, Actions).
2. Click on the collapsible triangle to the left of a folder or action.

3. View the list of actions in the Actions palette.
4. Choose an action you want to perform on the selected image.
5. Click on the Play Selection button at the bottom of the palette to perform the action selected in the palette. For example, in the figure below, I chose Sepia Toning from the Actions list, and the effect was applied to the image.

To load additional actions, open the Action palette's pop-up menu by clicking on the triangle button in the upper-right corner of the palette. Then choose Load Actions

To record an action, do the following:

1. If needed, select a layer or perform any preparation that's needed before you create the action.
2. Click on the New Action button at the bottom of the Actions palette. The New Action dialog box opens.
3. Enter a Name for the action in the Name text box, as well as choosing the action set file that will hold the action and specifying a function key shortcut for running the action, if desired.

4. Click on the Record button in the dialog box.
5. Perform one or more tasks on the current image.
6. Click on the Stop button at the bottom of the Actions palette to finish the action. The new action will appear at the bottom of the Actions palette.

ARRANGING IMAGES WITH THE LAYERS PALETTE

When you first open an image from your digital camera or scanner in Photoshop, it contains a background layer only. Photoshop creates a new layer for any text, shapes, and other features you add. You also can copy any part of the background image into a new layer. Each layer contains its own channel information. For example, if a document is in RGB color mode, each layer can have unique settings for each red, green, or blue channel. Create, delete, edit, and organize layers with the Layers palette. To use this palette, first open an image, and then do the following:

1. Click on the Create a New Layer button at the bottom of the Layers palette.
2. A new, empty layer appears in the Layers palette.
3. Select the background layer and drag it over the Create a New Layer button.
4. A copy of the image from the background layer is created in a new layer.

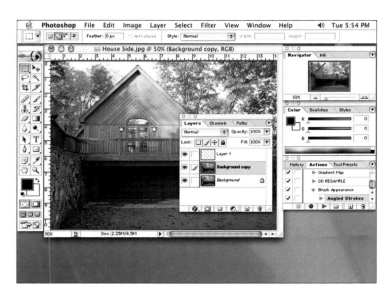

 For more information about working with Layers, see Chapter 8, "Combining Content with Layers."

CREATING MASKS WITH THE CHANNELS PALETTE

Channels display the color information for an image. For example, you'll find red, green, and blue channels in this palette if an image is in RGB mode. Here you can hide, display, or create channels and channel masks for an image. For more information about masks and channels, see Chapters 9, "Customizing Images with Masks," and 11, "Experimenting with Layers."

To use this palette, first open an image and then do the following:

1. Click on the Channels tab or choose Window, Channels to view the list of channels in the Channels palette.
2. Click the eye icon to hide one channel.

3. Choose a selection tool from the toolbox. Drag on the image to select an area of the image in the image window.

4. Click on the Save Selection as Channel button (the button showing a gray square with a white circle in the middle) at the bottom of the Channels palette.

5. An alpha channel named Alpha 1 appears in the Channels palette. An alpha channel is an 8-bit grayscale channel that can be used to store a mask.

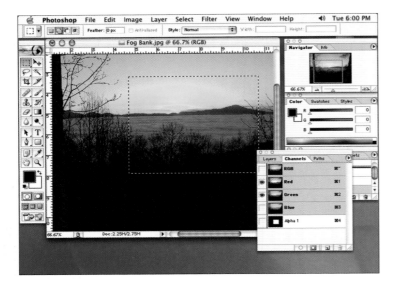

6. Click on the alpha channel in the Channels window to view the mask in the window. A mask enables you to edit, isolate, or protect certain parts of an image. For example, you can edit any part of the image within the white color of the mask, but you cannot edit any part of the image within the black color.

7. Click on the composite channel (the RGB channel in new JPEG images) to redisplay all the color channels in the image.

WORKING WITH THE PATHS PALETTE

The Paths palette contains a list of any line art, including fill or stroke paths, in an image. Use a pen or a shape tool to create a path in an image. A thumbnail of each path appears next to the name of each path. Create, delete, show, hide, or select a path from the Paths palette. The following steps show you how to add paths to an image.

1. Choose a pen or shape tool from the toolbox.
2. Click the Paths button on the options bar.
3. Draw an object or path in the window.
4. Display the Paths palette by clicking its tab or choosing Window, Paths.
5. Open the Paths palette menu and click Save Path.

6. Type a path name in the Save Path dialog box that appears; then click OK.

7. If you want to use the path as a selection, click the Load Path as a Selection button at the bottom of the Paths palette.

CHAPTER 5

CORRECTING IMAGES

CORRECTING IMAGES

YOU MIGHT THINK THAT A CERTAIN PICTURE LOOKS GREAT
WHEN YOU TAKE IT, BUT ONCE YOU TRANSFER IT TO YOUR
COMPUTER AND COMPARE IT WITH ANOTHER PICTURE OR TRY
TO COMBINE PARTS OF IT WITH ANOTHER PICTURE, YOU MAY
REALIZE YOU NEED TO DO SOME TWEAKING. PHOTOSHOP 7 IS
A GREAT TOOL FOR MAKING SMALL CHANGES TO AN ENTIRE
PICTURE OR TO A FEW PIXELS IN A PICTURE.

CORRECTING COLORS

An image can be too dark or too bright across the entire picture, or only in sections of the picture. You can use Photoshop 7 to manually or automatically adjust the tonal range of colors in a picture, or to correct a picture that's too blue. This section focuses on how to manually change colors in a picture. However, you can use the Auto Levels, Auto Contrast, or Auto Color commands on the Image, Adjustments submenu to make fast, automatic corrections.

CHANNEL MIXING— THE BIG PICTURE

Depending on how you plan to use a picture—as a stand-alone showpiece or combined with other images—you might need to make changes that affect the entire document. You can use the built-in filters and tools in Photoshop, like the channel mixer, to correct colors and make a good picture look better. The following steps show you how to change an image using the Channel Mixer command.

The Channel Mixer command enables you to combine a percentage of color from one channel to create part of another channel. You can use the channel mixer to adjust colors in a picture, swap or duplicate channels, or create a black-and-white, sepia, or other color-tinted image from a color image. Many of the effects created with the channel mixer can also be created with the Image, Calculations command, although you may find the channel mixer easier to use.

1. Open an image in Photoshop.
2. Open the Image menu, select Adjustments, and then choose Channel Mixer.
3. Notice that there is an Output Channel pop-up menu at the top of the Channel Mixer dialog box. Use it to choose which channel you want to mix in the image: Red, Green, or Blue.

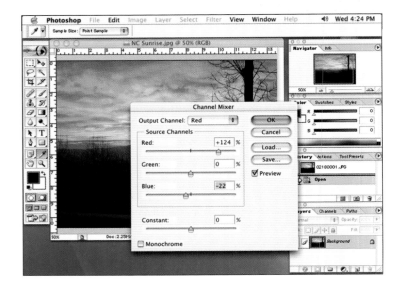

4. In the Source Channels area, drag the sliders to the left to lower the color value across the picture or to the right to increase the color value across the picture. Values range between −200% and +200% and can be selected in the text box or using the slider controls.
5. The Constant slider at the bottom of the window adjusts the opacity of the output channel. Negative values act as a black channel and positive values act as a white channel. Experiment using the Constant slider before and after making changes to each color channel.
6. Click on the Monochrome check box. Adjust the slider controls to adjust the amount of contrast in the grayscale image. You can use this option with each color channel to create a hand-tinted final image. Click on the OK button to save your changes.

 Open the Layer menu, select New Adjustment Layer, and then choose Channel Mixer or any other submenu item. Photoshop creates a special layer for the effect. Click on the eye icon in the Layers palette to turn the effect on and off. Note that if you use this approach, Photoshop prompts you to save the image file using the Photoshop file type if you try to close the image; you must save it to preserve the separate color correction layer.

REPLACING SPECIFIC COLORS

Make a blue sky gray, or green grass greener, by using a combination of selection tools and adjustment layers. Correcting or replacing colors can be a tedious, if not frustrating, task. Sometimes, it can be difficult to select or adjust a range of colors without ruining the original quality of a picture. The following steps show you how to experiment with replacing and changing colors using the Magic Wand selection tool:

1. Choose the Magic Wand tool from the toolbox.

2. Click the area of color to correct in the image window. (You also can click multiple locations to expand the marquee.) Photoshop surrounds the specified set of pixels with a dotted line, also known as a marquee.

Marquee

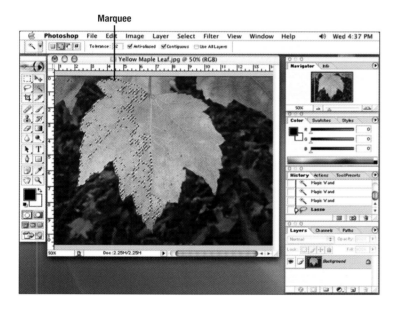

3. Open the Layer menu, select New Adjustment Layer, and then choose Hue/Saturation. Creating a new layer ensures that you can easily edit, add, or remove this color correction. The New Layer dialog box appears.

4. Type a name for the layer in the Name text box of the New Layer dialog box and then click OK. The Hue/Saturation dialog box opens.

5. Drag the desired sliders—Hue, Saturation, and Lightness—to the left or right to decrease or increase the hue, saturation, or lightness of the selected area in the image.

6. Click OK to finish creating the layer and to display the color correction.

7. To edit the Hue/Saturation adjustment layer, click the layer name in the Layers palette.

8. Open the Layer menu and choose Layer Content Options. This command opens the corresponding dialog box for the selected adjustment layer—in this case, the Hue/Saturation dialog box. .

9. Make any changes you like and then click on OK to save your changes to the Adjustment layer.

 You can convert an adjustment layer from one type to another. To do so, click on the layer name in the Layers palette. Open the Layer menu, select Change Layer Content, and then click the desired new layer type in the submenu that appears. Adjust settings as needed in the dialog box that appears and then click OK.

BALANCING COLORS

If you have a scanned picture or one taken under low-light conditions, the resulting image might have a subtle, unnatural brown, yellow, or green hue. Depending on the quality of the scanned or digital image and the colors in the image, the color change might be more obvious. You might want to correct the image by removing the color imbalance.

To see a color imbalance, you need to set your monitor to display millions or billions of colors (also referred to as 24-bit or 32-bit color). If your monitor is set to display 256 colors, the color imbalance won't be as noticeable. To change the color depth of your monitor in Windows XP, right-click the desktop and click Properties. Click the Settings tab and choose Highest (32 bit) from the Color Quality drop-down list. Click on OK. On a Mac OS X system, click the System Preferences icon on the dock. Click the Displays icon, open the Colors pop-up list, and click Millions. Choose System Prefs, Quit System Prefs to close System Preferences.

To correct a color imbalance, do the following:

1. Open the Layer menu, select New Adjustment Layer, and then choose Color Balance. (Alternately, choose Color Balance from the Image, Adjustments submenu to adjust color directly on the background layer.) The New Layer dialog box opens.
2. Type a name for the layer in the Name text box of the New Layer dialog box and then click OK. The Color Balance dialog box opens.

3. Select either the Shadows, Midtones, or Highlights option button in the Tone Balance area to select which tones will be affected by the color changes.
4. Adjust the Color Balance settings for the specified tones by moving the sliders along each scale as needed. Preview your changes in the image window.
5. Repeat Steps 3 and 4 as needed to set the color balance for other tones; then click OK to save your changes.

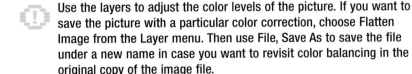

Use the layers to adjust the color levels of the picture. If you want to save the picture with a particular color correction, choose Flatten Image from the Layer menu. Then use File, Save As to save the file under a new name in case you want to revisit color balancing in the original copy of the image file.

ADJUSTING TONAL LEVELS

You can adjust the tonal range of dark and light colors to correct a photograph's contrast. For example, if a photo is comparatively lighter or darker than your other photos, you can correct all or part of the image using the Levels tools.

DEFINING TONAL RANGE

The tonal range of an image includes different levels of white and black values. Adjusting the limits of the white, or highlight, of an image, as well as the black, or shadow, of an image involves redistributing the midtone pixels of that image. Photoshop displays the tonal range using a histogram. Higher or taller bars in the histogram indicate more pixels in a particular black or white level of the image. View a histogram to find out how the pixels are distributed in a picture.

To view the histogram of an image, choose the Image, Histogram command. Choose a channel from the Channel drop-down menu. Then pass the mouse pointer over any part of the histogram to view a particular tonal range level. The numbers on the left and right sides of the histogram represent the low and high levels, respectively. The Histogram window also displays the mean, standard deviation, median, and pixel count of the selected image.

To adjust the tonal range, first open an image, and then use the following steps:

1. Open the Layer menu, select New Adjustment Layer, and then choose Levels. The New Layer dialog box opens. (Alternately, choose Image, Adjustments, Levels to adjust the tonal range directly on the background layer.)
2. Type a name for the layer in the Name text box of the New Layer dialog box and then click OK. The Levels dialog box opens.
3. View the histogram for the image in the Input Levels area of the Levels dialog box. In the Input Levels area, move the left slider to the right to reduce the tonal range of dark colors. (When the Preview check box is checked, you can preview your changes in the image window.)

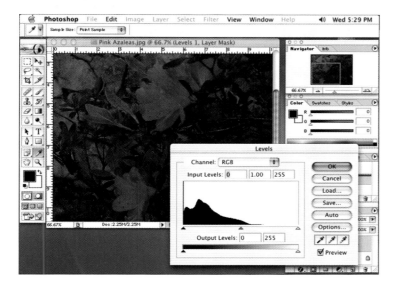

4. Move the right slider to the left to reduce the tonal range of the light colors.

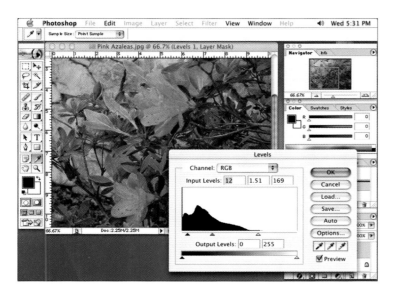

5. Drag the middle triangle to adjust the midtone levels for the picture.
6. View the intensity of light and dark colors in the histogram. Click OK to save your changes.

 Move the sliders toward the center if there are no extreme dark or light values in the histogram in the Levels dialog box. White space, which appears as a flat line in the histogram in the Levels window, can increase an image file's size even though you can't see any difference.

CHANGING CONTRAST AND BRIGHTNESS

The brightness and contrast controls in Photoshop work similarly to those on a computer monitor or television. Brightness levels can increase or decrease the amount of light, or white colors, in an image. Contrast affects both white and black, or highlights and shadows, in an image. Adjust brightness and contrast settings independently—or in tandem—to intensify or soften the colors in a picture. Here's how:

1. Open the Layer menu, select New Adjustment Layer, and then choose Brightness/Contrast. The New Layer dialog box opens. (Alternately, choose Image, Adjustments, Brightness/Contrast to adjust the brightness and contrast directly on the background layer.)
2. Type a name for the layer in the Name text box of the New Layer dialog box and click on OK. The Brightness/Contrast dialog box opens.
3. Drag the Brightness slider. This will adjust the brightness levels of the photo.

4. Drag the Contrast slider to increase or decrease the amount of light and dark contrast in the photo.
5. Preview your changes. Click on OK to save your changes.

 Another way to adjust the light in a photo is to use the Dodge tool in the toolbox (it lives with the Sponge and Burn tools). Modify the tool by changing its brush, range, and exposure settings in the options bar that appears below the menu bar after you've selected the tool. Click or drag on the image to lighten areas.

EMBELLISHING IMAGES

It's not uncommon to see a picture that looks truer than life on a Web site or in a magazine. I'm not talking about people with perfect proportions, or even Laura Croft proportions. I'm referring to photos that morph the head of one person onto the body of another and into a picture of outer space. Sure, this technique has been used in photographs as well as on television and in the movies, but let's find out how to create these effects in Photoshop. Such techniques can still be used to entertain and annoy your friends and relatives.

CORRECTING THE IMAGE WITH THE PATCH OR HEALING BRUSH

These two tools are new in Photoshop 7. They can be used not only to embellish an image but also to fix problems in an image, such as camouflaging unwanted elements in a photo or removing spots or scratches. I've found that the patch tool works best in the former situation, while the healing brush often works best in the latter.

Let's start with an example of the patch. Say I have a photo of Rika (a dog), in which a drain appears in the background. I can use the Patch tool to remove the drain. To use the Patch tool in such a situation, follow these steps:

1. Choose the Patch tool from the toolbox. If needed, Control+click (Mac) or right-click (Windows) the Healing Brush tool and then click Patch tool in the shortcut menu that appears.
2. Be sure to click the Destination option button on the options bar. This tells Photoshop that you would like to select the patch as the source and then move it over the destination (the area to fix).
3. Press and hold the Option key (Mac) or Alt key (Windows) while dragging to select the area to use as the patch. The patch should be approximately the same size and shape as the area to be patched.
4. Release the mouse button and Alt/Option key.

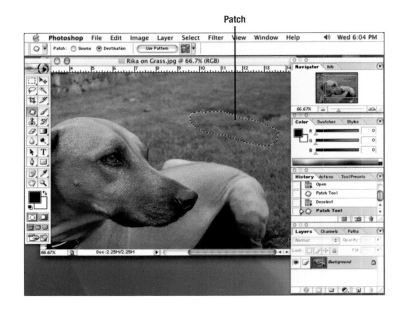

5. Drag the selected patch over the area you want to correct in the image.

The Healing Brush tool works in an almost identical fashion. Rather than selecting an area to use as a patch, however, you "load" the brush with an area of the image that has the color or pattern to use for the repair and then paint over the damaged area. This is ideal for fixing a heavily damaged photo, like the one shown here. To use the Healing Brush tool in such a situation, follow these steps:

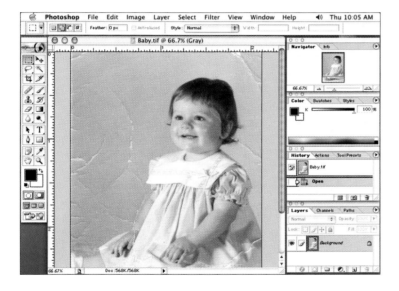

1. Choose the Healing Brush tool from the toolbox. If needed, Control+click (Mac) or right-click (Windows) the Healing Brush tool and then click Healing Brush Tool in the shortcut menu that appears.
2. Choose brush settings in the options bar and be sure that the Sampled option button is selected as the source. This tells Photoshop to load the brush with the image information that you select.

3. Press and hold the Option key (Mac) or Alt key (Windows) while dragging to select the area to use as the patch. The patch should be approximately the same size and shape as the area to be patched.
4. Release the mouse button and Alt/Option key.

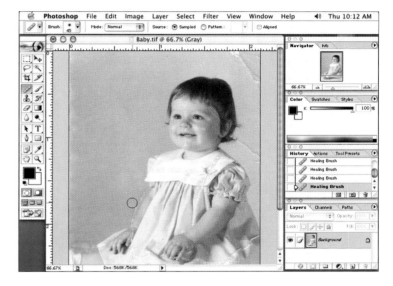

5. Click repeatedly on the area to correct in the image. In this example image, I've used the Healing Brush tool to correct much of the damage at the left side of the image.

 Typically, you will need to click repeatedly to correct some damaged areas. If, however, you click with the Healing Brush tool and don't like the result, undo the result immediately by pressing Command/Ctrl+Z. Also note that you can repeatedly change the brush size and resample with Option/Alt+click to repair various areas in the image.

USING THE CLONE STAMP TOOL

The Clone Stamp tool resembles a rubber stamp icon in the toolbox. You can use it to capture part of an image and apply it to any other part of the same document. To use this tool, do the following:

1. Select the Clone Stamp tool from the toolbox.

2. Adjust the brush size on the options bar as you prefer (a larger brush makes it easier to reveal the cloned material).

3. Press and hold the Option key (Mac) or Alt key (Windows) and click on the center of the area of the picture you want to use as the master image.

4. Release the mouse button and Alt/Option key.

5. Drag with the mouse in a different location in the image to "reveal" the cloned material in the new location. The master image remains unchanged, while you can apply its clone to any new location.

 Use the Clone Stamp tool to make all the faces in a crowd identical or to remove (or add) dust, spots, or glitches from a photo.

 If you're not sure whether cloning part of an image is the right thing to do, save a copy of the original image or create an adjustment layer before applying the Clone Stamp tool.

REPLACING COLORS IN AN IMAGE

If you have a photo with a faded blue sky, or if the clouds just wouldn't go away when you were taking pictures on the beach, you can use Photoshop to correct or replace areas of color in a picture. The following steps show you how to use the Magic Wand tool combined with the Levels and Replace Color menu commands to replace the colors in an image.

1. Open the image you want to edit and then select the Magic Wand tool from the toolbox.
2. Click on the color area(s) you want to edit. All instances of that color in the image are selected.

3. Choose Image, Adjustments, Levels. The Levels dialog box opens.

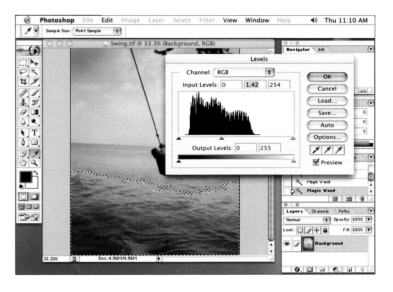

4. Adjust the levels of the selected area by dragging the left, middle, or right triangles in the Input Levels area. Then click on OK.
5. Choose Image, Adjustments, Replace Color. The Replace Color dialog box appears.

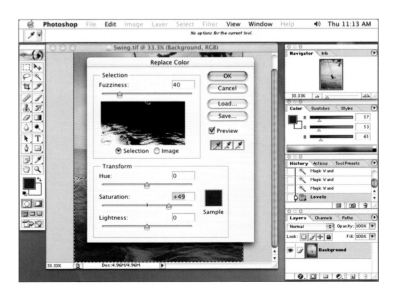

6. Click on the black square in the middle of the Replace Color dialog box and then drag the Hue, Saturation, and Lightness sliders to change the sample color.

7. Click on the plus or minus Eyedropper tool to add or subtract a color from the selection.

8. Click on OK to save your changes.

 One of the last things to do to correct an image is to use the **Unsharp Mask filter located in the Filter menu under the Sharpen submenu. This filter adjusts the contrast of the edge detail in a picture, creating the illusion of a clearer, more focused image.**

CROPPING AN IMAGE

The Crop tool resembles a rectangular frame with a thin diagonal line running across it. My dad, an architect, used a similar tool on his drawing board to frame part of an image. Photoshop's Crop tool works similarly to imaging crop tools in the real world. If you want to quickly remove fringe elements in a photo or improve its composition, use the Crop tool. Here's how:

1. Open the image you want to edit and then choose the Crop tool (C) from the toolbox.

2. Drag to specify the area you want to crop.

3. Click on any of the borders of the cropped area to enlarge or shrink the cropped region of the picture. Click and drag any corner handle to resize the cropped area.

4. Click on the Commit button (check mark button) on the options bar to complete the crop. Alternately, you can press Return (Mac) or Enter (Windows) to apply the crop. To exit the crop tool without saving any changes, click on the Cancel button on the options bar.

 When cropping an image, try to apply the same composition rules to the cropped image as you would when taking a picture with a camera. First, consider balance. Decide whether you want the shadows, light, shapes, or lines of the image to be symmetrical or informal design. Second, consider the rule of thirds. Place the main subject and any subordinate elements in the picture near one-third point intersections in the picture, breaking a picture up into nine equally shaped areas.

ROTATING AN IMAGE

You can use the Rotate Canvas commands, located in the Image menu, to change a picture's rotation by 180° or 90° clockwise or counter-clockwise. To rotate an image, open an image and then click on the Image menu. Then choose

Rotate Canvas and choose either 180°, 90° CW (clockwise), 90° CCW (counter-clockwise), Arbitrary, Flip Horizontally, or Flip Vertically. Photoshop will change the orientation of the image in the window.

Use the Rotate Canvas commands to turn a picture upside down or to create a mirror image effect. You can also combine the Arbitrary Rotate Canvas command with the Measure tool (which is located with the Eyedropper and Color sampler tools) to straighten the vertical alignment or flatten the horizontal alignment of any picture.

STRAIGHTENING AN IMAGE

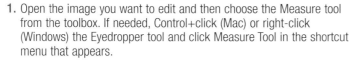

No matter how careful I am, I always take a crooked picture. Fortunately, I can straighten my photo using the Measure tool in Photoshop 7. Here's how to do it:

1. Open the image you want to edit and then choose the Measure tool from the toolbox. If needed, Control+click (Mac) or right-click (Windows) the Eyedropper tool and click Measure Tool in the shortcut menu that appears.

2. Draw a line between two vertical points on the image. Because the image is crooked, your vertical line should be slightly slanted as well.
3. Choose Image, Rotate Canvas, Arbitrary. The Rotate Canvas dialog box appears.
4. Photoshop 7 places an Angle value (calculated as the difference between the y axis and the position of the line you created with the Measure tool) in the Rotate Canvas dialog box. Click on OK.

5. View the straightened image and crop it if required.

 If you draw a straight line (versus a crooked one) with the Measure tool, Photoshop will not input a value into the Rotate Canvas dialog box. The Measure tool enables you to specify how far to rotate an image. Photoshop will rotate the image so that the line you draw with the Measure tool aligns with the horizontal and vertical access of the image window.

 After straightening an image, use the Crop tool to remove any white space along the border of the image. To find out how to use the Crop tool, see the section "Cropping an Image" earlier in this chapter.

CORRECTING THE HORIZONTAL AXIS

Alternatively, you can correct the horizontal axis of a picture using the Measure tool.

1. Open the image you want to edit and then choose the Measure tool from the toolbox. If needed, Control+click (Mac) or right-click (Windows) the Healing Brush tool; then click Patch Tool in the shortcut menu that appears.

2. Draw a (slightly slanted) horizontal line between two horizontal points of the image. For example, follow the slanted horizontal line in the image.
3. Choose Image, Rotate Canvas, Arbitrary. The Rotate Canvas dialog box appears.
4. Photoshop 7 places an Angle value (calculated as the difference between the x axis and the position of the line you created with the Measure tool) in the Rotate Canvas dialog box. Click on OK.

5. View the straightened image and crop it if required.

CHAPTER 6

ENHANCING IMAGES WITH FILTERS AND EFFECTS

PHOTOSHOP ENABLES YOU TO CLEAN UP, CORRECT, STYLIZE, OR DESTROY A PICTURE BY APPLYING FILTERS AND EFFECTS. MOST FILTERS AND EFFECTS ARE PLUG-IN FILES INSTALLED WITH PHOTOSHOP. PHOTOGRAPHER'S FILTERS, USED TO CORRECT DIFFERENT TYPES OF LIGHTING CONDITIONS, WERE THE INSPIRATION FOR NAMING PHOTOSHOP'S FILTERS. HOWEVER, PHOTOSHOP FILTERS GO BEYOND TRADITIONAL PHOTOGRAPHY FILTERS AND CAN BE USED TO CORRECT COLOR, DECONSTRUCT IMAGES, OR ADD A VARIETY OF STROKE-BASED AND OTHER KINDS OF SPECIAL EFFECTS TO AN IMAGE.

WHAT ARE PLUG-INS?

The folks at Adobe created the plug-in design in Photoshop to enable developers to create their own custom plug-ins. Today, many graphics applications, including Web browsers, follow the plug-in model as an easy way to add new features to an application. To install one, you often can simply designate a plug-in folder (where you've previously placed the plug-in files) for Photoshop using the Preferences dialog box, or place a plug-in file in the Photoshop Plug-Ins folder prior to starting Photoshop. In other cases, the plug-in features its own installer that places files in the appropriate folders for you.

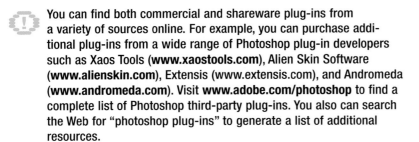

You can find both commercial and shareware plug-ins from a variety of sources online. For example, you can purchase additional plug-ins from a wide range of Photoshop plug-in developers such as Xaos Tools (www.xaostools.com), Alien Skin Software (www.alienskin.com), Extensis (www.extensis.com), and Andromeda (www.andromeda.com). Visit www.adobe.com/photoshop to find a complete list of Photoshop third-party plug-ins. You also can search the Web for "photoshop plug-ins" to generate a list of additional resources.

INSTALLING PLUG-INS

Adobe installs its Photoshop plug-ins to the Plug-Ins folder. The Plug-Ins folder is located in the Photoshop 7 folder on your hard disk. The following steps show you how to configure Photoshop to work with additional plug-in files:

1. Choose Photoshop, Preferences (Mac) or Edit, Preferences (Windows) and then select Plug-Ins & Scratch Disks.
2. Click on the Additional Plug-Ins Folder check box to check it. If needed, also click Choose. The Choose an Additional Plug-Ins Folder dialog box (Mac) or Browse for Folder dialog box (Windows) opens.
3. Navigate the hard disk and locate the Plug-Ins folder you want to use with Photoshop. If the Plug-Ins folder is on a CD-ROM drive, navigate to the Desktop and then select the CD-ROM disc. Select the folder containing the plug-in files.

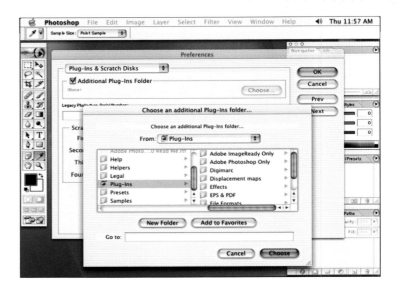

4. Click on Choose (Mac) or OK (Windows) to save the folder information to the Preferences dialog box. Click on OK to save your changes and exit the Preferences dialog box.
5. Exit Photoshop.
6. Drag and drop the files for any Photoshop plug-ins into the Plug-Ins folder that you specified.

USING PLUG-INS

Adobe installs dozens of plug-ins with Photoshop. The previous section showed you how to install more plug-ins. To use a plug-in, first open an image file and then do the following:

1. Click on the Filter menu to view the categories of plug-ins installed.

2. Drag the mouse pointer over a category to view a list of filters, also known as effects, for that category.
3. Select a filter.

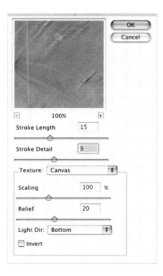

4. Adjust the Filter settings. Click on OK. Filter settings vary from filter to filter. If a filter does not have any custom settings, the effect will be applied to the image window, so you can skip this step.

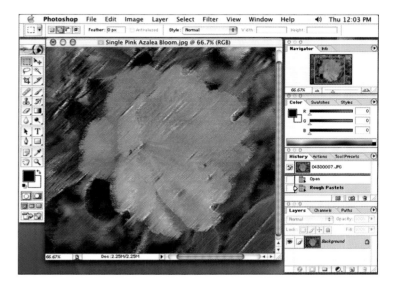

5. View the effect of the filter in the image window.

 The most recently used filter appears at the top of the Filter menu. Press Command+F on a Mac or Ctrl+F in Windows to access the most recent filter. Also remember that you can undo the filter effect by immediately pressing Command/Ctrl+Z.

FILTERS

Although it's easy to categorize all filters as effects, or vice versa, I categorize filters as plug-ins that affect the quality of a photographic image, such as sharpening, blurring, or color correcting an image. Effects, on the other hand, change a picture by adding a style, stroke, or distinctive visual element, like fur or metal, to an image. The following sections explain two different categories of filters.

CORRECTIVE FILTERS

You can apply sharpen or blur filters directly from the Filter menu, or tweak levels, contrast, and colors from the Image, Adjustments submenu.

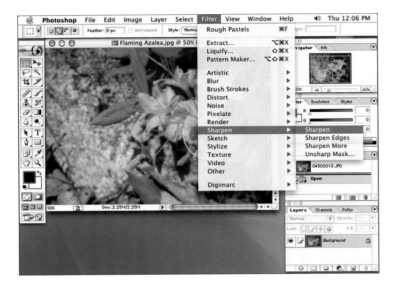

You also can create new adjustment layers to add filters one by one to an image. Choose Auto Levels, Auto Contrast, or Auto Color from the Image, Adjustments submenu if you want Photoshop to take its best shot at correcting image levels, contrast, or colors. Otherwise, choose the Levels, Curves, Color Balance, Brightness/ Contrast, Hue/Saturation, or Desaturate commands from the Image, Adjustments or Layer, New Adjustment Layer submenus to adjust the way your picture looks.

DESTRUCTIVE FILTERS

Some of the filters in Photoshop, such as the filters in the Pixelate submenu, break up an image, as opposed to making an image clearer. In some cases, for example, if you have a photo that includes some private or offensive information (such as a rude slogan on a T-shirt), you can use a filter on a specific area of an image to blur or decompose the offending pixels so the image details are no longer recognizable.

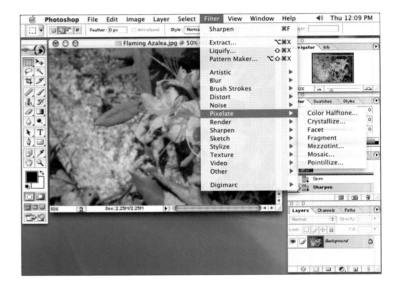

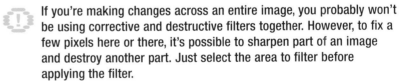

If you're making changes across an entire image, you probably won't be using corrective and destructive filters together. However, to fix a few pixels here or there, it's possible to sharpen part of an image and destroy another part. Just select the area to filter before applying the filter.

EFFECTS

Adobe includes a group of stroke, stylize, texture, and distort effects with Photoshop. You can apply all effects directly to a selected layer in the image. A subset of effects can be applied as a Layer, Layer Style submenu. Each Layer Style appears as a separate layer effect in the Layers palette. Layer effects are also called live effects because this type of effect doesn't directly affect the pixels in the image. Click on the eye icon to hide or show a layer effect in the image window. The stylize and distort effects are highlighted in the following sections.

STYLIZE

Choose Stylize from the Filter menu to choose from among Diffuse, Emboss, Extrude, Find Edges, Glowing Edges, Solarize, Tiles, Trace Contour, and Wind effects. Depending on the content of your picture, these effects might look great or might not make any noticeable change. The Find Edges effect is shown here.

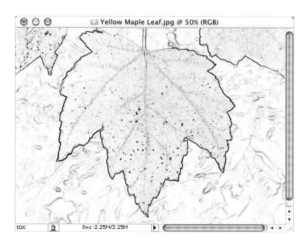

DISTORT

As with the other effects, the names of the distort effects won't give you an exact idea of what they can do to an image. Even so, you'll probably have the most fun with these filters. Choose from Diffuse Glow, Displace, Glass, Ocean Ripple, Pinch, Polar Coordinates, Ripple, Shear, Spherize, Twist, Wave, and ZigZag. Each effect has a corresponding panel, enabling you to customize the effect for a picture. The Diffuse Glow effect is shown here.

 A filter cannot be applied to an image in Bitmap, indexed-color mode, or to 16-bit images. If needed, change the image color mode to 8-bit or RGB by selecting the appropriate command from the Image, Mode submenu.

APPLYING EFFECTS AND FILTERS

Apply an effect to a single image, or experiment with multiple effects by moving an image to a layer or layer set, and then turning off all layers except one to view and compare effects. To create an experimental layer for viewing effects, copy and paste an image to a new layer and apply individual or combinations of effects to the image layer. To view a particular effect, click on the eye icon box to show a particular effect layer; then hide all the other layers. You can also turn effects on or off by selecting entries in the History palette.

BLUR FILTERS

When you're taking pictures, image clarity and focus are critical for capturing a clear, crisp picture. You can use blur effects, however, to create a soft focus, emphasize another part of the picture, or to de-emphasize a specific part of a picture—for example, a face, or if you're working with a screen capture, a password, or login name. To blur the entire image (I've chosen to apply a radial blur), do the following:

1. Open an image file. Open the Filter menu, choose Blur, and select Radial Blur.
2. Adjust the settings for this effect as needed in the Radial Blur dialog box.
3. Click on OK. Photoshop applies the effect to the image.

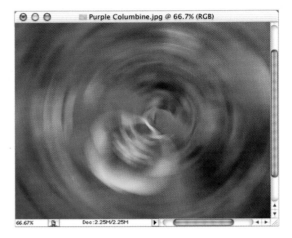

4. View the new image.

To blur a portion of the image (I've chosen to apply a motion blur), do the following:

1. Use a Lasso or other selection tool to select a particular area of an image.

2. Open the Filter menu, choose Blur, and select Motion Blur.
3. Adjust the settings as desired in the Motion Blur dialog box.
4. Click on OK. View the effect in the image window.

✅ Blur effect menu commands can blur a selected area or an entire image. To blur a small area of an image, choose the Blur tool from the toolbox. Press Shift+R to cycle through the tools that share toolbox space with the Blur tool or right-click to select one of them from a menu. Drag over the image to blur specific pixels. You might need to use the Zoom tool prior to selecting the Blur tool to get a closer look at the pixels you want to blur.

✅ After a filter or effect is selected from the Filter menu, it appears as the top-most menu item in the Filter menu. Press Command/Ctrl+F to re-apply the last filter applied to an image from the Filter menu.

SHARPEN FILTERS

Depending on the type of digital camera used to create a source image, you might want to try to improve the clarity of an image with Photoshop's sharpen effects. Don't set your expectations too high, though; the sharpen filter can't increase the amount of pixelation or hard edges in digital

pictures. The resulting image may not appear to be any clearer than its original.

If you see large, coarse, or squarish-looking pixels in an image, you're looking at pixelation. Applying the sharpen filter to this type of image will not make it any clearer. You may want to try applying the Unsharp mask with different settings to see if this filter helps decrease the pixelation.

A sharpen filter increases the contrast between neighboring pixels. If the image lacks the pixel information to increase the contrast or clarity of all or part of an image, the sharpen filter won't change the original image. You probably won't notice any difference after applying a sharpen effect to a blurry picture. The following steps show you how to apply sharpen effects to the image window:

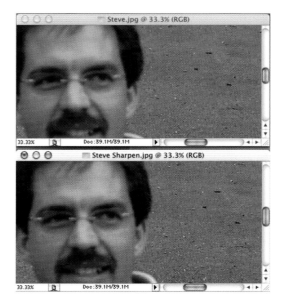

1. Open an image file. Open the Filter menu, select Sharpen, and choose Sharpen.
2. If you do not see any change in the image, select the Zoom tool (Z) and zoom in on the image. The original image is shown on the top and the image after applying the sharpen effect is shown on the bottom.
3. Press Command/Ctrl+Z to undo the effect. Alternatively, select Undo from the Edit menu.

4. Choose Sharpen More from the Sharpen submenu. The effect should appear in the History panel.
5. View the updated image.
6. Choose Filter, Sharpen, Unsharp Mask. The Unsharp Mask dialog box appears.
7. Adjust the settings as needed in the Unsharp Mask dialog box. Amount enables you to assign a value between 1 and 500 to determine how sharp to make the image. Choose a number between 1 and 250 pixels to define the radius of how sharp the edges should be made. Select a number between 0 and 255 for the Threshold setting to tell Photoshop how it should recognize edges in the image. Preview the changes in the Unsharp Mask window.
8. Click on OK to apply the filter to the image window.

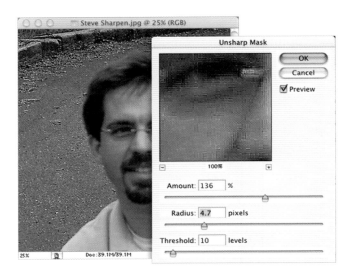

 Applying sharpening effects across an entire picture can over-emphasize edges and alter parts of the picture that were fine before the sharpen effect was applied. Compare the image before and after applying several doses of the sharpen effect. Click on a previous state in the History palette to undo any accidental abuse of the sharpen effects.

Apply several filters to a picture to create effects that result in a better-looking picture. For example, select all or part of an image that contains pixelation, or lots of jagged edge pixels. Choose

Median, Gaussian Blur, and Unsharp Mask effects in succession to improve the clarity of a digital image. View the image after applying all three effects. Use the History panel to compare before and after states of the picture and save the one that looks best.

Adobe provides the Sharpen effects in menu and tool forms. Use the menu commands to apply the effect across an entire picture or to a selected area of the picture. If you only need to edit a comparatively small area of pixels, press Shift+R to cycle through and select the Sharpen tool in the toolbox. Click and drag this tool over the image to sharpen specific pixels. You might need to use the Zoom tool to benefit from this tool.

TEXTURE EFFECTS

Experiment with non-traditional photographic effects by adding a texture effect. Choose from Texturizer, Stained Glass, Patchwork, Mosaic Tiles, Grain, or Craquelure in the Filter menu's Texture submenu. To apply such an effect, do the following:

1. Open an image file. Open the Filter menu, select Texture, and choose Craquelure. The Craquelure dialog box opens.
2. Adjust the Craquelure settings as desired.
3. Click on OK and then view the changes in the document window.

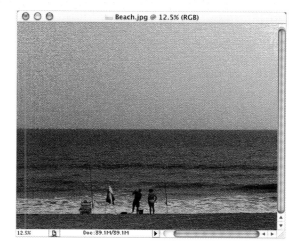

ARTISTIC AND SKETCH EFFECTS

Some effects, such as Artistic and Sketch effects, combine the foreground and background colors with settings in the effect window. To apply such an effect, do the following:

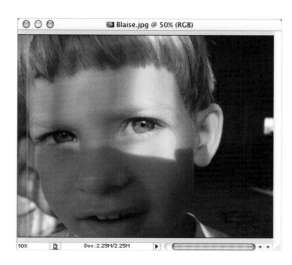

1. Open an image file. Open the Filter menu, choose Artistic, and select Smudge Stick. The Smudge Stick dialog box opens.

2. Adjust any of the smudge settings as desired in the dialog box.

3. Click on OK and then view the effect on the image.

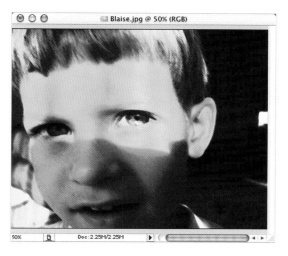

 You can view your picture beyond the bounds of the document window. Change the document view of the front-most image by pressing the F key or by choosing a view mode from the toolbox. Pressing the F key once will grow the image to fill the screen below the menu and toolbars. Pressing F a second time hides the menu bar. The third time brings you back to the document window view.

TINT AND FADE EFFECTS

There are a few ways to adjust the color tint of a picture. One way is to add a layer, use the paint bucket to apply a solid color to it, and then adjust the opacity in the Layers palette. See Chapter 11, "Experimenting with Layers," to find out more about adding a tint using layers. This example shows you how to add a tint with the Neon Glow and Fade effects. Try these steps:

1. Open an image file. Open the Filter menu, select Artistic, and choose Neon Glow. The Neon Glow dialog box appears.
2. Adjust the Glow Size, Glow Brightness, and Glow Color settings as needed; then click on OK.

3. Choose Fade Neon Glow from the Edit menu. The Fade dialog box appears.
4. Drag the slider to set the opacity.
5. Click on OK. View the Fade effect in the document window.

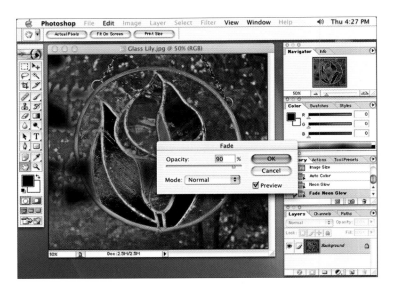

HALFTONE EFFECTS

Halftone effects can serve two purposes: they create a neat looking "pop art" effect, and they reduce the number of colors used in an image. If you don't want to pay for full-color printing costs, or you simply want to keep images on your Web site as small as possible, consider using halftone effects on your images. The following steps show you how to apply two kinds of halftone filters to a picture:

1. Open an image file. Open the Filter menu, select Pixelate, and choose Color Halftone. The Color Halftone dialog box appears.

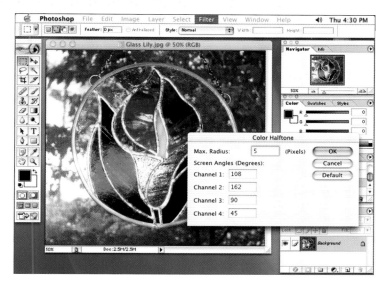

2. Adjust the Max. Radius size as needed to define how many pixels are used to create the halftone dots. Also enter a new value between 1 and 256 into any of the channel text boxes to adjust the screen angle of the halftone dots.
3. Click on OK to apply the changes. Wait for Photoshop to render the effect.
4. View the color halftone effect in the document window.

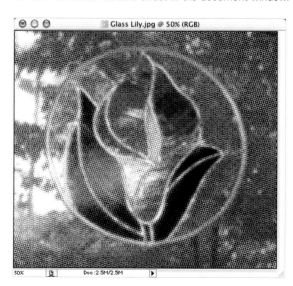

5. Alternatively, open the Filter menu, select Sketch, and choose Halftone Pattern. The Halftone Pattern dialog box opens.
6. Choose a Pattern Type for the halftone and adjust the Size and Contrast settings by dragging the slider controls.
7. View the halftone image in the document window.

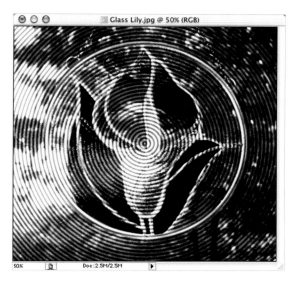

 Halftone effects reorganize the pixels in an image into spot-shaped cells, or halftone cells. A halftone image doesn't contain the clarity of a traditional photograph image, but can give a simple image a distinct look.

COMBINING EFFECTS

Combining effects can be tricky. You can use layers to view how one effect will look, but because each effect is based on the current picture, it's not easy to determine which effect to add when, and with what settings, in order to create a particular look from a group of effects.

There are a couple of ways you can experiment with effects without ruining the original picture. Obviously, you can create a copy of the original, and add and undo effects until your picture evolves into something you want to save. Memory permitting, you can add as many effects as you like. If you never choose the Save command, you can always close the image without saving the changes.

If you have plenty of hard disk space, you can add layers with different sets of effects to an image. Then save the file as a Photoshop file. Keep in mind that a 1MB JPEG image can easily grow beyond 20MB if it's saved as a Photoshop file.

APPLYING STROKE EFFECTS

Although Photoshop has a set of stroke-related features for drawing on an image, this section focuses on stroke effects, which can add brush strokes to a digital photo. Stroke effects can be found in a couple of Filter submenus: Brush Strokes and Sketch. The Sketch effect uses the colors in the color well to create a particular effect, whereas the Brush Strokes effect works solely with the image's pixels.

BRUSH STROKE EFFECTS

When you choose a Brush Stroke effect, a preview appears in the dialog box for the effect, enabling you to adjust the settings for that effect before you apply your choices. Use the Hand tool to move the preview image around to see how the effect applies to different areas of the image. The following steps show you how to apply the Crosshatch and Sprayed Strokes effects to an image.

1. Open an image file. Open the Filter menu, select Brush Strokes, and choose Crosshatch. The Crosshatch dialog box opens.
2. Drag the slider controls to adjust the Stroke Length, Sharpness, and Strength settings for this effect.
3. Click on OK to apply the first effect.
4. Open the Filter menu, select Brush Strokes, and choose Sprayed Strokes. The Sprayed Strokes dialog box opens.
5. Adjust the Stroke Length, Spray Radius, and Stroke Dir. Settings; then click on OK.
4. View the effects in the window.

 If you don't like a particular effect or combination of effects, simply click on a previous effect in the History palette. The document window will revert to the effect settings chosen in the History palette.

SKETCH EFFECTS

Select a foreground color in the toolbox and then select a sketch effect to apply the effect based on the selected color. The following steps show you how to apply the Bas Relief effect to an image:

1. Open an image in Photoshop.

2. Choose the desired foreground color.
3. Open the Filter menu, choose Sketch, and select Bas Relief. The Bas Relief dialog box opens.
4. Adjust the Detail, Smoothness, and Light Dir. settings as needed; then click OK.
5. View the effect in the document window.

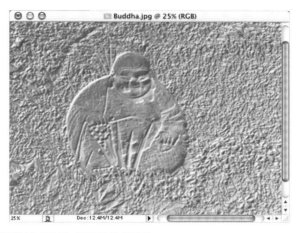

STYLIZE EFFECTS

Most of the stylize effects work with edge patterns in an image to create a special effect. Naturally, it's not always obvious what a stylize effect can do. However, if you adjust the contrast or levels of an image prior to applying edge-related effects, you can force some effects to stand out a little more. The following steps show you how to apply the extrude effect to an image:

1. Open an image file.

2. Open the Filter menu, select Stylize, and choose Extrude. The Extrude dialog box opens.
3. Adjust the Type, Size, Depth, and other settings. Click on OK and view the effect in the document window.

ADDING 3D EFFECTS

Convert part of an image into a three-dimensional object by applying the 3D Effect Render filter to a picture. This effect opens a 3D Transform and includes a toolbox, in addition to a preview window and tool options. Choose a square, sphere, or cylinder 3D tool from the toolbox. Drag in the miniaturized grayscale preview image to create the 3D object. Use a selection tool to place the 3D object in the 3D Transform window. Edit the 3D shape with the Direct Selection tool. Do the following steps to create a 3D effect in a picture:

1. Open an image file. Open the Filter menu, choose Render, and select 3D Transform.
2. Choose a 3D tool, like the sphere, from the toolbox at the left side of the 3D Transform window. Then drag to create the sphere or other shape in the image preview window. Place it over the part of the image to which you want to apply the 3D effect.

3. Click on the Trackball tool (right tool on the second row from the bottom) and then drag on the 3D image area in the preview to specify the amount of 3D.
4. You can move the sphere with the Pan Camera tool (left tool on the second row from bottom). This places the 3D image in its own separate area in the document window.
5. Click on OK and view the 3D effect in the document window.

Combine the 3D effects with other pictures. Use layers, masks, and channels to create your own image compositions.

LIQUIFYING IMAGES

Use the Liquify tool to create interesting effects or to reconstruct, freeze, or thaw part of an image being previewed. Freeze and thaw tools work similarly to masks. Frozen pixels, which are usually marked by a special color such as red, cannot be edited, whereas thawed pixels can. The Liquify command appears near the top of the Image menu, located above the listing of filter categories (along with the Extract and Pattern Maker commands).

The following steps provide a brief tour of the effects in the Liquify command:

1. Open an image file. Open the Filter menu and choose Liquify.

2. Click on the Warp tool, located at the top of the toolbox. Drag it over the image and watch the pixels distort in the direction of the mouse pointer as you drag it.

3. Choose one of the two Twirl tools from the toolbox. Move the mouse pointer over an area to distort; then press and hold down the mouse button; watch the tool twirl the pixels.
4. Use the Turbulence, Pucker, and Bloat tools to apply additional distortions.
5. Click on OK to apply your changes to the image.

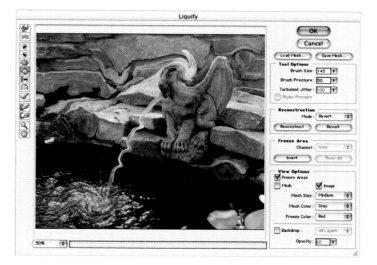

 Press Command/Ctrl+Shift+X to open the Liquify window. Change the brush size and pressure and other settings between tool selections to enhance the desired effect.

CHAPTER 7

CREATING OBJECTS AND GRADIENTS

CUSTOMIZE AN IMAGE BY CREATING OR SELECTING AN IMAGE OBJECT IN THE IMAGE WINDOW. YOU CAN ADD A BITMAPPED OR VECTOR OBJECT TO AN IMAGE. BECAUSE YOU'RE EDITING DIGITAL PICTURES, THIS CHAPTER FOCUSES ON HOW TO WORK WITH BITMAP GRAPHICS USING THE SELECTION AND DRAWING TOOLS. YOU CAN CREATE VECTOR OR BITMAP GRAPHICS IN PHOTOSHOP 7 USING THE SHAPE AND DRAWING TOOLS IN THE TOOLBOX. USE THESE TOOLS TO CREATE CUSTOM GRAPHICS AND MASKS, ENHANCE A SPECIFIC COLOR, OR APPLY A GRADIENT TO PART OF A PHOTO. (A GRADIENT IS A TYPE OF COLOR CHANGE WHERE ONE COLOR BLENDS INTO ANOTHER WITHIN A PARTICULAR AREA, SUCH AS WITHIN AN IMAGE OBJECT.) YOU CAN COMBINE VECTOR GRAPHICS WITH BITMAP GRAPHICS TO CREATE GREAT-LOOKING PICTURES.

See Chapters 9, "Customizing Images with Masks," and 12, "Creating Custom Masks," for more information about masks.

DRAWING WITH PHOTOSHOP TOOLS

Even if you're not an artist, you can use Photoshop's drawing tools to follow the lines in a photo to create a custom shape. The Pen tool enables you to create a line that can match any photographable shape. You can draw directly on a layer and then copy and paste the image to a new layer or to a different image window. You can also use the shape tools, Pencil, Brush, and Paint Bucket tools to add or edit graphics.

You'll find a great group of selection tools, plus a powerful set of bitmap editing tools, such as the Smudge tool, in the toolbox. Access or edit foreground and background colors from the toolbox, or from the Color or Swatches palettes. At the bottom of the toolbox is a button that takes you directly to ImageReady, which contains even more tools organized similarly to those in Photoshop.

CREATING OBJECT PATHS

Don't be thrown off by such an ambiguous name. An object path, also referred to as a path or path object, exists as a series of points creating a line. You can use the shape tools or Pen tool to create and edit paths. However, only shapes are created as vector graphics—resolution-independent graphics that preserve detail and clarity if scaled to a larger or smaller size.

Paths created with the Pen tool or with a shape tool appear in the Paths palette. Click on a layer in the Layers palette; then view any paths stored in that layer in the Paths palette. Add, remove, and group vector graphics to help create effects localized to specific objects in a picture. The following steps show you how to create a path object with the Pen tool.

1. Select the Pen tool in the toolbox.

Clicking again sets the second point and follows the curve established by the handles for the first point

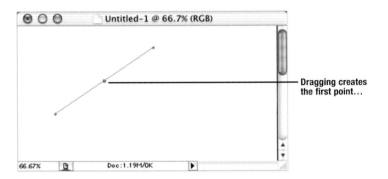

Dragging creates the first point...

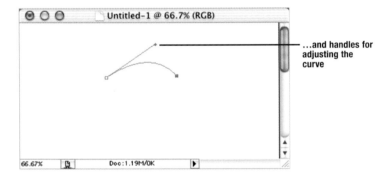

...and handles for adjusting the curve

2. Click in the image window to create the first point of the path. If you drag to create the first point, handles appear so you can set how much the line will curve between the first point and the next point that you add. Click a second time to create the second point in the path. If you drag to create the second point, you can set the curve of the line to that point. Press the Delete key to remove the previously created point. Click on the first point to close the path, or click on the Move tool (V) to de-select the Pen tool. Create a line that completely surrounds an object in the image window by clicking along the borders of the object. This creates a connect-the-dots effect.

3. Be sure to click on the starting point to close the path object. (When you are back at the starting point, a small circle appears along with the pen mouse pointer.)

4. To edit the path when needed, press and hold Command/Ctrl; then drag to move an anchor point as desired. Simply click on an anchor point to delete it.

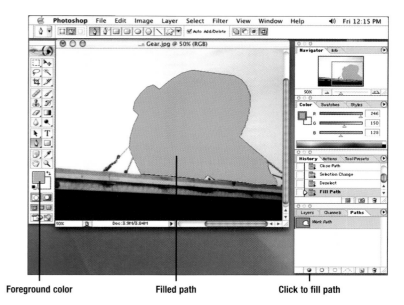

Foreground color   **Filled path**   **Click to fill path**

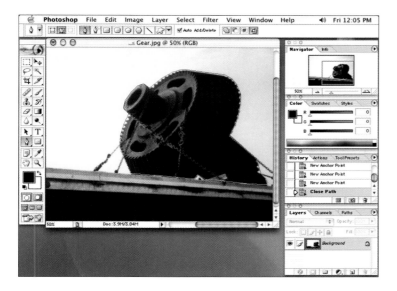

5. Choose a new foreground color.

6. Display the Paths palette by clicking the Paths tab or choosing Window, Paths.

7. Click the Fill Path with Foreground Color button at the bottom of the Paths palette.

8. The path you create initially appears as a work path. It's a good idea to save the path so that you can use it again. To do so, click on the Paths palette menu button and click Save Path.

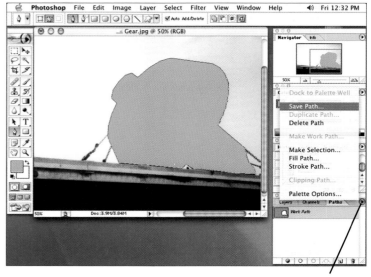

**Paths palette
menu button**

Every palette window in Photoshop has a common set of icons and buttons similar to the ones you'll find in the Paths palette. For example, there's a palette menu (right arrow) button in the upper-right corner of every palette window. If you click on this button, you'll see a pop-up menu offering commands for that palette. Most palettes also include a button at the bottom of the window that looks like a document; use this button to create a new item in the palette, such as a new layer. Most palettes also include a Delete (trash) button at the bottom for deleting the selected item (such as the selected path), as well as a couple of custom buttons.

9. Type a name for the path in the Name text box of the Save Path dialog box that appears and then click on OK. The path appears with its new name in the Paths palette.
10. To load the currently-selected path as a selection at any time, select the path name in the Paths palette and then click the Load Path as a Selection button at the bottom of the Paths palette.
11. Add a new fill layer or adjustment layer to blend in colors, gradients, or effects to the path object. Select the layer containing the object path by clicking the layer in the Layers palette. Choose Layer, New Fill Layer, or choose Layer, New Adjustment Layer. Choose the type of layer to add in the submenu that appears. Adjust settings in the dialog box that appears and click OK. Be sure the new layer appears above the object path layer in the list of layers in the Layers palette. The following example shows a path filled with a pattern.

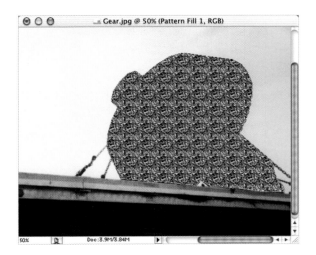

Press P to select the Pen tool in the toolbox. Press Shift+P to cycle between the Pen and Freeform Pen tool.

Combining a path with a new fill or adjustment layer in this way enables you to display or hide the path effect at will by clicking the eye icon beside the layer in the Layers palette.

To create a path using one of the shape tools (the tools that appear when you Control+/right-click on the Rectangle tool), choose the desired tool and then be sure to click the Paths button on the options bar. If the Shape Layers or Fill Pixels button is selected instead, the tool will not create a path (vector), it will create a new object (bitmap), either on a new layer or on the current layer.

EDITING GRAPHICS WITH BITMAP TOOLS

Images are bitmaps, which is a fancy name for a group of pixels. Bitmap tools, such as the Smudge and Blur tools, let you create or edit pixels. Other tools, like the Levels command, enable you to adjust the tonal range of pixels across an image object. If you zoom into a digital photograph, you'll notice a huge matrix of pixels. With thousands or millions of colors to choose from, it's pretty tough to just go in and tweak a pixel with the Pencil tool. Because bitmap images can be so complex, tools like the Clone Stamp, Nudge, Smudge, and Blur tools are invaluable image-editing tools. See Chapter 5, "Correcting Images," to find out how to use the Clone Stamp tool.

LEVELS TOOL

The Levels tool is available as an adjustment layer (which is probably the best way to use this kind of tool), as well as from the Image, Adjustments submenu. Alternatively, press Command/Ctrl+L to open the Levels dialog box. If an object or gradient doesn't quite match the tonal range of the rest of the picture (or if you want to make the selection stand out a bit more), try applying a levels adjustment to see whether it results in any improvement. The Levels tool enables you to adjust the highlight and shadow (white and black) levels that represent the tonal range of a picture.

The following steps show you how to adjust the tonal range levels of a selected bitmap image object:

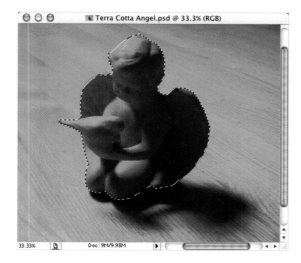

1. Open the image to adjust and select a particular area to edit using the selection tool of your choice in the image window. (Don't forget that you can load a path you've created previously as a selection.)
2. Choose Layer, New Adjustment Layer, Levels. (Alternately, choose Image, Adjustments, Levels to perform the edit on the current layer.)
3. Type a name for the layer in the Name text box of the New Layer dialog box; then click OK. The Levels dialog box opens.
4. Select a specific channel to adjust, if needed, using the Channel pop-up menu. To adjust all the channels, leave RGB selected.
5. Adjust the levels using the sliders at the bottom of the Input Levels histogram. The left slider adjusts the darker levels, the right slider adjusts the lighter tones, and the middle slider adjusts the mid-range tones.
6. Click OK to apply the changes.

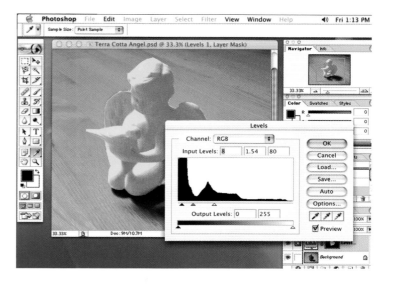

SMUDGE TOOL

Make fine-tuned adjustments to an object or gradient using the Nudge, Smudge, and Zoom tools. Smear pixels around in an image with the Smudge tool. If you need to make more exact edits, use the Zoom tool to zoom into the pixels. Then zoom back out (hold down the Alt/Option key and click on the image with the Zoom tool) to see whether you created a desirable effect. The following steps show you how to use the Smudge tool:

1. Choose the Smudge tool (it's the hand with a pointed finger icon) in the toolbox. You can Control/right-click the Blur tool and then click Smudge Tool in the shortcut menu that appears, or press Shift+R to cycle through the Sharpen and Blur tools to get to the Smudge tool.
2. Choose Brush, Mode, and Strength settings on the options bar.
3. Drag the mouse in the image window.

4. Undo a smudge by selecting an earlier instance of the Smudge tool in the History palette. Or open the Edit menu and choose the Undo Smudge tool command.

WORKING WITH FOREGROUND AND BACKGROUND COLORS

You can use the toolbox, Color palette, and Swatches palette to select foreground and background colors for use with various tools. Use the Eyedropper tool to choose a specific color in an image to serve as the foreground or background color, for example. Edit the foreground or background colors by clicking the Set Foreground Color or Set Background Color squares in the toolbox. Click or Option/Alt+click a color on the color ramp at the bottom of the Color palette, or click or Command/Ctrl+click a color on the Swatches palette. You can choose from thousands or millions of colors to work with. This range of selectable colors is limited, however, to the amount of dedicated video or graphics memory installed in your computer, and to the number of colors set for your display under Mac OS X or Windows.

Photoshop uses color-management settings to define the range of colors that make up the RGB color mode or any of its other color modes, such as CMYK. The biggest problem that color management solves is how to provide a consistent definition of the way a color should look on a monitor, camera, video tape, printer, or other image-related computer peripheral. Without color management, a yellow in Photoshop might appear as an orange or green color on a different computer or printer.

Color management is a complex subject, and although it's definitely a topic worth reading about, I'm recommending you leave the color-management settings as the Photoshop defaults. Unless the colors in an RGB image are wrong, don't change the color-management settings. The section in Chapter 3 titled, "Viewing Color Settings" explains how to calibrate your monitor to work best with Photoshop's colors.

If you see an alert icon in the Color palette after choosing a color, that means the color falls outside the allowable colors for the current color mode and other settings. Choose another color to avoid problems with printing or displaying the image.

If you display the Color Settings dialog box (choose Photoshop, Color Settings on a Mac or Edit, Color Settings on a Windows machine), you should see sRGB IEC61966-2.1 as the default choice for the RGB pop-up menu in the Working Spaces section. If you save an image file with this default color setting, most colors will translate correctly if the image file is opened with another graphics application, such as Macromedia's Fireworks.

Mac operating systems include the ColorSync color-management system. You can synchronize Photoshop to work with ColorSync by choosing ColorSync Workflow from the Settings pop-up menu in the Color Settings dialog box (Photoshop, Color Settings). On a Windows PC, you can choose an alternate color-management system (ColorSync is not available) from the Settings drop-down menu in the Color Settings window. Note that you typically only need to change color synchronizations for professional color output. Your printing vendor can give you more guidance about what color management system to use.

CHOOSING A COLOR

Changing or selecting a color is a fairly simple task. First, click on Set Foreground Color or Set Background Color square at the bottom of the toolbox. The Color Picker dialog box opens. Click on a general color in the vertical color bar near the center of the dialog box and click on a color in the Select Foreground (Background) Color area at the left side of the dialog box. Click on OK, and the specified foreground or background color becomes active.

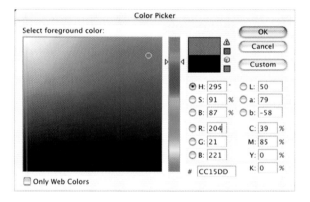

You can choose one of two methods to use the Color palette to choose colors. For the first method, click either the Set Foreground Color or Set Background Color square in the palette (click Cancel to close the Color Picker dialog box, if it opens); then drag the R, G, and B, sliders to create the color. You also can use the mouse to select a color in the Color palette. Click on the desired foreground color in the color ramp (the band of colors along the bottom of the palette). Option/Alt+click on the desired background color in the color ramp.

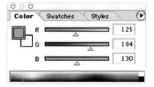

Finally, you can select and edit colors using the Swatches palette. Click the swatch with the desired foreground color, or Command/Ctrl+click the desired background color. To sample a new color from the image, choose the Eyedropper tool in the toolbox and then click the desired color for the new swatch in the image. Click on the Create New Swatch of Foreground Color button at the bottom of the Swatches palette to add the new swatch. Control+/right-click any swatch and then click Delete Swatch in the shortcut menu that appears to remove the swatch from the palette. The Swatches palette enables you to create, edit, group, or delete a custom set of colors, which can be saved to a file and used with other image files. To work with various sets of swatches, click on the Swatches palette menu button in the upper-right corner of the palette.

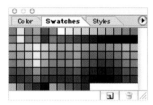

EXAMPLE: APPLYING A COLOR WITH THE SWATCHES PALETTE

This example shows you how to use the Swatches palette along with the Paint Bucket tool to fill a selection of an image with a new color. If you want, you can substitute another method of selecting a foreground color for the fill.

1. Open an image file and use the method of your choice to select the area to fill with a new color.

2. Click on the Swatches palette or choose Window, Swatches. The Swatches palette becomes active.

3. Click on a different color in the Swatches palette. The color becomes the current foreground color.

4. Select the Paint Bucket tool from the toolbox. If needed Control+/right-click on the Gradient tool and then click Paint Bucket Tool in the shortcut menu that appears.

5. Click in the selected area to fill it with the new color. You may need to click, multiple times to fill non-contiguous parts of the selection, such as the spaces within the letters O, A, and R in this example

6. Choose Select, Deselect to finish recoloring, if needed.

 You can copy and paste a specific area of a picture and save it to its own layer. Then edit specific colors before moving it back to the original image.

UNDERSTANDING GRADIENTS

A gradient gradually blends two or more colors. A basic gradient blends the current foreground color and background colors. You apply a gradient with the Gradient tool in the toolbox. You can create, define, and apply a gradient to an image or a selection.

Photoshop offers five different gradients: Linear, Radial, Angular, Reflected, and Diamond. After you've selected the Gradient tool, a button on the options bar represents each type of gradient. Simply click on the gradient to apply it. The linear gradient creates a layered blend of colors, whereas the radial and angle gradients blend the colors in a circular pattern. As you might expect, the diamond gradient blends its colors in the shape of a diamond. Two or more linear gradients blend outward in the reflected gradient.

Choose from any of the pre-installed gradients or create your own in the Gradient Editor window. Gradients can be used to blend images together in a picture, or enhance an image.

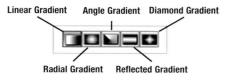

Linear Gradient   Angle Gradient   Diamond Gradient

Radial Gradient   Reflected Gradient

APPLYING A GRADIENT

A gradient can be applied across an entire image or to a selected area of an image or object. Use the Magic Wand, Lasso or shape selection tools (found when you Control+/right-click on the Rectangular Marquee tool) to choose the specific part of the image to customize with a gradient.

By default, the gradient uses the current foreground and background colors. It's easiest to choose the desired foreground and background colors prior to selecting the Gradient tool. Follow these steps to apply a gradient to a selection in an image:

1. Open an image and use the desired selection tool from the toolbox to select the area to which you want to apply the gradient. (Don't forget that you can load a path you've created previously as a selection.)
2. Choose the desired foreground and background colors for the gradient.

3. Choose the Gradient tool in the toolbox. The gradient options appear on the options bar.
4. Choose the type of gradient to apply by clicking the appropriate button on the options bar.
5. Drag on the image within the selection. The starting point for your drag operation defines the center of the gradient. The angle of the stroke, or line that appears when you drag, defines the angle of the radius of gradient. The length of that line determines the radius size of the gradient. The diamond gradient works a little differently than the other types of gradients. The line drawn defines a corner location and shape of the diamond gradient.

6. View the gradient in the image window.

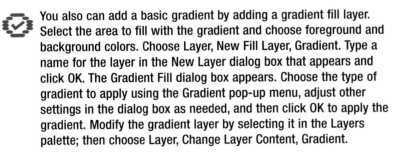

Press G to select the Gradient tool in the toolbox. Press Shift+G to cycle between the Gradient and Paint Bucket tools.

You also can add a basic gradient by adding a gradient fill layer. Select the area to fill with the gradient and choose foreground and background colors. Choose Layer, New Fill Layer, Gradient. Type a name for the layer in the New Layer dialog box that appears and click OK. The Gradient Fill dialog box appears. Choose the type of gradient to apply using the Gradient pop-up menu, adjust other settings in the dialog box as needed, and then click OK to apply the gradient. Modify the gradient layer by selecting it in the Layers palette; then choose Layer, Change Layer Content, Gradient.

CREATING A CUSTOM GRADIENT

After you've applied a gradient, you can edit it and even save the edited gradient as your own custom gradient. To begin the process, first choose the Gradient tool in the toolbox. Then click the Click to Edit the Gradient choice (it's the preview of the current gradient), located near the left end of the options bar, to open the Gradient Editor window.

Click here to display the Gradient Editor dialog box

Once you've opened the Gradient Editor dialog box, you can perform a variety of activities. You can apply a different gradient by clicking on one of the Presets at the top of the dialog box. You can click the color stops at the bottom of the preview bar to edit the foreground or background color (the Color option under Stops becomes active when you do this, so that you can change the color). You can add more colors by adding a color stop. You can then type a new gradient name and save your custom gradient.

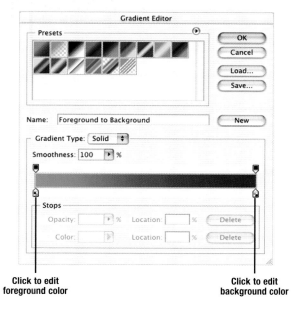

Click to edit foreground color

Click to edit background color

The following steps present an example of how to customize gradient colors and save the custom gradient:

1. With the layer holding the gradient selected in the Layers palette, choose the Gradient tool in the toolbox.
2. Click the Click to Edit the Gradient choice (it's the preview) on the options bar to open the Gradient Editor window.
3. If needed, drag one of the color stops along the bottom of the preview bar to make room for the new color. Then click along the bottom of the bar to add a stop for a third gradient color. (You can add new stops between existing stops or to the left or right of existing stops if there's space available on the bar.)

4. The new stop should be selected. (If not. click it to select it.) Then double-click the Color box and the bottom of the dialog box to open the Color Picker dialog box.
5. Use the Color Picker as described earlier in this chapter to select a new color and click on OK.
6. Type a name for the custom gradient in the Name text box, midway down the dialog box.
7. Click the New button to the right of the Name text box to save the new, custom gradient.

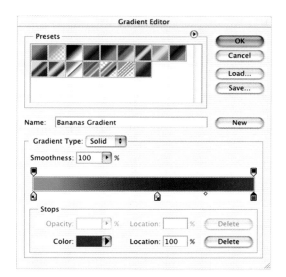

8. Click on OK to save the new gradient.
9. Reapply the gradient as described in the earlier section "Applying a Gradient."

 If you create a number of custom gradients in the Gradient Editor dialog box, you can save them as a set. First, create the custom gradients as desired. All the gradients show in the Presets area will be saved in the set, so you can delete unneeded gradients if you want. To do so, Control+/right-click a preset; then click Delete Gradient. When only the needed gradients appear, click the Save button to display the Save dialog box. Type a name for the gradient set in the Save As text box (leave the .grd extension in place), specify a save directory using the Where pop-up menu, and click Save. You can use the Load button back in the Gradient Editor dialog box to load your custom gradients at any time. To redisplay the default gradients (or choose another set of gradients shipped with Photoshop), click on the menu button (with the right arrow on it) in the Presets area; then click Reset Gradients.

CHAPTER 8

COMBINING
CONTENT
WITH
LAYERS

COMBINING CONTENT
WITH LAYERS

LAYERS LEND PHOTOSHOP ITS MAGIC. LIKE A TRANSPARENT
SHEET OF PAPER, EACH LAYER CAN HOLD DIFFERENT IMAGE
CONTENT. WHEN STACKED ON TOP OF ONE ANOTHER, THE
LAYERS (TRANSPARENT SHEETS) OVERLAY ONE ANOTHER TO
FORM THE FINISHED IMAGE. LAYERS ENABLE YOU TO MAKE
CHANGES TO ONE ELEMENT IN AN IMAGE WITHOUT AFFECTING
OTHER IMAGE DATA. ALL LAYERS SHARE THE SAME
RESOLUTION, CHANNELS, AND IMAGE MODE (SUCH AS RGB
IMAGE MODE). YOU CAN MOVE, ADD, DELETE, AND DRAW ON A
LAYER WITHOUT AFFECTING THE IMAGE CONTENT IN OTHER
LAYERS.

Any image file from a digital camera or scanner that you open in Photoshop contains one layer—the background layer. You add additional layers into the image file—such as text layers, shape layers, and fill and adjustment layers—to build the image content. As you add layers to the image file, you can turn any layer on or off in the Layers palette. Turning a layer off hides its content. The remaining active layers (marked as visible in the Layers palette) remain visible in the image window. When you copy or paste image objects from another image or application, they appear on a new layer. As you complete an image in Photoshop, you can merge selected layers or flatten all layers into one.

You view, edit, and delete layers from the Layers palette; many of the commands located in the Layers palette can also be found in the Layer menu. This chapter covers layer basics. See Chapter 11, "Experimenting with Layers," for more advanced layer topics.

> To use layers, you must save a file in the Photoshop (PSD) format. The TIF and JPEG formats native to most scanners and digital cameras cannot include layers. The Background layer in an image file holds the main image content, such as the photo you actually shot with a digital camera or scanned. By default, there are certain operations you cannot perform on the Background layer. For example, you cannot apply certain filters to the Background layer. The section called "The Background Layer," later in this chapter, explains how to work around this issue.

WORKING WITH THE LAYERS PALETTE

Any layers created for an image file can be viewed, hidden, copied, merged, locked, edited, or deleted using the Layers palette. When you add a layer to an image file, it appears as the top-most layer (first in the list) in the palette window. However, you can drag layers to reorganize them in the Layers palette, which adjusts how the content appears in the image window to correspond with the new layer order. With Photoshop 7, you can create layer sets to group specific layer settings with a selected set of layers. To

view the Layers palette at any time, click the Layers tab or choose Window, Layers.

> Although Photoshop will technically let you create up to 8,000 layers, the number of layers you can create is limited to the amount of your computer's physical memory, the amount of free space on your system's hard disk, and the Memory Usage setting specified in Photoshop preferences. To adjust the latter setting, choose Photoshop, Preferences, Memory & Image Cache (Mac) or Edit, Preferences, Memory & Image Cache (Windows). Increase the value for the Maximum Used by Photoshop setting, and then click OK.

THE BACKGROUND LAYER

The Background layer is sort of sacred in Photoshop, but don't take my word for it. Try to find layer properties or apply a blending mode for the Background layer, and you'll find that these settings are disabled in the Layers palette. You must double-click on the Background layer to adjust mode and opacity settings.

The background layer always appears as the bottom-most layer. Its stacking order cannot be changed. However, you can copy and paste the image from the Background layer to another layer or image window in order to manipulate the layer content.

You can make a copy of the Background layer, or copy the Background layer to a new layer, in the Layers palette. To work around this problem, you can copy the Background layer. To do so, drag the Background layer over the Create a New Layer (document) button at the bottom of the Layers palette. Then hide the original Background layer by clicking the eye icon beside it. Once you've hidden the Background layer, you can perform any needed operations on the copy you made of that layer.

LAYERS PALETTE BUTTONS

A note in the last chapter touched on the fact that most Photoshop palettes have standard buttons and features. Because layer operations will form the core of your editing activities in Photoshop, take a moment now to become really familiar with the Layers palette. The following steps show you how to use the buttons in the Layers palette:

1. Open an image file.
2. Click on the Create New Fill or Adjustment Layer button on the bottom of the Layers palette. The button has a half-black, half-white circle. A menu of adjustment layer choices appears.

3. Click the Levels choice in the menu. The Levels dialog box appears, and a new layer appears in the Layers palette.
4. Adjust the levels for the image and then click OK. To find out more about how to adjust the controls in the Levels window, go to "Adjusting Tonal Levels" in Chapter 5, "Correcting Images."
5. Click on the Background layer in the Layers palette. That layer becomes the active layer.
6. Click on the Create a New Set (folder) button at the bottom of the Layers palette to create a new layer set. Drag the new Levels 1 layer into the layer set folder in the Layers palette.
7. Click on the eye icon next to the Levels 1 layer to toggle its display off.
8. Click on the empty check box next to the box that held the eye icon. A link icon appears, linking the selected layer with the layer below it.
9. Clear the link and click the box for the eye icon to redisplay the Levels 1 layer.

10. Save the image as a Photoshop file to preserve the new layer.

 Control+/right-click in any layer to view a shortcut (contextual) menu for the selected layer.

 To select a layer, click it in the Layers palette.

ADDING A NEW LAYER INTO AN IMAGE

To add a new, blank layer into an image, follow these steps:

1. Open the image in Photoshop. If it's an image that you've just scanned or imported from your digital camera, notice that the image has only the Background layer in the Layers palette. The Background layer contains the image content.

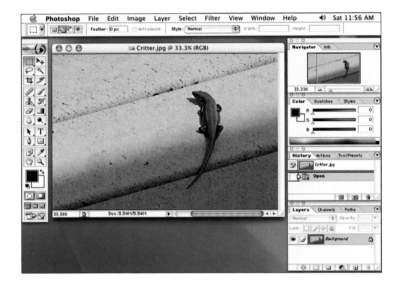

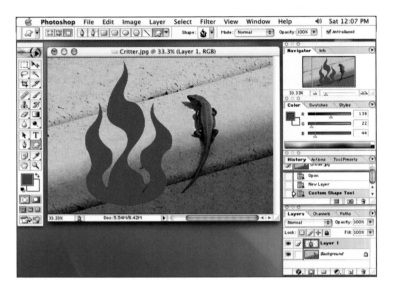

2. Click on the Create a New Layer button (located beside the Trash button) at the bottom of the Layers palette. Alternately, you can choose Layer, New, Layer or press Shift+Command/Ctrl+N to create a new layer.

3. A new layer appears in the Layers palette. You can now add content to the new layer, such as painted strokes or filled shapes. (Note that using the Text tools automatically adds a separate layer to hold the text.) The remaining steps give an example of adding content to the new layer.

4. Click the new layer in the layers palette, if needed. This makes the layer active, so the layer will hold the new content that you add.

5. Choose a tool, such as the Brush tool, or choose one of the shape tools, such as the rectangle tool.

6. Specify options for the tool on the options bar. For example, choose a brush size and shape for the Brush tool, or choose the Fill Pixels button on the options bar for a shape tool.

7. Specify a new foreground color using the method of your choice.

8. Click or drag on the layer to add the desired content.

9. To hide the content on the new layer at any time, click the eye icon beside the layer in the Layers palette.

 If you want to layer the content of a new layer behind what's on the Background layer, start by creating a new, blank layer. Copy the Background layer content to the new layer and delete the Background layer content. You can add and arrange additional layers as you prefer.

 All the functions handled from the Layers palette are also available via the Layer menu. You can create a new layer, add fill and adjustment layers, or make changes to layers. Grayed-out items in the Layer menu indicate that the option is not available for the currently selected layer.

LOOKING AT LAYER PROPERTIES, BLENDING STYLES, AND MERGING

Considering all the kinds of layers you can work with in Photoshop, it's surprising, and a little relieving, to find that most layers contain similar characteristics. You can create, edit, or delete a layer by choosing one of the many commands in the Layer menu or buttons on the Layers palette. Fill layers, adjustment layers, and regular layers (those you create to hold content) have properties, modes, and other settings that you can change. Layer properties include the layer name and color. You also can assign a blending mode, opacity setting or lock transparency, image, position, or all layer properties for the selected layer.

Blending modes consist of a base color (from the selected layer), blend color (from the layer below it), and the result color (the blended result appears in the image window). Blending modes only affect the layer directly below the selected layer. If there's no image below the selected layer, changing blending modes won't produce any visible change to the selected layer. Choose from Normal, Dissolve, Multiply, Screen, Overlay, Soft Light, Hard Light, Color Dodge, Color Burn, Darken, Lighten, Difference, Exclusion, Hue, Saturation, Color, or Luminosity blending modes.

The following list contains a brief description of each blending mode. You will find some or all of these blending modes in other command windows, such as the Apply Image or Calculations windows. You can also apply a blending mode to a tool by choosing the mode menu from the options bar for the selected tool.

* Normal—This is the default mode of a layer.
* Dissolve—Randomly replaces blend colors with base colors to create result colors.
* Darken—Selects the base or blend color (the darker of the two colors) as the result color.
* Multiply—Multiplies the base color with the blend color, usually resulting in a darker color.
* Color Burn—Darkens the base color (by adding contrast) to approach the blend color. No change occurs if you try to blend with white.

* Linear Burn—Darkens the base color (by curtailing brightness) to approach the blend color. No change occurs if you try to blend with white.
* Lighten—Selects the base or blend color (the lighter of the two colors) as the result color.
* Screen—Multiplies the inverse of the blend and base colors, usually resulting in a lighter color.
* Color Dodge—Brightens the base color (by curtailing contrast) to approach the blend color. No change occurs if you try to blend with black.
* Linear Dodge—Brightens the base color (by adding brightness) to approach the blend color. No change occurs if you try to blend with black.
* Overlay—Screens and mixes the base and blend colors and multiplies them to show the lightness or darkness of the color from the original layer.
* Soft Light—Depending on the blend color (dodges or burns depending on whether the blend color is lighter or darker than 50% gray), will lighten or darken resulting colors with an appearance like a soft spotlight.
* Hard Light—Depending on the blend color (screens or multiplies depending on whether the blend color is lighter or darker than 50% gray), will lighten or darken resulting colors with an appearance like a focused spotlight.
* Vivid Light—Depending on the blend color (whether the blend color is lighter or darker than 50% gray), dodges or burns the image (adjusting contrast) to lighten or darken resulting colors.
* Linear Light—Depending on the blend color (whether the blend color is lighter or darker than 50% gray), dodges or burns the image (adjusting brightness) to lighten or darken resulting colors.
* Pin Light—Depending on the blend color (whether the blend color is lighter or darker than 50% gray, with the blend color acting as the light source), will replace colors darker than a light source that's less than 50% gray or replace colors lighter than a light source that's more than 50% gray.
* Difference—Subtracts either the base from the blend color or vice versa, depending on which has the higher brightness value. Blending with white inverts the base colors. No change occurs if you blend with black.
* Exclusion—Creates result colors similar to Difference mode, but with lower contrast.
* Hue—Uses the luminance and saturation of the base color and the hue of the blend color to mix the final color.

* Saturation—Uses the luminance and hue of the base color and the saturation of the blend color to mix the final color.
* Color—Uses the luminance of the base color and the hue and saturation of the blend color to mix the final color.
* Luminosity—Uses the hue and saturation of the base color and the luminance of the blend color to mix the final color. This blending mode is the inverse of the Color blending mode.

Choose Layer Styles from the Layer menu or click the Add a Layer Style button at the bottom of the Layers palette to customize a layer's blending options with the layer below it or add a layer effect. You also can use the pop-up menu at the top of the Layers palette to choose a layer blending style. Combine two or more layers by choosing one of the Merge commands from the Layer menu. The following steps provide a brief overview of the adjusting layer blending, opacity, and more using the Layers palette and Layer menu commands:

1. Open an image file that has multiple layers or add new layers into an existing image. (Be sure to save the image in Photoshop PSD format to preserve the layers.)

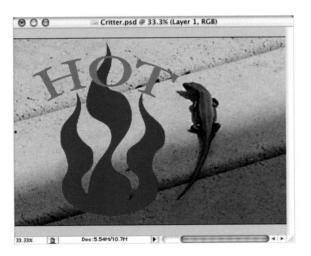

2. Select a layer in the Layers palette.
3. Choose Layer, Layer Style, Blending Options or click on the Add a Layer Style button at the bottom of the Layers palette and click on Blending Options. The Layer Style dialog box appears.
4. Open the Blend Mode pop-up menu at the top of the dialog box and choose the desired blend mode. Drag the Opacity slider to adjust the opacity of the layer. The lower the opacity level, the more transparent the selected layer becomes. Click OK to apply the layer settings. (To adjust the layer directly, use the pop-up menu at the top left of the Layers palette to choose the blending mode and then use the Opacity setting at upper-right to change the opacity.)

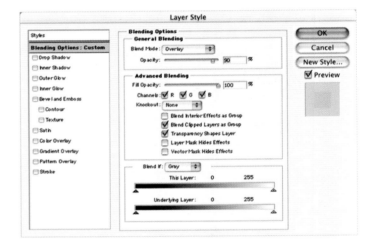

5. The Layers palette offers four lock settings for each layer. You can lock the layer's transparency (transparent pixels), content (image pixels), position, and all three. (All three settings are locked on the Background layer by default.) Applying lock settings prevents unwanted changes on the layer. Choose the lock settings for the current layer by clicking the appropriate Lock button on the Layers palette. In the image below, the Layer 1 layer has been locked; previously, the Overlay blending mode and reduced opacity were applied to the layer, resulting in the gradated blend of the flame object.

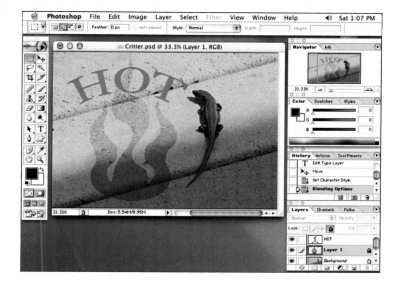

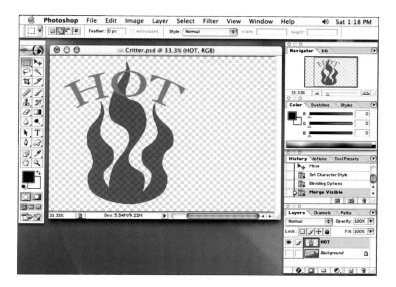

6. Choose a layer in the image; then choose Layer, Group with Previous. This links the layer to the next layer below it. The linked layer (the one that was first selected) takes on the characteristics of the layer below, including blending style and opacity. In addition, transparent areas on the layer below override pixels in the same position on the linked layer, making them transparent. This means that the content from the linked layer "disappears" from transparent areas on the layer below.

7. Choose Edit, Undo Group with Previous to remove the grouping.

8. If you want to merge certain layers, it's best to start out by hiding those you don't want to merge. To do so, click the eye icon beside each layer to hide them in the Layers palette.

9. Choose Layer, Merge Visible. This combines the content of the merged layers. Unlike when you grouped layers, no content disappears, and the content from each individual layer retains its previous blending characteristics.

10. Choose Edit, Undo Merge Visible to separate the layers and then click the eye icon box beside any hidden layer to redisplay it. .

 Double-click on an unlocked layer in the Layers palette to open the Layer Style dialog box.

 Merge a layer with the viewable layer directly below it by choosing Merge Down (which becomes Merge Layers if you select a layer) from the Layer menu.

LAYER MASKS

Adjustment and regular layers can contain layer masks in the Layers palette. Layer masks enable you to hide or reveal specific pixels in a layer or layer set. If a layer contains a layer mask, a layer mask icon will appear beside the name of that layer in the Layers palette. Follow these steps to create a layer mask in an image:

1. Add the layer that you want to mask. In this example, I'll apply a mask to a gradient layer.

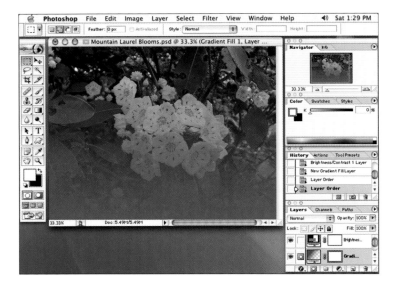

2. If the layer is an adjustment layer, it includes a layer mask by default. You need to delete that mask. To do so, Control+/right-click on the layer mask thumbnail (the white box just to the left of the layer name in the Layers palette) and then click Discard Layer Mask. This removes the original layer mask.

3. Click on the layer to mask in the Layers palette, if needed; then select all or part of the content in the layer you want to mask using the selection tool of your choice. The content that you select will still appear after you apply the mask (this may seem a bit backwards). Content that is *not* selected will be hidden by the layer mask.

4. Click on the Add a Mask button (gray rectangle with a white circle in the middle) at the bottom of the Layers palette to create the new layer mask on the selected layer. For more information about layer masks, see Chapter 11, "Experimenting with Layers."

 When you're selecting the content for your layer mask, don't forget that you can use the Select, Inverse command to invert the current selection.

LAYER MATTES

When you select the content for a layer mask, if you enter a Feather value greater than 0 and leave the Anti-Aliased check box checked on the options bar, a new option becomes available on the Layer menu when the layer holding the finished mask is selected. This command, the Matting command, defines how the edges of the masked layer content combine with the content from other layers.

The Layer, Matting submenu offers the Defringe, Remove Black Matte, and Remove White Matte options. For more information on how to use the Matting command, see Chapter 12, "Creating Custom Masks."

WHAT'S IN A LAYER SET?

A layer set appears as a folder on the Layers palette. Use the layer set to store layers with content that is related in some way. You can drag any layer except the background layer into a layer set to add that layer to the set. Because a layer set is not an image, you can't apply any effects or edit the set. However, you can adjust a layer set's opacity level, blending mode, and whether the red, green, or blue channels appear in the image window. Choose Layer Set Properties to change the name of a layer set, assign a color label to it, or determine the color channels you want to use. Like regular layers, the order of the layers stored in a layer set affect the image appearance; the bottom layer in the set is affected by any layers above it. The following steps show you how to create a layer set:

1. Open an image file. Click on the Create a New Set (folder) button at the bottom of the Layers palette, or open the Layer menu, choose New, and select Layer Set.
2. A layer folder appears in the Layers palette list. Click on the triangle beside the folder icon to collapse or expand the contents of the layer set folder.
3. Double-click the name on the new layer, type the name you prefer, and then press Return/Enter to rename the layer.

4. Drag a layer to the folder icon to add it to the set. Drag an item away from the folder to remove it from a set.

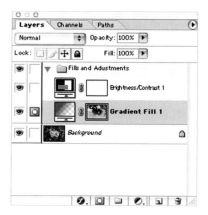

It's easiest to move the mouse pointer over the layer name to drag the layer.

USING ADJUSTMENT AND FILL LAYERS

Create layers to experiment with color correction and effects for a single image, or with multiple images you want to merge into one picture. Adjustment layers enable you to toggle specific level, color, and filter settings in a particular layer. Create a solid color or gradient fill layer to enhance the colors in a picture.

CORRECTING COLORS

Adjustment layers enable you to place adjustable levels, curves, color balance, brightness/contrast, hue/saturation, selective color, channel mixer, gradient map, invert, threshold, and posterize settings within separate layers. Make small adjustments to a tint or hue of a picture by adding a fill layer to an image. Try different level settings, or turn on different combinations of adjustment layers to tweak a picture until it looks just right.

ADJUSTMENT LAYERS

Add an adjustment layer to an image to actively edit color and level settings for that image. Click on the eye icon to turn any adjustment layer on or off. If you decide you don't want to use the adjustment layer, delete it by dragging it to the Delete Layer (trash) icon at the bottom of the Layers palette. The following steps show you how to add an adjustment layer to an image:

1. Open an image file containing one or more layers. Choose Layer, New Adjustment Layer, and then choose the type of adjustment layer to create.
2. Enter a layer name in the New Layer dialog box, if desired, and then click on OK to create the new layer.
3. View the adjustment layer settings. Check the Preview check box to view any changes you make in the image window.

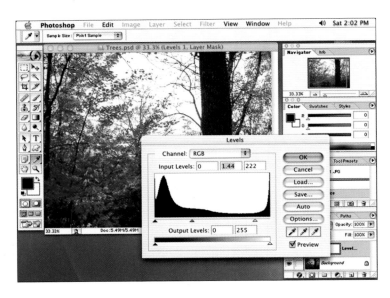

4. When you're ready to save your changes, click on OK.

COLOR LAYERS

Enhance photos by adding semi-transparent layers of colors. Make a blue sky bluer, or a sunset rosier, by adding a fill layer to an image. For a similar effect, add a color gradient layer to add color more dynamically across an image. The following steps show you how to add a solid color fill layer:

1. Open an image file. Open the Layer menu, select New Fill Layer, and choose Solid Color.
2. Enter a name for the layer in the New Layer dialog box; then click on OK to create the new layer.
3. Choose a color for the fill in the Color Picker dialog box; then click OK.

4. Adjust the opacity for the new layer by changing the Opacity setting in the Layers palette.

 Gradient and fill layers work best if you have a picture with a neutral background like a white wall or blue sky. Add several fill layers to find the best combination of colors for the image you're working with.

PREVIEWING COLOR ADJUSTMENTS

The Variations command enables you to preview various combinations of color and tone corrections and to select the appearance you prefer for your image. The following steps show you how to use the Variations commands to adjust the colors in an image:

1. Open an image file. Choose Image, Adjustments, Variations. The Variations dialog box opens.
2. Open the Image menu, select Adjust, and choose Variations.
3. Choose the Shadows, Midtones, Highlights, or Saturation option button to determine which tones to adjust.
4. Click on one or more of the thumbnail images to change the colors of the image, using the Current Pick thumbnail image to view the results of your selections.

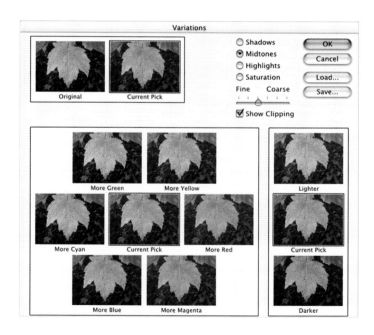

5. Lighten or darken an image by clicking on the Lighter or Darker image on the right side of the window.
6. Click OK to apply your changes.

FLATTENING ALL LAYERS

Because most image formats don't preserve layers created by Photoshop, there will come a time when you want to save a JPEG image, and Photoshop won't let you save it until you flatten all the layers. The Flatten Image command merges all layers into a single layer—the Background layer. Only use the Flatten Image command when you've finalized all layer edits. If you plan to continue working on an image but need a flattened version as well, your best bet is to save a copy of the file in Photoshop PSD format, and then perform the following steps:

 If a layer is hidden, its changes won't appear in the final background layer. Click the eye icon box to redisplay the layer, if needed.

1. Open an image file containing one or more layers.
2. Open the Layer menu and choose Flatten Image. Whether you have one layer or 800, the Flatten Image command will combine all layers into the background image.
3. Notice that there is now only one layer, the Background layer, in the Layers palette.

 Make a mistake? Press Command/Ctrl+Z to undo the Flatten Image command. Alternatively, choose a previous state in the History palette.

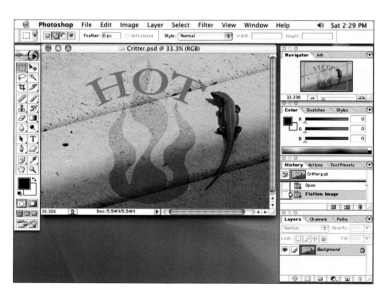

CHAPTER 9

CUSTOMIZING IMAGES
WITH MASKS

A MASK IN PHOTOSHOP ENABLES YOU TO ISOLATE, EDIT, HIDE, AND DISPLAY INFORMATION IN THE LAYER BELOW THE MASK. ANY AREA COVERED BY THE MASK IS PROTECTED FROM BEING EDITED. YOU CREATE MASKS USING SELECTION TOOLS, AND CAN EDIT THE MASK USING ADDITIONAL TOOLS LIKE PAINTING TOOLS. YOU CAN CREATE MASKS ON LAYERS, AS WELL AS CREATING SPECIAL TYPES OF MASKS CALLED ALPHA CHANNELS. THIS CHAPTER CONTAINS SEVERAL SETS OF STEPS THAT SHOW YOU HOW TO CREATE A MASK AND USE MASKED INFORMATION.

DEFINING A MASK

You can create several different kinds of masks in Photoshop. The fastest way to create a mask is with the Quick Mask tool; however, alpha channel and layer masks provide the most flexibility. You create a layer mask on a specific layer to hide some or all of the layer's content. You create alpha channel masks using the Channels palette. Each image can have up to 24 alpha channels.

An alpha channel contains 8 bits (or 256 shades of gray), and defines transparency information of an RGB image. An RGB image is a 32-bit image made up of Red, Green, and Blue channels, or 24 bits of color information. In Photoshop an alpha channel is used to store a channel mask.

Like alpha channels, each layer can have its own 8-bit mask, called a layer mask. All masks are bitmap graphics, except for a Layer Clipping. A Layer Clipping is a sharp-edged vector graphic mask that can be applied to an image layer. You must use a Shape tool from the toolbox to create a Layer Clipping. To find out how to create a layer clipping, see Chapter 11, "Experimenting with Layers."

To create an alpha channel or layer mask, use a selection tool to define the area to mask. After you create the mask, the layer or channel information will be visible in the white area of the mask. Black areas of the mask hide layer and channel information.

Because masks use 8 bits a channel, the image you're working with must be in the 8-bit mode rather than the 16-bit mode. To convert an image to 8-bit mode, choose Image, Mode, 8 Bits/Channel.

You cannot create layer masks on the Background layer or copy the masked information from the Background layer. If you want to mask and copy the content from that layer, copy the layer by dragging it over the Create a New Layer button at the bottom of the Layers palette and then hide or deleting the original Background layer. Also, you must save the image you're working with to the Photoshop (PSD) file format, which supports layers and channels. Native camera or scanner file formats (TIFF or JPEG) don't support layers.

CREATING, HIDING, AND SHOWING LAYER MASKS

As you saw briefly in Chapter 8, you can use layer masks to hide part of a layer. The position of the layer holding the layer mask affects how other fill or gradient layers interact with it. Layer clipping (vector) paths and layer (raster) masks are the two types of layer masks that can be created in Photoshop. Both appear in the Layers palette to the right of the thumbnail picture of an image layer. The following steps show you how to create a basic layer mask:

1. Open the image file that holds the information to mask.
2. In the Layers palette, drag the Background Layer over the Create a New Layer button at the bottom of the Layers palette. This creates a new layer named Background copy.
3. Control+/right-click on the original Background layer; then click Delete Layer in the menu that appears. Click Yes in the confirmation dialog box to finish deleting the original layer. (If you prefer to preserve the Background layer, you can click the eye icon beside it to hide it, instead. The point is that you can't create a layer mask on the Background layer, so you need to be working on a copy of that layer.)

4. Select the new image layer by clicking on the layer in the Layers palette, if needed.

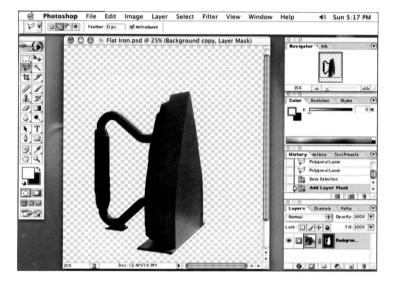

5. Use the selection tool of your choice to select part of the image in the image window. The area you select will be revealed by the mask.

6. Open the Layer menu, select Add Layer Mask, and choose Reveal Selection. Or click the Add Layer Mask button at the bottom of the Layers palette. The layer mask appears in the Layers palette, and the masked information is hidden. If the layer with the mask is the only layer in the image, the hidden areas become transparent (the gray and white checkerboard in the image window).

7. To temporarily turn off the layer mask, Control+/right-click the layer mask thumbnail (not the thumbnail for the layer content itself) and then click Disable Layer Mask in the menu that appears.

This book presents keyboard shortcut combinations for both Mac and Windows. Where a particular key differs, I present the Mac key first, a slash, and then the Windows equivalent. In this case, Control+/right-click means to Control+click on the Mac or right-click in Windows.

8. To reapply the layer mask, Control+/right-click the layer mask thumbnail and then click Enable Layer Mask in the menu that appears. (Alternately, you can Shift+click to disable and enable the layer mask.)

Do not choose the Apply Layer Mask command when you Control+click or right-click the layer thumbnail. Doing so deletes the layer content hidden by the layer mask.

You may use a combination of selection tools to create the mask selection. And don't forget that you can use the Add to Selection and Subtract from Selection buttons on the options bar to adjust whether the selection tool currently adds pixels to or deletes them from the selection. You also can choose Select, Inverse to select the layer areas not currently selected and vice versa.

MASK A LAYER USING A SELECTION FROM ANOTHER LAYER

While each mask you create applies only to the current layer, in some cases you create masks to blend content from multiple layers. For example, you might want to hide a gradient or fill layer except where it appears over text. Or, you may want to apply an adjustment layer change only to the area revealed by the mask. The following steps illustrate how to use a selection from one layer to create a mask on another layer—in this case, a mask that hides a pattern layer except where it overlays text on a text layer:

1. Open the image file that holds the information to mask.

2. In the Layers palette, delete any existing mask for the layer that holds the content you eventually want to mask, such as the pattern layer in this example. (Remember, fill and adjustment layers by default include a mask that allows the whole layer to appear.) To remove the mask, Control+/right-click it and then click Discard Layer Mask in the menu that appears.

3. Click on the eye icon beside the layer that holds the content you eventually want to mask, which hides the layer. While this step isn't necessary, it sometimes makes it easier to make the selection on which to base the mask from another layer. In fact, you can hide any additional layers as necessary.

4. Click on the layer that holds the content on which you want to base the mask, such as the layer with text in this example. This selects the layer.

5. Use the selection tool or tools of your choice to make the selection on which you want to base the mask.

6. Redisplay the layer on which you want to create the mask (the pattern layer in this example) by clicking the box for the eye icon.

7. Select the layer on which you want to create the mask by clicking the layer name in the Layers palette.

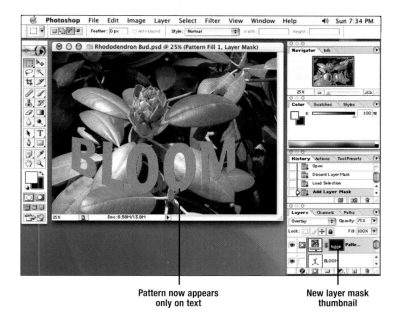

**Pattern now appears
only on text**

**New layer mask
thumbnail**

8. Click the Add Layer Mask button at the bottom of the Layers palette. Photoshop applies the new mask immediately.

If you want the mask to use a soft blend effect, use the Feather text box on the options bar for the selection tool you use to make the selection that will become the mask. Increasing the Feather text box entry softens the edge of the selection. You also can use the commands on the Select menu to modify the selection.

If a layer holds text or a small drawn object, there's a quick way to select just that content on the layer. Open the Selection menu and choose Load Selection. In the Load Selection dialog box, make sure that (Layer Name) Transparency appears as the Channel pop-up menu selection and then click OK.

EDITING OR DELETING A LAYER MASK

After you've created a layer mask, you can edit the mask to increase or decrease the area revealed by the mask. To do so, use the painting and shape tools, as well as the Eraser and Paint Bucket tools. Painting with white or adding a white shape increases the area revealed by the mask. (This is why white automatically becomes the foreground color when you select a layer that holds a mask.) Painting with black or adding a black shape decreases the area revealed by a mask. If you dislike the effect created by a layer mask or don't like the mask adjustments you've made, you can delete the mask at any time and start over. The next set of steps describes how to alter or delete a layer mask.

1. Open the image file that holds the mask.
2. In the Layers palette, click on the layer that holds the mask to alter or remove.

3. Use the painting or shape tool of your choice on the image. Use white as the foreground color to increase the area revealed by the mask. Use black as the foreground color to decrease the area revealed by the mask. In this example, I've used the Brush tool to paint in white on several of the leaves, revealing the pattern on them, as well as on the text.

4. To delete a layer mask, Control+/right-click on the mask thumbnail for the layer in the Layers palette and then click Discard Layer Mask in the menu that appears. Photoshop removes the mask immediately, redisplaying all the content on the layer.

 You also can use the techniques described in this section to edit a quick mask.

PREPARING A CHANNEL TO DEFINE AN ALPHA CHANNEL

An alpha channel is a special type of mask stored in the Channels palette. In certain situations, you may find it easier to create an alpha channel, because you can use a copy of a particular color channel in the Colors palette to help isolate the content on which you want to base the mask. In color images, sometimes one of the separate color channels (R, G, or B rather than the composite channel that contains all three colors) presents a more definite outline of the area to select. Plus, you can use tools to enhance that area and help with the selection process that precedes saving the alpha channel. The following steps show you how to duplicate a channel in the Channels palette and emphasize the image to make it easier to create an alpha channel:

1. Open an image.
2. Display the Channels palette by clicking the Channels tab or choosing Window, Channels.
3. Click on the Red, Green, and Blue channels in turn. You want to identify and select the channel that best isolates the part of the image you eventually want to save as the alpha channel. The idea is to choose the channel that shows strong outlines and contrast.

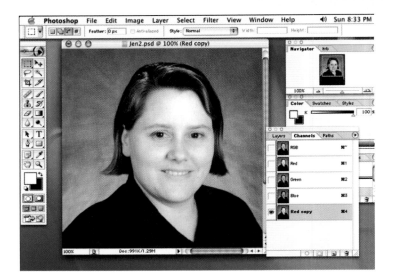

4. Drag the desired channel to the Create New Channel button (which looks like a document) at the bottom of the Channels palette. This copies the specified channel. Now, you can work with tools to emphasize the image content you'd ultimately like to select.

5. You can use filters, effects, and drawing tools to work with the area you intend to mask. For example, open the Filter menu, choose Other, and select the High Pass filter. Adjust the radius of the pixels to see whether the edges of the image mask are any easier to see; then click OK.

6. Choose Image, Adjustments, Levels. Drag the Input Levels sliders toward the center of the channel's histogram image and then click OK. Now the edges of the area to mask are better defined.

If an image looks more or less the same across all channels, you might want to create a copy of the image in its own layer and adjust the levels for that layer so that the edges of the area you want to edit stand out a little more. Then pick a channel you want to use to create the mask.

SELECTING THE CHANNEL CONTENT AND CREATING THE ALPHA MASK

Selecting part of an image that you want to convert to an alpha channel can be one of the most challenging things you do in Photoshop. If the edges of the image you want to turn into a mask are clearly defined, use one of the selection tools, such as the Magic Wand or Lasso, to select the area that you want to define as a mask. Again, you can use a combination of selection techniques, such as choosing Select, Color Range to make the initial selection, and then using the Lasso or Polygonal Lasso tools to refine the selection. You also can use the Add to Selection or Subtract from Selection buttons on the options bar for a selection tool to help use the tool to refine the selection. The following steps review how to select the mask area and add the alpha channel mask:

1. Use the selection commands and tools of your choice to select content on the channel copy you created and enhanced earlier. The Magnetic Lasso tool also works well for selecting areas on the channel.

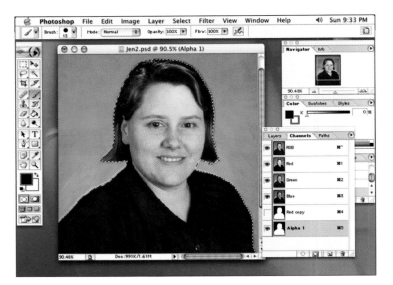

2. Use the Levels and Brightness/Contrast commands in the Image, Adjustments submenu to lighten the selected area (the area to be revealed by the mask). Then choose the Select, Inverse command and use the Levels and Brightness/Contrast commands to darken the area to be hidden by the mask. Finally, use the Brush tool or any other tools, as needed, to refine the areas to mask, painting in white to increase the area revealed by the mask or in black to decrease the area revealed by the mask.

3. You can stop right there and use your channel copy as the channel mask. Press the ~ (Shift+`) key to hide and reveal the composite channel and rubylith area versus the mask. At this point, you've created a regular channel mask. Any file format that supports the color mode for the image should preserve the channel information.

4. As one last step, however, you may want to save the mask as an alpha channel. (This helps you better distinguish the mask channel from, say, a channel you're using to tint the image.) Click the Save Selection as Channel button at the bottom of the Channels palette. The Alpha channel appears.

5. Press the ~ key. The image colors appear, and the alpha channel appears (by default) as a red rubylith area mask in the image.

6. Click the eye icon to hide the channel mask and/or alpha channel mask that you've created; otherwise, you'll see only the mask when you return to the Layers palette and want to work with the image.

 Once you've created a channel or alpha mask, you can edit it anytime you like. Then press ~ to view the masked area (in black and white) in the image window. Edit the mask by using the painting and shape tools as described earlier. Use the Paint Bucket or the Erase tool to change image pixels to a solid black or white color. You also can invert the channel or alpha mask. Use the Magic Wand tool to select the white or black area in the mask; then choose Image, Adjustments, Invert.

 Only the Photoshop (PSD), PDF, PICT, Pixar, TIFF, and Raw formats support alpha channels.

CREATING A QUICK MASK

Creating a layer or channel mask can take quite a bit of time. The fastest way to create a mask is to use one of the selection tools combined with the Quick Mask button, which is conveniently located in the toolbox. It's the button containing an icon of a gray rectangle with a white circle in its center, located below the foreground and background color squares. The Standard Mode button is located to the left of the Quick Mask button. Use these buttons to hide or show a quick mask in an image. Note that you can use the Quick Mask button to create a mask on either a layer or a channel.

A quick mask is created in the same way as any other mask. First, you must pick a selection tool. Then you have to select part of the image you want to turn into a mask. Here's how:

1. Use the method you prefer to select the part of the layer or channel the mask will reveal.

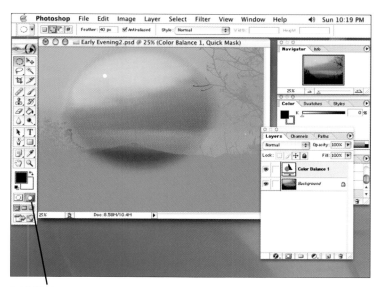

Quick Mask button

2. Click on the Quick Mask (Edit in Quick Mask Mode) button near the bottom of the toolbox. A red rubylith covers the hidden area of the image. A Quick Mask channel appears in the Channels palette, if it's displayed.

COPYING MASK CONTENT TO ANOTHER IMAGE

Cleaning up a mask can be a tedious process, especially when you have a lot of rough edges in the original image. After the mask is completed, you can copy the image content revealed by the mask to another image file. It's basically a drag-and-drop process.

1. Open the image to which you want to copy masked information.
2. Open the image that holds the mask. Be sure to move and size this image window so that you can see the window for the image you opened in Step 1.
3. Apply the mask (quick mask, layer mask, or alpha channel) using the appropriate method. For example, you can Shift+click the mask thumbnail in the Layers palette, or select the channel mask or alpha channel in the Channels palette, and then press ~.
4. Load the mask as a selection using the applicable method. For a layer mask or quick mask, choose Select, Load Selection. The mask channel should appear as the selection for the Channel pop-up menu; click OK to load it. If you're working with a channel or alpha mask on the Channels palette, click the Load Channel as selection button at the bottom of the palette.

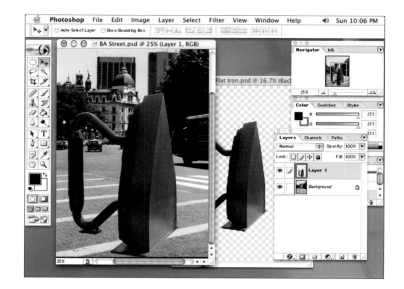

5. Press and hold Command/Ctrl plus ~ and drag the masked image to the window for the image you opened first. When you release the mouse button and keyboard keys, the masked information appears in the other image window on a new layer. (If the image is fairly large, you might need to wait for Photoshop to process the masked image before it appears in the second image window.)

For best results, the destination image should be at least as large as the file holding the masked information. Otherwise, all of the copied information won't display in the destination image. Use the Image, Image Size command to resize an image.

WORKING WITH THE FINAL IMAGE

You can continue to edit the content after copying it to another image window. The following steps note a few examples of how to work with the copied content in the destination image:

1. If needed, use the Move tool to position the copied content on the new layer.
2. Command/Ctrl+click on the layer containing copied content in the Layers palette. This shortcut selects the layer content.

3. Apply a filter to the selection. For example, here I've apply the Sponge filter to the copied content.

CHAPTER 10

MAKING IMAGES STAND
OUT WITH CHANNELS

PHOTOSHOP CREATES COLOR INFORMATION CHANNELS WHEN IT
OPENS AN IMAGE FILE. FOR EXAMPLE, YOU CAN WORK WITH A
PICTURE'S COLOR INFORMATION IN RGB (RED, GREEN, AND
BLUE), THE OPTIMAL FORMAT FOR DISPLAYING IMAGES
ONSCREEN. YOU CAN CONVERT IMAGES TO CMYK (CYAN,
MAGENTA, YELLOW, AND BLACK), THE COLOR FORMAT USED
FOR PRINTING. THE CHANNELS PALETTE DISPLAYS A CHANNEL
FOR EACH COLOR IN THE IMAGE, PLUS A COMPOSITE (COMBINED
RGB OR CMYK) CHANNEL. BECAUSE IMAGES FROM A SCANNER
OR DIGITAL CAMERA USE THE RGB FORMAT BY DEFAULT, THIS
BOOK FOCUSES ON RGB RATHER THAN CMYK, EVEN THOUGH
BOTH TYPES OF CHANNELS WORK SIMILARLY. AN RGB IMAGE
FILE FROM A SCANNER OR DIGITAL CAMERA TYPICALLY
CONTAINS 32 BITS OF INFORMATION; 8 BITS EACH FOR THE RED,
GREEN, AND BLUE CHANNELS, AS WELL AS AN UNSEEN 8-BIT
CHANNEL (AN ALPHA CHANNEL) CONTAINING TRANSPARENCY
INFORMATION. IF AN IMAGE HAS MULTIPLE LAYERS, EACH LAYER
CONTAINS ITS OWN SET OF RGB CHANNEL INFORMATION.

Of the three channels in an RGB image, the Red channel tends to show warmer, red colors. Red colors appear as white if the Red channel is the only visible channel in the image window. The Green channel usually highlights the elements that make a picture sharp. The Blue layer tends to capture junk elements of an image, such as graininess or scratches.

Each time you add a layer to an image, Photoshop adds another set of RGB channels to the image file, thus increasing its file size. To work with the colors on a particular layer, select the layer in the Layers palette and then display the Channels palette. In addition, each layer can have its own color settings. For example, you can have a grayscale image layer in the same image file that also contains a full color image. (You have to copy the grayscale layer from a grayscale image to achieve this.) As was covered in Chapter 9, you can use channels to create masks and to manipulate selected areas of an image to create sophisticated, great-looking, high-resolution images. This chapter contains a series of steps that show you how to work with channels to make image corrections.

 If you want to have your images printed professionally, or include those images in a full-color document that will be professionally printed, you typically must convert the image to CMYK color mode. Some print vendors automatically convert RGB color information in an image file to CMYK information. Other print vendors require you to create your own CMYK image file in order to print. In any case, check with the print vendor you intend to use in advance for guidance about how to prepare your images in Photoshop.

WORKING WITH CHANNELS

Each channel in an RGB image contains roughly one-third of the color data for an image. You can create additional channels in color images. You can duplicate the Red, Green, and Blue channels automatically created by Photoshop. You can edit a channel to make a channel

mask or add an alpha channel, as described in the last chapter. You also can create a spot color channel if you want to print a solid ink color over a portion of the image. (The printing vendor uses a separate print plate for each spot color in the image.) Each image can hold up to 24 channels, including the default channels, added color channels, alpha channels, and spot color channels. Duplicating a channel or creating a new channel to apply a color correction or create a mask enables you to preserve the original color information in the image. You can choose whether or not to display the added channels by using the eye icon beside each channel in the Channels palette.

You copy a channel by selecting it in the Channels palette and dragging onto the Create New Channel button (it has a document on it) at the bottom of the Channels palette. When you copy a channel in an RGB file, the image's file size will grow by one third. If you plan to save images with editable channel information, be prepared to have plenty of hard disk space to store these larger files. Check the bottom of the image window to monitor the current file size (the right value) versus the original file size (the size before you added a channel).

As was noted in Chapter 9, you must save the image in the Photoshop (PSD), DCS 2.0, PICT, TIFF, or Raw file format in order to work with and preserve channel information.

NAVIGATING THE CHANNELS PALETTE

You manage channels with the Channels palette. Create, split, or merge channels by choosing pop-up menu commands or by clicking on a button at the bottom of the palette. View a thumbnail image of each channel mask as you work. The following steps provide a brief tour of the features in the Channels palette:

1. Open an image file.
2. Display the Channels palette by clicking its tab or choosing Window, Channels.

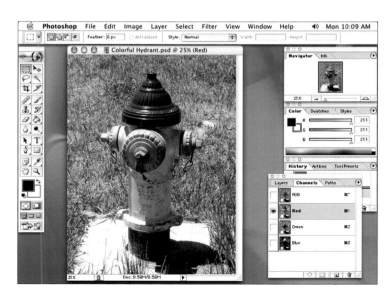

3. To view a single color channel in the image window, click on the channel in the Channels palette or press the channel's Command/Ctrl+key equivalent, which appears to the right of each channel in the Channels palette. For example, press Command/Ctrl+1 to view the Red channel.
4. To redisplay all the channels, click on the composite channel (the RGB channel for an RGB image) in the Channels palette or press Command/Ctrl+~.

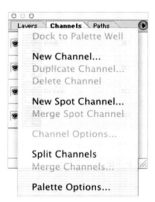

5. Click on the palette menu (arrow) button at the upper-right corner of the Channels palette to view a pop-up menu of commands for working with the palette or a selected channel.
6. Choose Palette Options. The Channel Palette Options dialog box opens. You can use it to change the size of the thumbnail image that appears for each channel in the Channels palette.
7. Press Esc to close the dialog box.

HIDING, DISPLAYING, AND DUPLICATING CHANNELS

Each channel color has unique characteristics. For example, the Red channel tends to store the broadest range of contrast values, whereas the Green channel tends to store more image detail information. Each channel's contents also depend on the contents of the picture. Therefore, the Blue channel might hold a bunch of noise and jitter in one picture, but store more image-related data in a picture of a blue sky or screen. When you view each

of the channels, you can identify which one you need to alter to improve the image appearance. If you want to use a channel to define a mask, pick the channel that most clearly distinguishes the edges of the object and duplicate that channel as described in the last channel.

By comparing two channels with a single channel, you can see which colors bring together different aspects and objects in a picture. You can duplicate multiple channels and then merge them later to create a custom channel. The following steps show you how to hide and show channels, as well as how to duplicate a channel, using the Channels palette:

1. Open an image file and display the Channels palette.

2. Hide the Red channel in the Channels palette by clicking on its eye icon. (You can show or hide multiple channels by dragging the mouse pointer through the eye icon column in the Channels palette.) View the Green and Blue channels in the image window.

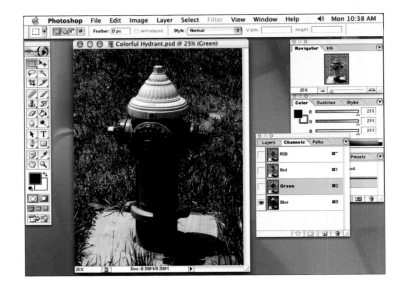

3. Click on the eye icon for the Green channel to hide it. The Blue channel appears alone, as a grayscale image.
4. Select the channel you want to duplicate. (For example, hide both the Red and Blue channels and select the Green channel.)

5. Drag the selected channel onto the Create New Channel button at the bottom of the Channels palette. A copy of the selected channel appears immediately in the Channels palette.

You may need to click on the channel name in the Channels palette to ensure that you're viewing that channel's grayscale information in the image window.

Note that copying a color channel in the image will tint the image unless you convert the channel to a channel mask as described in the preceding chapter, hide the channel, or otherwise adjust the channel for color correction purposes.

ADJUSTING CHANNEL CONTENT

You can apply effects or adjust the tonal range in an original or duplicated channel to improve the image appearance. The following sections discuss some of the changes you can make to a channel.

Many of the channel changes you make will have a subtle effect on the appearance of an image. If you want to make a very dramatic change to the image's appearance, you'll have to choose extreme settings for the color correction you apply.

CLEANING UP A CHANNEL

Channels aren't really dirty by nature. When I use the phrase "cleaning up a channel," I'm referring to the process of working with the channel content to improve the appearance of the image. This can be accomplished by applying a combination of selection tools, filter effects, and level adjustments to a particular channel.

For example, consider the image below. Let's say I like the colors in the image except for the red portions. They seem too dingy, and I want to brighten them up. I can do so directly on the Red channel for the image, as follows.

1. Hide all channels but the Red channel in the Channels palette. (You can show or hide multiple channels by dragging the mouse pointer through the eye icon column in the Channels palette.) Click the name of the Red channel in the palette, if needed, to select the channel. Only the Red channel content appears in the image window.

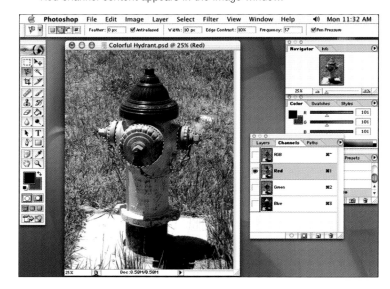

2. Use a selection tool to choose the areas to color correct. In this example, I used the Magnetic Lasso tool and clicked the Add to Selection button on the options bar so that I could select multiple non-contiguous areas to correct—the red valves protruding from the front and sides of the hydrant.

3. Choose Image, Adjustments and then choose the command for the color correction you want to make. In this case, I want to improve the brightness of the selected red areas, so I'll choose Brightness/Contrast.

4. Adjust the settings in the correction dialog box as needed and then click OK.

5. Choose Select, Deselect to remove the selection.

6. Click on the composite (RGB) channel in the Channels palette to redisplay the image colors. If you compare the image above to the one before Step 1, you can see a dramatic improvement in the brightness of the red areas that were selected in the Red channel. The red values in the remaining areas of the image have not been corrected. Also, contrast the image above with the image below, in which the whole Green channel has been intensified using the Image, Adjustments, Levels command.

If you want to make this type correction on a duplicate channel in order to have a reusable mask, first display only the channel that holds the information you want to select. Then select the areas that you want to correct using the tool of your choice. Choose Select, Save Selection. Type a name for the new channel in the Name text box of the Save Selection dialog box and click OK. Now you've created a channel mask based on the selection. Then, any time in the future, you can choose the channel mask in the Channels palette and click the Load Channel as selection button at the bottom of the Channels palette. Next, hide the duplicate channel and display only the channel that holds the information you want to adjust. Use the appropriate command on the Image, Adjustments submenu to make the desired changes.

ADDING A LIGHTING EFFECT

You can add light or shade to an image by applying light-enhancing or detracting filters from the Filter menu. One filter in particular, the Lighting Effects filter, enables you to choose one of the color channels in the image to texturize the lighted image. The following steps explain how to work with this filter:

 It's a good practice to save a copy of your original image so that you can be free to experiment with channels and lighting effects.

1. Open the image file to alter.
2. Copy the Background layer and then delete it, leaving the copied layer in the image. (This step is necessary because many filters don't work on the Background layer.)
3. If the image contains a selection, choose Select, Deselect. Otherwise, the desired filter won't be available.
4. Open the Filter menu, select Render, and choose Lighting Effects. The Lighting Effects dialog box opens.

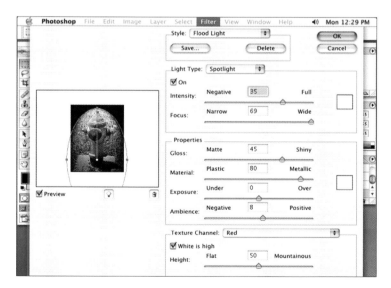

5. Choose a light Style from the pop-up menu and adjust any properties to modify the light source. For example, drag the light boundary in the Preview area to adjust the light direction.
6. Choose the channel to use to texturize the image from the Texture Channel pop-up menu.

7. Click on OK to apply your changes to the picture.

DODGING AND BURNING
A CHANNEL

If you want to make a less specific color correction to an image, you can use the Dodge and Burn tools to lighten or intensify the apparent saturation of the color on a channel, as illustrated next.

1. Open the image that holds the content you want to adjust.
2. Display the Channels palette and hide all channels but the channel to adjust. (For example, hide all but the Blue channel.) Also be sure to select the channel to adjust by clicking the channel name. Only the selected channel's content appears in the image window.
3. Choose the Dodge or Burn tool from the toolbox, adjust its settings (such as Brush) in the options bar, and then use the tool on the image to apply the dodge or burn effect to the desired areas of the channel.

4. Click the eye icon for the composite (RGB) channel in the Channels palette to redisplay all the image channels and view the resulting changes. For example, if you compare the image above with the image before Step 1, you can see that I've burned in the top of the hydrant on the Blue channel to intensify the Blue color there.

When you're using the Dodge or Burn tool on a single channel, it's a good idea to click the eye icon beside the composite channel from time to time so that you can see the effect of the changes you're making. Then hide all but the channel you're editing to continue your work, if needed.

USING FILTER EFFECTS WITH CHANNELS

You can choose the Red, Green, or Blue channel and apply Filter menu effects to that single channel. Or, you can select part of the channel and apply the filter to it alone. Applying a filter to one or more channels enables you to apply a very specific, and in some cases, very subtle effect.

ADDING EFFECTS TO A CHANNEL SELECTION

You may experience instances where you want to isolate an area of color in an image and apply a filter to that area and color only. This capability gives you dramatic flexibility in editing your images in Photoshop. The steps are as follows:

1. Open the image that holds the content to filter.
2. Display the Channels palette and hide all channels but the channel to adjust. (For example, hide all but the Green channel.) Also be sure to select the channel to adjust by clicking the channel name. Only the selected channel's content appears in the image window.

3. Using the selection tool or method of your choice, select the area to which you want to apply the filter.
4. Open the Filter menu, choose a filter category, and then click on the name of the filter to apply. (For example, choose Filter, Distort, Diffuse Glow.) The dialog box with the filter's settings opens.
5. Adjust the filter settings as desired; then click on OK to apply the filter.

6. Click the eye icon for the composite (RGB) channel in the Channels palette to redisplay all the image channels and view the resulting changes.

 You can load a previously-created alpha channel mask as the selection, or you can load a selection saved in another copy of the image file. To do the latter, open the file that contains the saved selection to use and then open the file where you want to load the selection. Choose Select, Load Selection to open the Load Selection dialog box. Make sure the document holding the selection appears as the Document pop-up menu choice and select the name of the channel holding the selection to load from the Channel pop-up menu. Click OK to load the selection in the second document.

ADDING EFFECTS TO AN ENTIRE CHANNEL

In contrast, you can apply a filter effect to a full channel selected in the Channels palette. Click on the RGB channel, or on any of the original Red, Green, or Blue channels in the Channels palette. Then apply an effect from the Filter menu. The following steps show you how to apply two different effects, plastic wrap and trace contour, to the Red, Green, and Blue channels of an image:

1. Open the image that holds the content to filter.
2. Display the Channels palette and hide all channels but the channel to adjust. (For example, hide all but the Green channel.) Also be sure to select the channel to adjust by clicking the channel name. Only the selected channel's content appears in the image window.
3. Open the Filter menu, choose a filter category, and then click on the name of the filter to apply. (For example, choose Filter, Distort, Ocean Ripple.) The dialog box with the filter's settings opens.
4. Adjust the filter settings, as desired, and then click on OK to apply the filter.

5. Click the eye icon for the composite (RGB) channel in the Channels palette to redisplay all the image channels and view the resulting changes. In this case, I've applied the Ocean Ripple filter to the Green channel only.

 You can apply multiple filters to a channel or a selection on a channel to create even more stunning color effects.

PART 3

CREATING COMPLEX IMAGES

CREATING COMPLEX IMAGES

TAKING A GROUP PHOTO OR COMPOSING AN IMAGE WITH ALL THE RIGHT ELEMENTS CAN BE AS TOUGH AS HERDING CATS. SOMETIMES, THE PICTURE YOU WANT TO TAKE ISN'T PHYSICALLY POSSIBLE. ALTHOUGH A PICTURE CAN BE A GREAT COMPOSITION RIGHT OUT OF THE CAMERA, YOU CAN USE PHOTOSHOP TO COMBINE ALL KINDS OF CONTENT FROM DIFFERENT PICTURES INTO ONE IMAGE FILE. YOU CAN ADD ONE OR DOZENS OF SELECTIONS TO AN IMAGE WINDOW, AS WELL AS CORRECT COLORS IN LAYER SETS OR ACROSS LAYERS. YOU ALSO CAN COMBINE LAYERS, CHANNELS, AND MASKS, AND APPLY FILTERS AND EFFECTS TO CREATE SOPHISTICATED IMAGES AND ANIMATIONS.

EXPERIMENTING
WITH LAYERS

BLEND LAYERS TOGETHER, COMBINE THEM INTO SETS, PUT
THEM INTO GROUPS, AND THEN MERGE SOME AND FLATTEN
THEM ALL TO CREATE A NEW, IMPROVED PICTURE. THERE ARE
SO MANY THINGS YOU CAN DO WITH IMAGES. THE BEST WAY TO
PUT MULTI-LAYERED IMAGES TOGETHER IS TO EXPERIMENT WITH
A VARIETY OF DIFFERENT LAYER COMBINATIONS.

INTEGRATING LAYERS WITH BLENDING OPTIONS

When you paste a selection from one image into another, it appears on its own layer. You can then blend the layers together in Photoshop to make their content appear seamless. There are two primary ways to do the blending. As noted in an earlier chapter, you can modify each layer by choosing an alternate layer blending style option. Instead of choosing layer blending options, you also can blend layers by applying feathering options to masked copied layer content, as well as specifying a blending mode or opacity setting for content added to a layer with a fill, paint, or shape tool and the Fill and Stroke commands on the Edit menu. The next sections show you how to add content from one image into another and then apply a layer style blending option to control how the layers blend.

 The Apply Image and Calculation commands on the Image menu offer even more dynamic blending options, such as saving the resulting blended image as a channel or file. Chapter 13 covers these commands for blending content.

COMBINING CONTENT FROM SEPARATE IMAGES

Images have different balances of light and dark colors in addition to the range of millions of colors that make a picture what it is. When you combine content from two images, you can adjust blending option settings for each layer to make the two pictures blend more seamlessly or to emphasize the content on one layer over another. The following steps show you how to copy a selection from one image into another image, thus creating a new layer.

1. Open the image into which you want to copy content.
2. Open the image that holds the content to copy. If necessary, arrange the image windows so that both are visible. This will facilitate copying between the images using drag and drop.

3. Select the content to copy using the selection tool or method of your choice. Remember that you can use a combination of tools and methods, such as selecting a color range and then adding to the selection by using the Magic Wand tool.
4. Click the Move tool on the toolbox; then press and hold the Option/Alt key and drag the selection into the window for the destination image. Alternately, you can copy and paste the selection into the first image. The copied selection will appear in its own layer in the Layers palette of the first image.

5. Use the Move tool (V) to position the copied selection in the image window. You also can reselect the selection by choosing Select, Load Selection, making sure that Layer (X) Transparency appears as the Channel choice, and clicking OK. Then you can use the commands on the Edit, Transform submenu to work with the new content—flipping it, sizing it, and so on.

6. Repeat the process as needed to place and position additional copies of the selection (or additional selections) in the destination image.

When you're moving selected content between images, the destination image should be at least as large as the copied content. Otherwise, you'll definitely have to select and resize the copied content in the destination image.

To move the contents of a whole layer to another image, drag the layer from the Layers palette in the source image, drop it into the window for the destination image, and then use the Move tool to position the layer content in the destination image. Both the source and destination images need to have the same resolution for the layer content to copy correctly.

APPLYING BLENDING OPTIONS

Double-click on a layer thumbnail in the Layers palette to open the Layer Style dialog box, which holds various layer settings such as layer blend modes and styles. The Blending Mode pop-up menu enables you to select a blending option that controls how the content on the selected layer blends with the layer below it. You can adjust the Opacity setting for the layer to produce a ghost effect. The lower the Opacity number, the more the current layer fades and blends with other layers. The Advanced Blending area of the dialog box offers another group of blending features, such as selecting a particular channel to blend or knock out. Another way to blend layers is to adjust the slider settings in the Blend If area. The following steps show you how to blend two image layers together using the Layer Style dialog box.

1. Double-click on the thumbnail for a layer you've added in the Layers palette. The Layer Style dialog box opens.

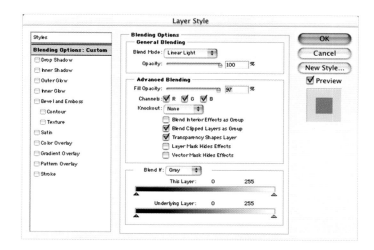

2. Choose an alternate mode from the Blend Mode pop-up menu.

3. Adjust other settings as needed and click OK. The Layer Style dialog box closes, and Photoshop applies the specified blending choices in the layer. As you can see in the example here, Layer 1 now uses the Linear Blend mode. Layer 2, which holds the copied flowers on the right, uses its original default blend mode.

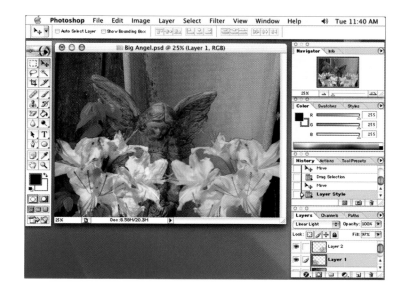

To preview the Blend Mode selection and other changes you've specified in the Layer Style dialog box, drag the dialog box so that you can see the image.

 To link two layers in the Layers palette, click on a layer you want to link. Then click on the box immediately to the left of another layer. A link icon should appear in the box, indicating that layer is linked to the previously selected layer in the Layers palette. Select a linked layer. Open the Layer, Align Linked menus and choose from align the top, bottom, left, or right edges, or horizontal or vertical centers to align the linked layers.

WORKING WITH LAYER SETS

You can group image layers and any related effects in a Layer Set folder. Because the order of the layers in the Layers palette affects how the layer content "stacks" in the image, layer sets enable you to quickly reorganize layered images and related effects. You can simply drag a Layer Set folder to a new position within the Layers palette to reposition all the layers in the set. Turn off sets of effects or layer adjustments with a click of the mouse. The next several sections illustrate how to use layer sets and masks to create an image that combines color and grayscale content, and then move it all to a second image window.

LOCALIZING EFFECTS WITH LAYERS AND LAYER SETS

Don't like the color of that shirt or dress? Want to use grayscale instead of color to emphasize a specific element in a picture? You can use layers and layer masks to isolate effects in an image. Then create a layer set to group the layers that create the effect. For example, let's say you want to isolate part of an image to eliminate an unwanted background. Then say that you want part of the content that remains to appear in grayscale and part of it in color, to create a "colorized" effect. The following steps illustrate how to use layers, masks, and a layer set to create just such a hybrid image.

 As was noted in earlier chapters, it's a good practice to make a copy of your image file before you experiment with techniques such as those presented here. That way, you'll always have a "clean" copy of your image to use for other purposes.

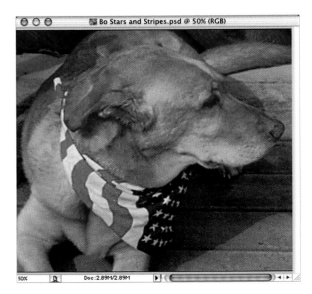

1. Open the image to alter.
2. In the Layers palette, drag the Background layer over the Create a New Layer button (document icon) at the bottom of the palette. A copy of the Background layer appears in the Layers palette.
3. Click the eye icon beside the original Background layer to hide it. This leaves only the Background copy layer visible and selected, so that your changes will apply to the layer copy.
4. Use the selection tool or method of your choice to select part of the layer content. The selection at this point should include both the content to convert to grayscale and the content to appear in color.

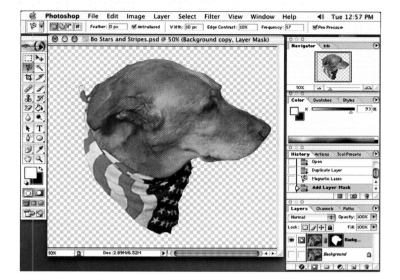

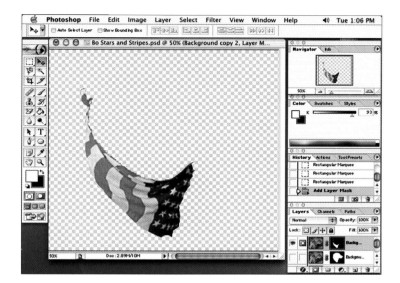

5. Click the Add Layer Mask button at the bottom of the Layers palette. Photoshop immediately applies the mask and displays only the masked content in the image.

6. Create another new layer by dragging the Background copy layer over the Create a New Layer button at the bottom of the Layers palette. The new layer, Background copy 2, appears at the top of the palette.

7. Select the Background copy 2 layer, if needed, and then choose Select, Load Selection. In the Load Selection dialog box that appears, make sure that Background copy 2 Mask is the Channel selection and click OK.

8. Control+/right-click on the Background copy 2 layer mask in the Layers palette and then click on Discard Layer Mask. This removes the mask for that layer, but leaves the layer selected.

9. Use the selection tool or method of your choice to reduce the selected area so it contains only the content to appear in color.

10. Click the Add Layer Mask button at the bottom of the Layers palette. Photoshop immediately applies the mask. To see the impact of this mask, click the eye icon beside the Background copy layer (the first layer copy you made) to hide it temporarily. When you've finished observing these changes, redisplay the layer by clicking in the eye icon box.

11. Click on the Create a New Set (folder) button at the bottom of the Layers palette. A new layer set named Set 1 appears in the Layers palette.

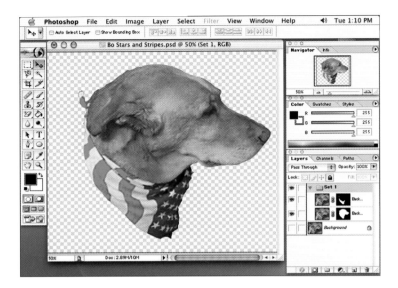

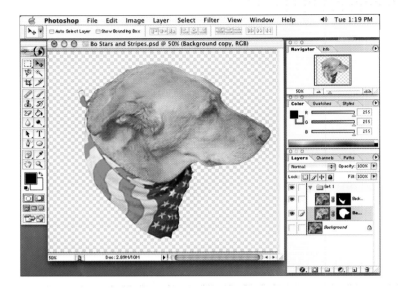

12. Drag the two layers you created and masked over the layer set folder. The listings for the two layers appear indented at the left, indicating that they are now part of the Set 1 layer set. . Make sure that you drag the Background copy 2 layer above the Background copy layer in the layer set. This is because Background copy 2 holds the image information that will be in color, so you want it to appear in front of the other content you'll convert to grayscale; otherwise, the grayscale content will hide the color content.

13. Click on the first layer you created, Background copy, to select it.

14. Choose Image, Adjustments, Channel Mixer. The Channel Mixer dialog box opens.

15. Check the Monochrome check box and then click on OK. Assuming the original Background layer is still hidden as instructed in Step 3, the final image combining grayscale and color should now appear. The layers composing the image appear within the Set 1 layer set.

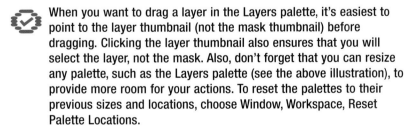

When you want to drag a layer in the Layers palette, it's easiest to point to the layer thumbnail (not the mask thumbnail) before dragging. Clicking the layer thumbnail also ensures that you will select the layer, not the mask. Also, don't forget that you can resize any palette, such as the Layers palette (see the above illustration), to provide more room for your actions. To reset the palettes to their previous sizes and locations, choose Window, Workspace, Reset Palette Locations.

If you're not sure which layer holds a particular portion of the image, Control+click (Mac) or Ctrl+right-click (Windows) on the desired portion of the image. A pop-up label appears to identify the layer holding that portion of the image.

You can include adjustment, fill, and gradient layers in a layer set, as well.

COPYING LAYER SET CONTENTS TO ANOTHER DOCUMENT

Part of the beauty of a layer set is that it functions as a unit. After you create a layer set to hold numerous content and adjustment layers, you can copy them to another image file as a unit If you instead copied each individual layer to another image, you'd likely have to spend time repositioning and adjusting the content for each individual layer. It's faster to copy the layers as a set, as detailed here.

1. Open or create the image to which you want to copy the layer set content.
2. Open the image that holds the layer set to copy. Open the image that holds the content to copy. If necessary, arrange the image windows so that both are visible. This will facilitate copying between the images using drag and drop.

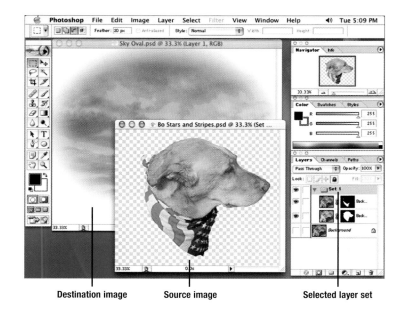

Destination image   **Source image**   **Selected layer set**

3. Click the layer set folder icon in the Layers palette to select the layer set.
4. Drag the layer set from the Layers palette in the source image and drop it onto the image window for the destination image.

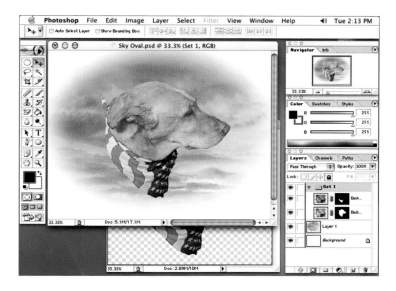

5. In the destination image, leave the layer set selected and use the Move tool to position the layer set contents and finalize the image.

 You can make additional changes to the layer set as needed in the destination image.

MERGING LAYERS IN A SET

When you think you no longer need to manipulate the individual layers in a layer set, you can flatten the layer set, which combines the layer set contents into a single layer. Merging the layers in a set shrinks the size of the Photoshop file, although the numbers of pixels in the image remains unchanged. The following steps show you how to merge the layers in a layer set.

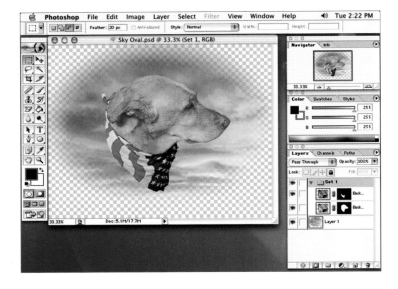

1. Open the image that has the layer set to merge. Note the current file size listed at the bottom of the image window (it's the right value).
2. Click on the folder icon for the layer set that holds the layers to merge in the Layers palette. This selects the layer set.

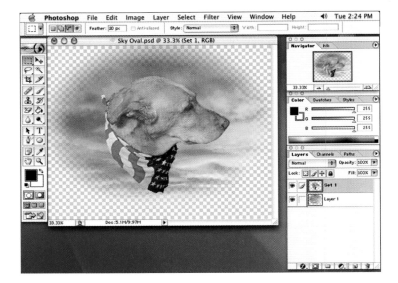

3. Open the Layer menu and choose Merge Layer Set. The layer set condenses into a single layer, which uses the set name as the name for the new layer. Observe the right file size value at the bottom of the image window again. It should now display a substantially smaller value.

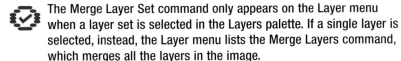 The Merge Layer Set command only appears on the Layer menu when a layer set is selected in the Layers palette. If a single layer is selected, instead, the Layer menu lists the Merge Layers command, which merges all the layers in the image.

There are several ways to retain image clarity, yet shrink the size of a file. One way is to convert an RGB image to indexed color and then choose a GIF or JPEG file format. Use ImageReady to preview image quality and file size differences between GIF, JPEG, and PNG file formats before saving the final image.

ADJUSTING A LAYER WITH A FILTER

Depending on how you want to compose a picture, you might want content from a specific layer to blend in with another layer, such as the Background layer. Or you might want to add another filter effect to a layer to tone its content down and make it stand out. The following steps show how to apply a filter to an image layer.

1. Open the image file containing the layer to filter.
2. Select the layer to filter in the Layers palette.
3. Open the Filter menu, choose a filter category, and choose the desired filter.

4. Adjust the filter settings in the dialog box that appears and then click OK to apply the filter. View the effect in the image window. In the example shown here, the Lighting Effects filter was used to place a spotlight effect on the foreground subject in Layer 1. In addition, the Pointillize filter applied to the Background layer broke it up into dots to make it subtler.

To have a clearer look at the impact of any filter you apply to a layer, hide the other layers in the image by clicking their eye icons. If you have plenty of memory and hard drive space, you can copy any layers you want to experiment with by dragging the layer over the Create a New Layer button at the bottom of the Layers palette. Also remember that some filter choices are not available when you select the Background layer.

If the layer was created using a layer mask, remember that you can edit the layer mask at any time by loading the layer mask as a selection, using one of the selection tools to add (reveal) or delete (hide) pixels, discarding the old mask, and saving the new mask.

CHOOSING A LAYER STYLE

You may instead want to apply a layer style to control how layer content appears where it adjoins the content of other layers. Typically, the available layer styles actually emphasize the edges of the content on a layer, lending an "artificial" effect in the image. For example, you can add a drop shadow, inner shadow, outer glow, or inner glow to a layer's content. Follow these steps to apply a layer style to a layer.

1. Open the image file that holds the layer to which you want to apply a style.
2. Double-click on the layer thumbnail for the layer in the Layers palette. The Layer Style dialog box opens.
3. Click on a style name in the list of Styles at the left side of the dialog box. You must click on the style's name—not its check box—to display the options for the layer style in the dialog box.

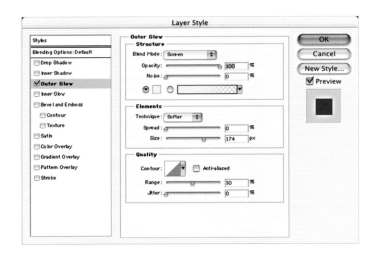

4. Adjust the settings for the selected style in the center of the Layer Style dialog box. Of course, the available settings depend on the style you selected in Step 3.
5. Click on OK and view the effect of the selected layer style on the layer. This example illustrates the Outer Glow layer style applied to the content of Layer 1.

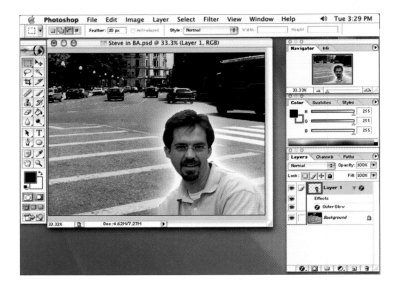

 Create a copy of the Background layer in order to apply a layer style to it. After copying the Background layer, click its eye icon to hide it.

 You also can apply the layer styles via the Layer, Layer Style submenu. To temporarily hide layer styles, choose Layer, Layer Style, Hide All Effects. Layer, Layer Style, Show All Effects redisplays the effects.

WORKING WITH LAYER ADJUSTMENTS

You can use any of the commands on the Image, Adjustments submenu to adjust the appearance of a single layer. For example, you can experiment with levels, curves, color balance, brightness and contrast, hue/saturation, and gradient map. You also can Invert, posterize, and view the threshold image for the layer, too. Use different effects on different layers to create the image you like best. Follow these steps to adjust the content of a layer in the image.

1. Open the image file that holds the layer to adjust.
2. Click on the layer thumbnail for the layer to adjust in the Layers palette.

3. Choose Image, Adjustments and then choose the desired adjustment in the submenu that appears. If a dialog box appears, adjust the settings as needed and then click OK. The effect of the selected layer adjustment appears on the layer. In this example, the Background layer has been inverted.

ADJUSTING THE IMAGE WITH FILL LAYERS

You can adjust the way an image appears to be lit by adding an adjustment layer, a semitransparent fill layer, a semitransparent two- or three-color gradient layer, or a semi-transparent pattern layer. Apply a fill or gradient directly to a layer that holds limited or masked content, or experiment by adding a separate layer you can hide and display in the Layers palette. Add several adjustment, fill, and gradient layers and rearrange them in different orders on the Layers palette to experiment with different color effects in your image. If you like a specific combination of fill and image layers, you can place them together in a layer set and merge them. The following examples illustrate how to experiment with additional layers to create image color combinations:

✱ In the top image here, the Brightness/Contrast adjustment layer appears only above the Background layer in the Layers palette. So the adjustment applies to the Background only. If you move the adjustment layer above all the image layers, as in the bottom image here, the adjustment applies to all the layers below it in the list.

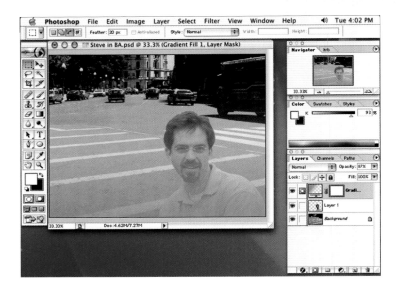

❋ In this example, the solid fill color layer affects the Background layer only, because that's the only layer below it in the Layers palette. Because it uses 50% Opacity, you can still see the content of the Background layer content, which appears tinted. If you dragged the fill layer to the top of the list in the Layers palette, it would also cover the content of Layer 1.

❋ In this example, the top image includes a two-color gradient. You could move it under Layer 1 in the list so it doesn't overlay the Layer 1 contents.

✳ This final example includes both a gradient and Hue/Saturation adjustment layer. The gradient layer applies to the Background layer only, because it's below Layer 1 in the Layers palette. Due to its position at the top of the list in the palette, the adjustment layer applies to both Layer 1 and the Background layer.

 If you want to move one or more fill or adjustment layers above a layer set in the Layers palette, you'll need to create a new layer set to hold the fill or adjustment layers and then move the new set in the list.

CREATING A LAYER CLIPPING GROUP

A layer clipping group (not to be confused with a layer clipping path) enables you to easily create a mask affecting multiple layers. You use the Layer, Group with Previous command to create the layer clipping group. The shape of the content in the bottom layer defines the mask shape. That content can be text, a shape drawn by itself on the layer, content copied to the layer, or masked content on the layer. The following steps show you how to create a layer clipping group.

1. Open the image file that holds the layers to group.

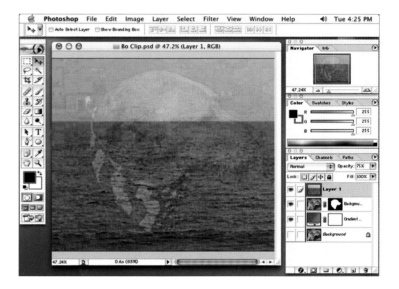

2. Drag the layers to place them in the appropriate order, with the layer that will define the shape of the layer clipping group below all layers that you will group.
3. Select the layer that will be the top layer to group in the Layers palette.

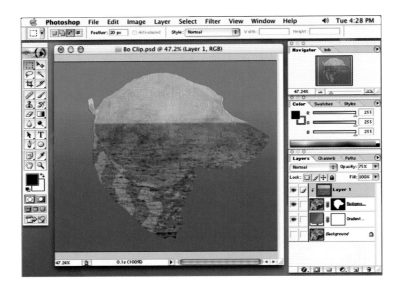

4. Choose Layer, Group with Previous. If you need to add additional layers to the group, click the next layer and choose the command, working your way down the list of layers to group. The results of the clipping group appear in the image.

CREATING CUSTOM MASKS

A MASK ENABLES YOU TO SELECT A SPECIFIC SET OF PIXELS IN AN IMAGE, WHILE PROTECTING ALL THE OTHER PIXELS FROM BEING EDITED. YOU LEARNED IN CHAPTERS 9 AND 11 HOW TO CREATE QUICK MASKS, CHANNEL MASKS, ALPHA CHANNEL MASKS, AND LAYER MASKS. THIS CHAPTER FOCUSES ON SOME ADDITIONAL TECHNIQUES YOU CAN USE TO CREATE MASKS AND ENHANCE MASKED IMAGES, SUCH AS EXTRACTING AN IMAGE OR USING A MATTE WITH THE MASK.

EXTRACTING AN IMAGE

The Extract command doesn't create a mask, but it does enable you to erase unneeded parts of a layer to the transparent background, creating roughly the same effect as a mask. This Photoshop feature tries to separate the foreground object from the background image. The Extract command does a particularly good job when you're working in an image that has indistinct edges. After you choose this command, you can define the edges of your mask using the Edge Highlighter and Fill tools in the Extract dialog box. It can take a while to use this technique, but it's a great alternative to manually defining a mask. The following steps show you how to extract an object from the rest of an image:

1. Open the image file that holds the content to extract.
2. In the Layers palette, drag the layer that holds the information to extract over the Create a New Layer button at the bottom of the palette. This copies the layer so that you can perform the extract operation on the copy.
3. Click the eye icon beside the original layer (the layer you copied) to hide it. Also hide other layers as needed, so that you'll be able to review the effects of extracting the image after you finish the process. Make sure that the layer copy is selected in the Layers palette.
4. Choose Extract from the Filter menu. The Extract dialog box opens.

Edge Highlighter tool   **Fill tool**

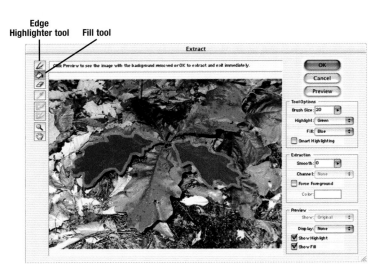

5. Click on the Edge Highlighter tool at the left side of the dialog box, if needed, and draw an outline around the edges of the area you want to extract. Green is the default highlight color. With a wide brush size like this, note that the edges of the extracted content will be somewhat broken up. Choose a smaller Brush Size at the right side of the dialog box to achieve a sharper result.
6. After you've surrounded the area you want to mask, click on the Fill tool. Click inside the highlighted area. It should fill with a blue color.
7. Click on the Preview button to preview the extracted image in the Extract dialog box.
8. When you're ready to extract the image, click OK in the Extract dialog box. The extracted image appears in the image window. You can then apply effects or color corrections to it, redisplay other layers as needed, and continue finalizing the image file.

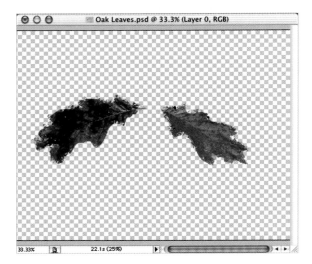

It's often easier to use the Edge Highlighter tool if you stroke the outline of the area you want to select rather than dragging continuously. You also can zoom in to help you work. If you make a mistake with the Edge Highlighter tool, use the Eraser tool to remove the error.

When you use a layer mask, recall that you can disable the mask whenever needed to redisplay the hidden areas of the layer. This is not true when you extract the image, a process that erases the pixels outside the extracted area.

ADDING A MASK TO A SELECTION

You've seen earlier that you can load a layer mask as a selection in the image file. In addition to using that approach, you can load a layer mask as an addition to the existing selection in an image, thus increasing the size of the overall selection.

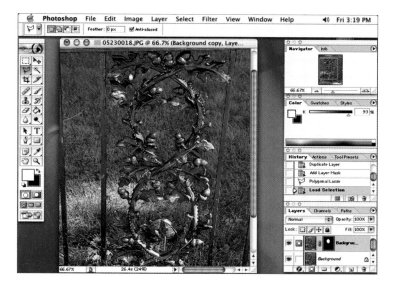

4. Click the Add Layer Mask to Selection choice in the menu that appears. Photoshop immediately increases the size of the selection to include the mask shape.

After you Control+click or right-click on the layer mask thumbnail, you can use the Subtract Layer Mask from Selection command to remove the layer mask area from the current selection. Or you can use the Intersect Layer Mask with Selection option to revise the selection to include only the area contained by both the selection and the mask.

1. Use the selection tool of your choice to make a selection on the desired layer.
2. Select the layer that holds the mask to load as a selection in the Layers palette by clicking the layer thumbnail.
3. Control+/right-click on the mask thumbnail.

CREATING A GRADATED MASK

To achieve a really sophisticated effect in a layered image, you can gradate a mask to make it semi-transparent and gradually reveal the layer contents. The fastest way to achieve this effect is to work with the layer mask's channel in the Channels palette.

1. Select the layer that holds the mask that you want to gradate by clicking its layer thumbnail in the Layers palette.
2. Display the Channels palette by clicking its palette tab or choosing Window, Channels. The channel for the selected mask will be selected there.
3. Click the eye icon box beside the channel mask to make sure it's displayed. Then click the eye icon beside the composite (RGB) channel to hide the individual color layers. You want only the channel mask to appear in the image window.

4. Make sure that black and white are selected as the foreground and background colors.
5. Click the Load Channel As Selection button at the bottom of the channels palette.
6. Choose the Gradient tool on the toolbox.

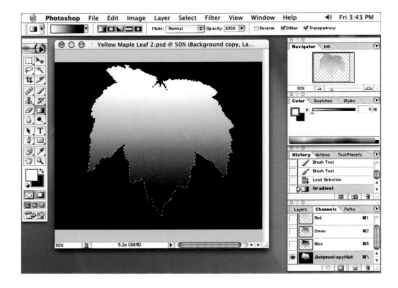

7. In the image window, drag within the unmasked (white) area of the image to gradate the area.
8. Click the eye icon box beside the composite channel to redisplay the image color information. Click the eye icon beside the channel mask to hide that channel.

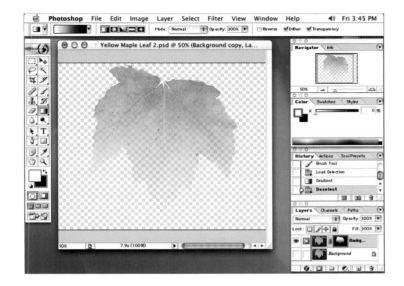

9. Return to the Layers palette by clicking the Layers tab or choosing Window, Layers. Remove the selection by choosing Select, Deselect. Then you can see the effect of the gradient in the image areas revealed by the mask. If you check the mask thumbnail in the Layers palette, you can see that the reveal (white) portion of the mask is now gradated. Once you've created a layer with this type of mask, you can copy the layer to another image file to create an image that contains objects with subtle blends like this.

FREEZING, WARPING, AND RECONSTRUCTING THE PICTURE

You can apply filter effects to a masked image just as you would apply an effect to all or part of any non-masked image. You might have noticed that some effects must be applied to a layer or background image in order to be accessible, whereas other effects and filters, such as adjustment layers, can be toggled on and off in the Layers palette. Reconstruct and Freeze tools work similarly to

adjustment layers, except that these tools appear only in the Liquify dialog box. If you want to experiment with image distortion effects, you can apply several different distortion effects to an image in the Liquify window. Then undo any of them using the Reconstruct tool. The following steps show you how to apply distortion effects in the Liquify window and to revert them using the Reconstruct tool:

1. Open an image file. If the image file contains multiple layers, select a layer containing an image.

Effect tools   Reconstruct tool   Freeze tool

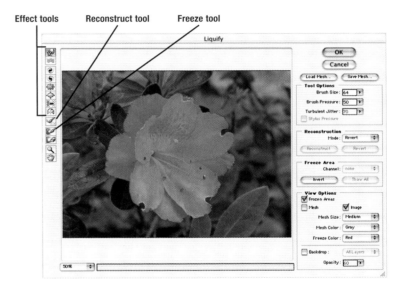

2. Choose Liquify from the Filter menu. The Liquify dialog box opens.
3. Choose the Freeze tool. Select the area you want to protect by clicking on it or dragging the mouse over it. A red tint covers the areas you freeze in the image.

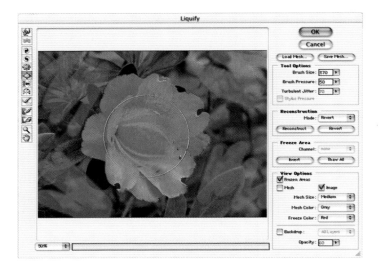

4. Click on an effect tool, such as Warp, Turbulence, Twirl, Pucker or Bloat, located on the left side of the Liquify dialog box. Click and drag in the image to apply a distortion effect.
5. Click the Reconstruct tool..
6. Click on any part of the image that you previously warped with an effect tool. The Reconstruct tool restores the image to its original, unwarped state.

> **!** If an area of the image is really warped, position the mouse pointer over it and then press and hold the mouse button for several seconds. This technique reconstructs the pixels a bit more quickly.

CREATING A VECTOR MASK

A vector mask works just like a layer mask, enabling you to hide part of a layer's content so that you can edit only the content revealed by the mask or combine content from a number of layers to create a more complex image. Vector masks differ in how you create them and how you edit them. To create a vector mask, you first create a work path in the image by using either the pen tool or a shape tool,

as described in Chapter 7. Then you save the work path as a vector mask. Vector masks offer two advantages over layer masks. First, vector masks create a more crisp edge, so you should create this type of mask when you want a sharp image. Second, you can edit vector masks more cleanly and precisely.

1. Open the image file that holds the content to mask.
2. In the Layers palette, duplicate the Background layer (if it holds the content to mask) by dragging the layer over the Create a New Layer button at the bottom of the palette. This copies the layer so that you can perform the extract operation on the copy.
3. Click the eye icon beside the original Background layer to hide it. Also hide other layers, as needed, so that you'll be able to review the effects of extracting the image after you finish the process. Make sure that the layer copy is selected in the Layers palette.

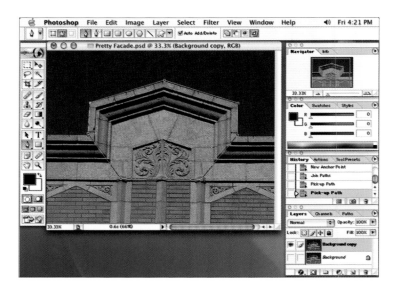

4. Use the Pen tool or the shape tool of your choice to select a path on the layer. Before you create the selection, make sure you click the Paths button on the options bar to specify that you want to create a path, not edit the image.

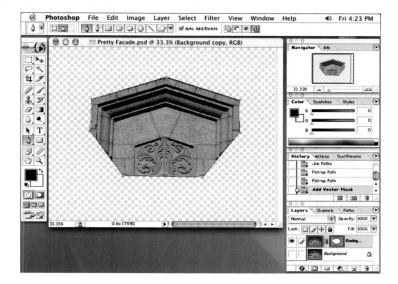

5. Open the Layer menu, select Add Vector Mask, and choose Current Path. Photoshop applies the mask immediately in the image window and displays a thumbnail for the vector mask in the Layers palette.

EDITING A VECTOR MASK

You can edit the vector mask at any time using the pen or shape tools. By editing the vector mask, you can reveal more or less of the layer content.

1. In the Layers palette, hide and display layers as needed to accommodate your editing; then click vector mask thumbnail for the mask you want to edit.
2. Choose the Pen tool or the shape tool of your choice.

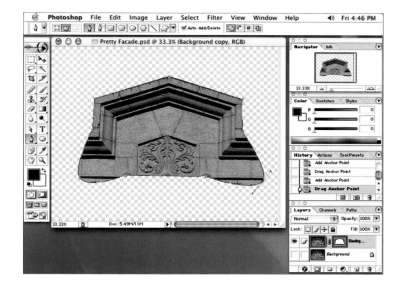

3. Command+Option+Shift+click or Ctrl+Alt+Shift+click the visible portion of the image to display the vector mask anchor points and enable it for editing.
4. Change the path on the layer. For example, here I clicked with the Pen tool to add a new anchor point at each lower corner and then used Command/Ctrl+drag to move the anchor point.
5. When you finish working with the vector mask, press Esc to deselect it.

TWEAKING MASKS
WITH MATTES

Although you can use the Feather command to smooth the edges of a mask when you make the selection on which the mask is based, in some cases, a matte provides a better solution. If you've created a masked image containing a border of unwanted pixels surrounding the mask, you may be able to shrink the edges of the mask, removing the halo surrounding the mask by using the Defringe matte command. Photoshop provides three different matte commands to help blend the edges of a mask with the rest of the picture: Defringe, Remove Black Matte, and Remove White Matte. The following steps show you how to defringe a mask and use the Remove the Black Matte command if you need for the mask content to blend into a white background image:

1. Select the layer containing the mask in the Layers palette.
2. Open the Layer menu. Select Matting and choose the Defringe command.

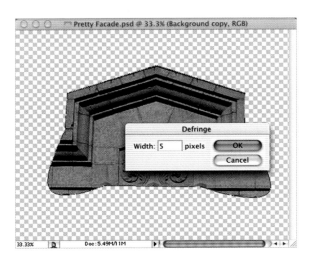

3. Type a number in the text box to determine how many pixels are removed from the edges of the masked image. Then click OK. The edges of the masked image will be blended in with any contrasting colors in the background layer.

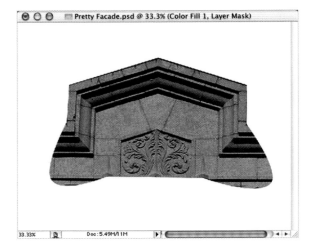

4. To blend the masked image with a black or white background, choose Remove Black Matte or Remove White Matte from the Layer, Matting submenu. In this example, the masked image will be placed over a white background. Choose Remove Black Matte command from the Layer, Matte menus to blend the mask edges into a white background.

 Another way to smooth mask edges is to adjust layer blending options for the masked layer and the layer directly below it in the Layers palette. For more information about layer blending options, see Chapter 11, "Experimenting with Layers."

FINE-TUNING YOUR LAYER
OR CHANNEL MASK

A good mask can take a lot of time to get just right, especially when the image being masked contains many detailed or fuzzy edges. A bad mask is generally a sloppy one, making the overall image look disjointed. One way to tell whether a mask is effective is to compare the contents of the masked layer to its proposed background picture. Try to find the edges of the masked image or any other characteristics of the image that might make the image look out of place in the picture. If you find a stray or incorrectly colored pixel, you can use the Brush or Pencil tools, plus some menu commands, to correct your mask.

Since you can modify a mask after it's created, the initial selection area you create does not have to exactly match the object you want to mask. Try to capture the core shape of the mask the first time you apply the selection tools to an image window or channel when you create the mask. Once the mask is created, use the Brush or Pencil tools to fine-tune, or re-shape, the masked area. As you apply black or white to the masked or unmasked areas of the image, the shape of the mask changes. Additionally, if you used the Magic Wand tool or the Select, Color command to select the area from which you created the mask, you may end up with some unwanted semitransparent areas. If you use the Image, Adjustments, Levels command to reduce the gray areas in the mask first, doing the cleanup work with the Brush and Pen tools will move along even faster. Work with adjusting a mask now.

1. Open the file that holds the mask.
2. Click on the layer thumbnail for the layer holding the mask in the Layers palette.
3. Display the Channels palette by clicking its tab or choosing Show, Channels.
4. Click the eye icon box beside the channel for the layer mask to display it.

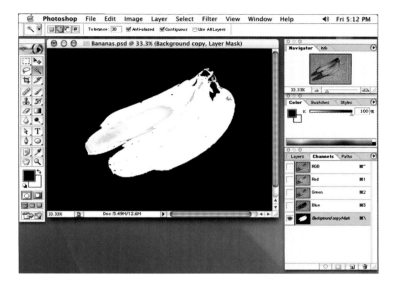

5. Click the eye icon for the composite (RGB) channel so you see the mask contents only in the image window.
6. Choose Image, Adjustments, Levels.

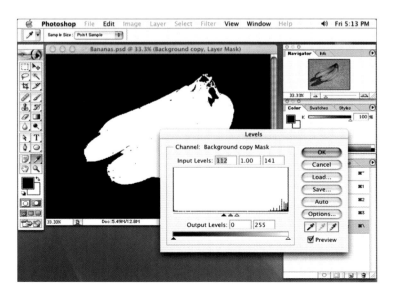

7. Drag the Input Levels sliders toward the center to reduce the gray areas in the image and then click OK.

8. Use the Brush or Pencil tool with black as the foreground color to define the areas you want the mask to hide. If you apply black around the edges of the mask, the size of the mask shrinks. If you apply white to the fringes of the masked image, the mask will grow in size.

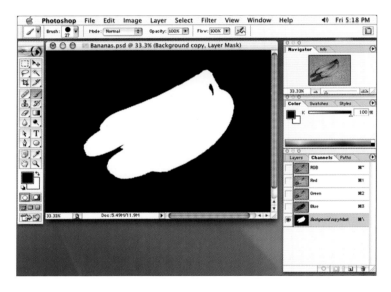

9. When you've made all the needed changes to your mask, click the eye icon box for the composite channel to redisplay the image colors, click the eye icon to hide the mask channel, and then return to the Layers palette by clicking its tab or choosing Window, Layers.

USING A MASK FROM ONE IMAGE IN ANOTHER IMAGE

Each mask not only provides you with a quick way to make a selection in the current image, but you also can load a mask from one image as a selection in another image. From there, you can edit the selection or even save it as a mask in the new image file. This technique saves you some work and also enables you to add interest to what might otherwise be a rather bland shot.

1. Open the image file that holds the mask you want to use as a selection.

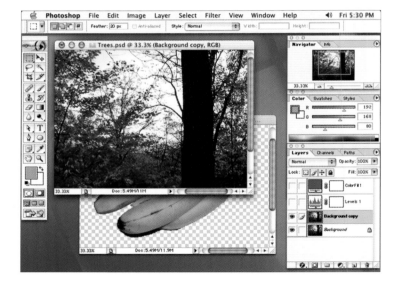

2. Then open the image where you want to use the mask as a selection.

3. Choose Select, Load Selection. The Load Selection dialog box opens.

4. Open the Document pop-up menu and choose the name of the source document (the document that holds the mask).

5. Open the Channel pop-up menu and choose the name of the mask that you want to load as a selection.

6. Click OK. The selection appears in the destination image.

7. Click the layer where you want to create a mask in the Layers palette for the destination image.

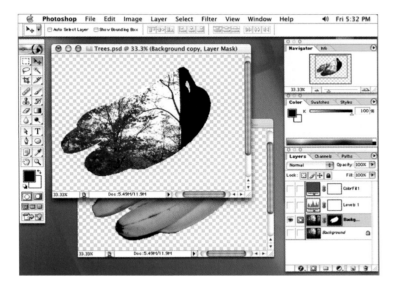

8. Click the Add Layer Mask button at the bottom of the Layers palette and then hide any layers as needed to see the mask results.

CHAPTER 13

EXPERIMENTING WITH CHANNEL OPERATIONS

THE TERM CHANNEL OPERATIONS CAN CONJURE UP VISIONS OF REMOTE CONTROLS AND TV SCREENS WITH PICTURE-IN-PICTURE. IN THE CONTEXT OF PHOTOSHOP, HOWEVER, CHANNEL OPERATIONS REFER TO TASKS THAT YOU PERFORM WITH CHANNELS, SUCH AS COMPOSITING IMAGES WITH CHANNELS AND USING THE CALCULATIONS OR DUPLICATE COMMANDS.

ALL THE CHANNEL, LAYER, AND MASK EXAMPLES IN THIS BOOK REQUIRE THE IMAGE TO BE IN RGB COLOR MODE. (AS MENTIONED BEFORE, RED, GREEN, AND BLUE ARE THE CHANNELS THAT MAKE UP AN RGB IMAGE.) TO CONVERT AN IMAGE TO RGB COLOR, CHOOSE IMAGE, MODE, RGB COLOR.

CREATING A CUSTOM CHANNEL

You can select and copy image channels in the Channels palette. Drag the channel to copy to the Create New Channel button at the bottom of the Channels palette to create a copy of a channel. Although an image might initially consist only of the RGB channels, when you copy one of those individual channels, you can view the new channel individually or combine it with other channels. The following sections show you how to customize a single channel or all three channels.

 If you have duplicate channels in the Channels palette (for example, if you've duplicated the Red channel), displaying both the original and duplicate channels might make the image's colors a little too intense (too red in this example). Click on the eye icon beside one of the channels to hide it and return the image to a more normal color balance.

CONVERTING TO MONOCHROME AND TINTING AN IMAGE

One way to convert a color image to a grayscale image is to choose the Image, Mode, Grayscale command. This menu command removes the color information from an image file, reducing it to a single Gray channel. The Channel Mixer dialog box provides a more dynamic way to view a color image as monochrome without removing the Red, Green, and Blue channels. You can display the Channel Mixer dialog box by choosing the Image, Adjustments, Channel Mixer command.

The Channel Mixer dialog box enables you to convert a layer or convert the Red, Green, or Blue channel into monochrome. You also can convert the whole image from RGB color to monochrome and then modify the Red, Green, and/or Blue channels to create an image with a custom tint.

 A grayscale image has one color channel, the Gray channel. A monochrome image retains separate Red, Green, and Blue channels, even though no color information is displayed in the composite channel.

Before you start this process, it's a good idea to duplicate the Background layer (or the layer you want to convert to grayscale), and then to make your changes to the layer copy. This approach enables you to work with the image in grayscale without losing its color information, which would be removed by the Image, Mode, Grayscale command. After you've created and converted the new layer, you can toggle its display on or off (using its eye icon in the Layers palette) to view the image in color or grayscale. The following steps show you how to create a grayscale image and then tint the image by adjusting individual channels:

1. Open the image file that you'd like to view in monochrome.
2. Copy the layer to convert to grayscale (typically the Background layer) by dragging it over the Create a New Layer button at the bottom of the Layers palette.

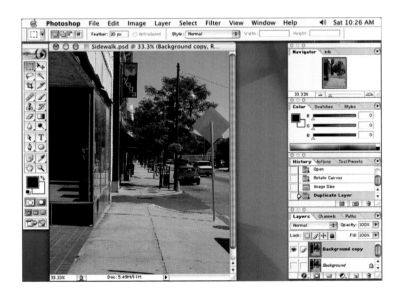

3. Hide the Layer you copied by clicking its eye icon in the Layers palette. Also hide additional layers as needed.

4. Open the Image menu, select Adjustments, and choose Channel Mixer. The Channel Mixer dialog box opens.

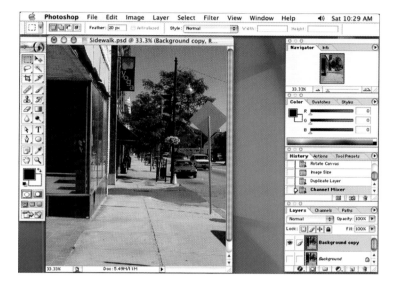

5. Click the Monochrome check box at the bottom of the dialog box to convert the new layer to monochrome and then click OK. The layer content appears in grayscale, as specified. (At this point, if you want to work with a true grayscale image, you could copy the layer to a new file as described in the next section and then choose the Image, Mode, Grayscale command to convert the file to a true grayscale image, without the individual color channels.)

6. To move on and tint the image, view the Channels palette by clicking its tab or choosing Window, Channels. The Red, Green, and Blue channels still appear in the palette, as well as the composite channel.

7. Click the eye icon beside two of the color channels to hide them, so you can work on the remaining channel. For example, if you want to tint the image with blue, hide the Red and Green channels. Also click on the channel you want to work with (in this case, the Blue channel), to ensure it's selected so that your changes will apply to the channel.

8. Choose one of the commands on the Image, Adjustments submenu to adjust the content of the channel. For example, you could choose Image, Adjustments, Brightness/Contrast.

9. Choose the applicable settings in the dialog box that appears and then click OK.

10. Make other adjustments as needed to the selected layer. You also can select other layers and adjust them, as well.

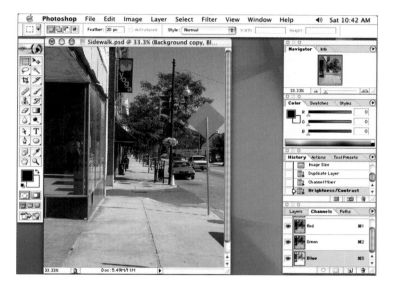

11. When you finish making channel adjustments, click the eye icon box beside the composite channel to redisplay all the channels. The grayscale or tinted image layer appears in the image window. In this example, I used the Image, Adjustments, Brightness/Contrast to increase the brightness and contrast for the Blue channel.

12. Redisplay the Layers palette by clicking its tab or choosing Window, Layers. Back in that palette, you can select the layer or layers you now want to appear in the image.

 When you're working with individual channels, it's a good idea to display the composite channel periodically so that you can check the impact of your changes on the overall image.

CREATING A NEW IMAGE
BASED ON A LAYER

For some operations, such as creating a duotone image (which will be described in the next section), the preferable technique is to work in a brand new image file. You can copy the image file and delete unneeded layers, if you want. However, if you've already prepared a layer that more closely approximates the image you ultimately want to create, you should instead create a new file by copying a layer.

1. Open the image file that holds the layer to copy.
2. Control+/right-click on the layer and click Duplicate Layer in the menu that appears. The Duplicate Layer dialog box opens.
3. Type a name you want the layer to use in the destination (new) file into the As text box.

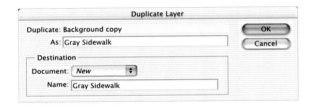

4. Open the Document pop-up menu and click New. This tells Photoshop that you want to place the duplicated layer into a brand new file. Photoshop moves the insertion point to the Name text box so that you can specify a name for the new destination file.

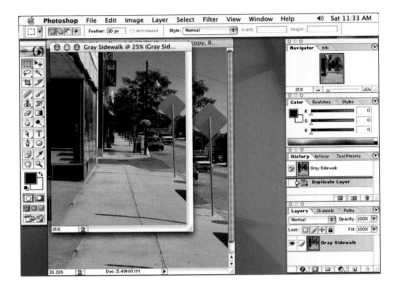

5. Click OK. Photoshop creates the new file copy and opens it in an image window.

CREATING A DUOTONE IMAGE

A duotone image might resemble the tinted image displayed in the "Converting to Monochrome and Tinting an Image" section, but you actually create a duotone very differently to prepare the image for a the commercial duotone printing process. (However, inkjet and color laser printers also print duotones just fine.) A duotone is a grayscale image to which you add a second printed color to tint the image overall. When your print vendor prints the duotone, it creates one print plate for the black-and-white information, and a separate color plate with the duotone color. (You can add two tint colors to create a tritone image, and three tint colors to create a quadtone image.) While a duotone effect often is much more subtle than a tint effect, it achieves the same richness in the image but provides for a cheaper professional print job for the document in which you use the image; it's cheaper to have a print vendor print a two-color document rather than a full-color document.

Remember, some tools and conversions aren't available for images using 16 bits of color information per channel, including creating a duotone. So convert the image to 8 bits per channel before you begin the following process.

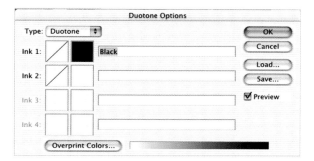

1. Choose Image, Mode, Grayscale. Even if you previously converted the channels in an image to monochrome, you must be working with a true grayscale image to convert it to a duotone. Grayscale images have a single Gray channel. In the dialog box that asks whether you want to discard color information, click OK.
2. Choose Image, Mode, Duotone. The Duotone Options dialog box appears.

3. Open the Type pop-up menu at the top of the Duotone Options dialog box and then click on Duotone in the list. The Ink 2 color setting becomes active. (Of course, you would click on Tritone or Quadtone to add more than one tint color to the image.)
4. Click on the white Ink 2 box. The Custom Colors dialog box opens.
5. Click on a color in the narrow band of colors near the middle of the dialog box. Photoshop will display a different selection of colors in the list at the left side of the dialog box. (You even can choose colors from a number of different color sets. To view colors in another set, make another choice from the Book pop-up menu at the top of the Custom Colors dialog box.)

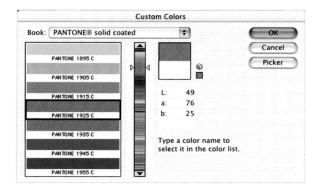

6. Click on a color in the list at the left side of the dialog box. The color you click on will become the active tint color. The image window previews the selected duotone tint.

7. Click on OK. The Custom Colors dialog box closes, returning to the Duotone Options dialog box.
8. Type a color plate name in the Ink 2 text box. (Enter Cyan, Magenta, or Yellow.) The name will tell Photoshop to use a separate color plate for the tint ink color. (If the duotone will be included in a document to be printed by a professional printer, it's best to write down the *Pantone Color* name, or leave it entered in the Ink 2 text box, so you can tell the printer the exact ink color to use for the second print plate.)

9. Click OK. The Duotone Options dialog box closes, and Photoshop displays the duotone.
10. If you decide you want to edit information for one of the colors in the duotone image (black or the print color for the duotone tint), you need to convert the image to a multi-channel image, which separates the two print colors into separate color channels. To do so, choose Image Mode, Multichannel. (If asked whether you want to flatten layers, click Yes to do so.) Photoshop separates the single duotone color channels into multiple channels, so you can preview individual colors.

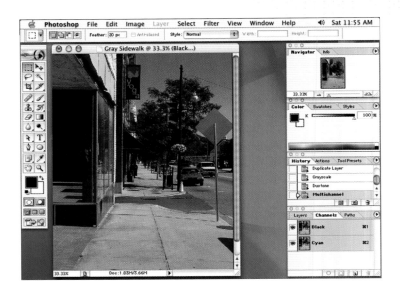

11. Display the Channels tab by clicking its tab or choosing Window, Channels. Edit the channels as needed.

CREATING A SPOT COLOR CHANNEL

Typically, you add spot color to enhance or colorize an area on a grayscale image, but you can really add spot color to any image that allows multiple channels. You can use an alpha channel to create the spot color, as described in the following example, or you can make another selection and then start with Step 4 to finish adding the spot color.

1. Convert the image to grayscale, if needed. Choose Image, Mode, Grayscale. In the dialog box that asks you to confirm that you want to discard color information, click OK.
2. Display the Channels palette by clicking its tab or choosing Window, Channels.

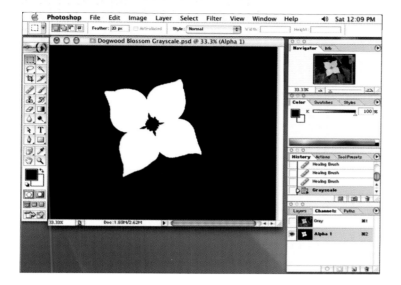

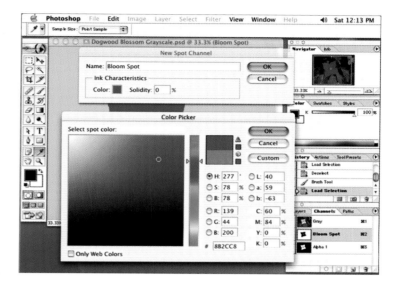

3. Click on the name of the alpha channel that you want to use to apply the spot color in the palette. The channel will be selected, and the Gray channel will be hidden.
4. Click on the Load Channel as Selection button at the bottom of the palette. The selection appears immediately in the channel.
5. Click on the Channels palette menu button and then click New Spot Channel in the menu that appears. The New Spot Channel dialog box opens.
6. Type a name for the spot channel in the Name text box. Your new name will replace the temporary name in the text box. Click on the Color box. The Color Picker dialog box will open.

7. Click on a color in the narrow band of colors near the middle of the dialog box; then click the desired color in the Select Spot Color box. The color you click on will become the active spot color. Click OK to close the Color Picker dialog box and return to the New Spot Channel dialog box.
8. Make a new entry in the Solidity text box, if needed. An entry greater than 0 will make the spot color more opaque. Click OK to close the dialog box and finish the spot color channel.

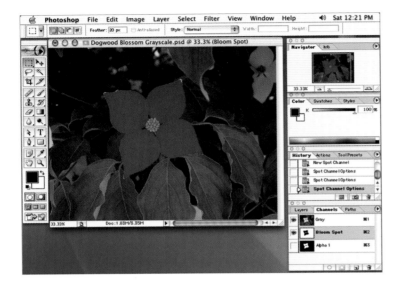

9. Display both the composite (Gray) and spot color channels, and hide the alpha channel. The image with spot color appears

10. If you were working in a grayscale image, choose Image, Mode, RGB Color. After you make this conversion, the image will print with the spot color. (If you skip the conversion, the image will still print in grayscale.)

FEATHERING AN ALPHA CHANNEL MASK

Once you create a mask such as an alpha channel mask, you don't have to use it "as is" to apply an effect or adjustment to a selection. You can use the Feather command to make the edges of the mask more diffuse, softening the boundaries of the area to which you apply an effect. Here's how:

1. Open the image that holds the alpha channel mask.

2. Display the Channels palette by clicking its tab or choosing Window, Channels.

3. Command/Ctrl+click on the alpha channel in the channels palette to load it as a selection on the composite channel.

4. Open the Select menu and click Feather to open the Feather Selection dialog box. Type a value into the Feather Radius text box to determine the range of pixels feathered on the selection border. Then click OK; the selection marquee adjusts to reflect the feather setting.

5. Apply the desired filter or color change to the selected area. The filter or color change diffuses at the selection border, as shown in the example here, where the Pointillize filter was applied to the feathered selection.

USING THE APPLY IMAGE COMMAND

Rather than moving a masked layer to another image to use its content there, you can blend masked content from one image with the content of all the channels of a target layer using the Image, Apply Image command. This approach can be less flexible than copying the masked layer from one image to another, but if you plan to flatten the image anyway, it may save some time.

Before you begin this process, make sure that the source and destination images are the same size. (Use the Image, Image command to check each file's dimensions.) For example, each of the image files must be 1,600×1,200 pixels.

1. Open the image file that holds the masked content you would like to copy (the source file).
2. Open the image file to which you want to copy the masked information (the destination file).
3. If the destination image has more than one layer, click on the layer thumbnail for the layer to which you want to apply the content from the source image. This selects the destination layer.
4. Choose Image, Apply Image. The Apply Image dialog box opens.

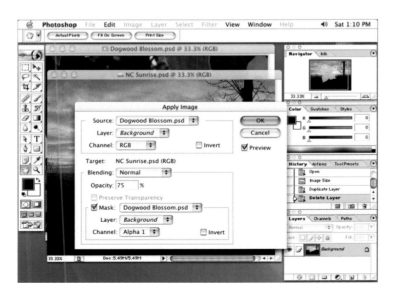

5. In the top area of the dialog box, make sure the first image's name appears as the Source. Choose the Layer and Channel that hold the information to copy.
6. In the Target area of the dialog box, choose a blending Mode (these modes are the same as those for blending layers) and enter an Opacity setting for the blended pixels. To copy information defined by a particular mask in the source image, click to check the Mask check box. Then choose the Layer and Channel that define the masked source content to apply.

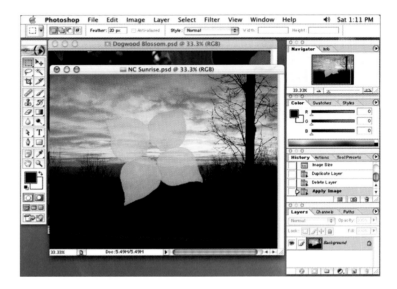

7. Click on OK to apply the source image content. If you examine the Layers palette in this example, you can see that no new layer was created. Instead, the content from the source image was applied directly to the Background layer.

 The Apply Image window can combine any two images, whether or not the source file has a mask.

USING CALCULATIONS WITH CHANNELS

You can blend masked or unmasked images without touching a pixel by using the Calculations command in the Image menu. The Calculations command can apply blend modes to single channels between two source image files, applying a mask if needed, resulting in a single grayscale channel.

The Calculations window enables you to control inter-channel operations between layers and channels, including alpha channels in the selected source images. You can apply this command to a single image file, or across two image files. Both images must be the same size (such as 1,600×1,200 pixels), and it might take a little time to determine the right combination of blending modes and calculation settings. However, the Calculations command can create some of the most unique channel effects in Photoshop. The following steps show you how to use the Calculations command to combine channels with a blending mode, creating a new, grayscale image:

1. Open the image files to blend.
2. Choose the Calculations command from the Image menu.

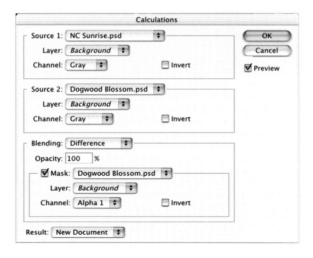

3. Select the appropriate images to use as Source 1 and Source 2. Which image you select as which will depend on the other settings you'll make, such as the Blending choice. In fact, you may have to come back and flip these choices (choosing the Source 2 image as the Source 1 image, and vice versa) to achieve the effect you're after.
4. Choose the Layer and Channel that holds the information to blend for each image.
5. Pick a blending mode from the Blending pop-up menu. Again the settings here are identical to the settings for blending layers, as described in Chapter 8, "Combining Content with Layers." Also specify the Opacity for the blend.
6. To copy information defined by a particular mask in the source image, click to check the Mask check box. Then choose the Layer and Channel that define the masked source content to apply.
7. Click on OK to apply the source image content. If you examine the Layers palette in this example, you can see that no new layer was created. Instead, the content from the source image was applied directly to the Background layer.
8. Open the Result pop-up menu and choose where to create the calculated channel. Selection places the combined information as a selection in the current document. (The last one you opened.) New Channel creates a new channel in the current document. New Document creates a new file to hold the calculated channel.
9. Then click OK. Photoshop performs the specified calculation and creates the new content in the specified destination. Following are two new images created with the Calculations command. The first shows two layers (each layer's Gray channel) simply blended by using the Screen Blending mode. The second example shows the same images blended again, this time with the mask from one channel applied.

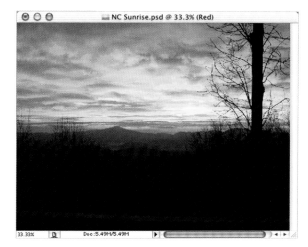

 Create a calculation between a layer and channel from the same image. Then save the result as a channel or selection to continue working with the image in progress.

ADJUSTING A CHANNEL'S CURVE

You can use the Curves command in Photoshop to adjust the tonal range of a layer or a single color channel. (You also can add a Curves adjustment layer by choosing Layer, New Adjustment Layer, Curves.) While the Curves command can come in handy for color balancing areas on a layer by adjusting its highlights, midtones, and shadows, you can use the command to create an even more dramatic impact by adjusting the curve of a single color channel.

1. Open the image file to adjust.

2. Display the Channels palette by clicking its tab or choosing Window, Channels.

3. Hide all channels but the channel to adjust in the channels palette; also click on the name of the channel to adjust to make sure that it's selected. For example, I'll adjust the Red channel in the image shown above.

4. Choose Image, Adjustments, Curves. The Curves dialog box opens. Along the diagonal line in the dialog box, the upper-right end represents the highlights, the middle represents midtones, and the lower-right end represents shadows. The horizontal gradient bar at the bottom represents the original channel colors, and the vertical gradient bar along the left represents the new color you select. Here, I've increased the intensity of mid-range highlights in the Red channel, while reducing the amount of red in the darker tonal ranges.

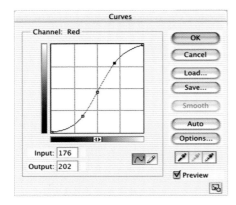

5. Adjust the highlight intensity or shadow intensity, if needed, by dragging either end of the diagonal line. To add curves within the diagonal, click to place curve points and drag them to the desired position.

6. Click OK to apply the curve change; then click the eye icon beside the composite channel to redisplay the image color and view the impact of the color curve change you made.

 When you're making a change like this that isn't previewed in the image window, keep your eye on the image thumbnail in the Navigator palette.

COMBINING IMAGES TO CREATE ANIMATION

DIGITAL IMAGES ARE GREAT TO LOOK AT AS A SINGLE PHOTOGRAPH, BUT THEY CAN BECOME EVEN MORE INTERESTING WITH A LITTLE ANIMATION. TO ANIMATE A PICTURE, YOU SIMPLY OPEN A PHOTOSHOP FILE IN IMAGEREADY, ADD A FEW FRAMES, EDIT A FEW LAYERS, AND APPLY SOME EFFECTS. THEN VIEW YOUR ANIMATION! IF YOU'RE CREATING ANIMATION FOR THE WEB, YOU FLATTEN THE FRAMES INTO LAYERS AND EXPORT THE FILE AS AN ANIMATED GIF.

ANIMATING WITH FRAMES

ImageReady uses frames to create animation. Each frame appears in the Animation palette and can have its own set of layers in the Layers palette. You can create keyframes to define the motion path of the animation. Then use the Tween command to add frames between two keyframes. You can adjust the timing of a frame by assigning a delay to it in the Animation palette. Use the VCR controls at the bottom of the Animation palette to view and step back and forth through the animation.

PREPARING THE IMAGE TO ANIMATE

ImageReady enables you to create an animation in a few different ways, depending on how complex an animation you want to create. To create a very basic animation, all you need is a Photoshop file with content on a single layer. In ImageReady, you can duplicate that content and move it around to create the animation. If you want to use the editing tools in Photoshop to prepare each animation frame in advance, you can prepare the content for each frame in a separate layer in Photoshop. For example, I wanted to create an animation where the image spins. In the Photoshop file (in the following illustration), I copied the Background layer and then deleted it, leaving the copy in place. I then copied that layer three more times, and then rotated the content of each copy (one 90° clockwise, one 180° clockwise, and one 270° clockwise). ImageReady can load the content of each layer as a separate animation frame.

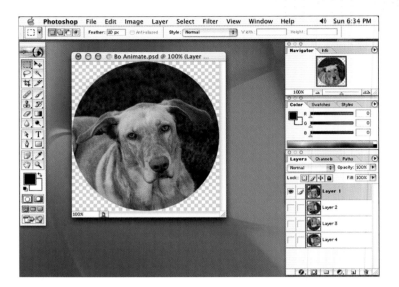

If you want to create an animation that's even more complex, you can save all the images in a single folder and then import them (as frames) into ImageReady.

RESIZING WITH THE IMAGE ASSISTANT

Although this chapter shows you how to create animation with ImageReady, you can resize an image in Photoshop before opening the file with ImageReady. Resizing a digital picture to a smaller size can help an animation play back faster, requires less memory while you're working in ImageReady, and reduces the final size of the animation file—the most important consideration if you're preparing the image for inclusion on a Web page or in a presentation.

One way to resize an image is to open the Image menu and choose the Image Size command. If you don't need to change the image resolution and only want to resize it, use Photoshop's Resize Image Assistant. The following steps show you how to resize an image file using the Resize Image Assistant:

1. Open the image file that holds the content to animate (and that you want to resize) in Photoshop.
2. Choose Resize Image from the Help menu.

3. Select the Online option button, because the animation will be viewed onscreen whether it's viewed via the Web or a presentation. Click on Next.

4. Type the desired width and height of the image; then click on Next.
5. Wait for the image to be resized. A preview of the resized image appears onscreen. If the image now meets your design needs, click on Finish. Otherwise, choose Back and type in a new width and height.
6. Save the resized image under the desired name. If you're preparing the animation for the Web, remember not to include spaces in the image name.

 You also can use the File, Automate, Fit Image command to resize an image file to a specific pixel width and height. To resize all your images to the same size, you can create an action, as described in the next chapter, and then use the File, Automate, Batch command to apply it to all the files stored in a folder you specify.

MAKING A FRAME FOR EACH LAYER

Once you've set up the layers and have adjusted the size of the image to animate, you can open it in ImageReady and quickly convert the layers to frames. This creates your first animation, in a matter of moments.

1. Open the image file to animate in ImageReady.

2. Click the Animation palette menu button and then click Make Frames from Layers.

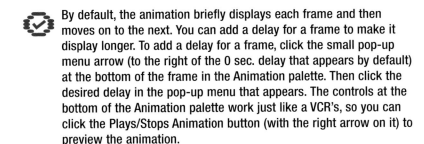

3. If needed, drag to position the frames in the correct order, and that's it! ImageReady can now play back the frames as a single animation. Jump ahead to the section titled "Viewing Animation" to learn how to play your animation file.

By default, the animation briefly displays each frame and then moves on to the next. You can add a delay for a frame to make it display longer. To add a delay for a frame, click the small pop-up menu arrow (to the right of the 0 sec. delay that appears by default) at the bottom of the frame in the Animation palette. Then click the desired delay in the pop-up menu that appears. The controls at the bottom of the Animation palette work just like a VCR's, so you can click the Plays/Stops Animation button (with the right arrow on it) to preview the animation.

If the Animation palette is not visible in ImageReady, choose Window, Animation to display it.

ANIMATING BY DUPLICATING AND ADJUSTING FRAMES

Using this next method, you can convert a simple, one-layer image (in this case, with a layer mask applied) to multiple frames to create the animation. After you create a frame duplicate, you use the Move tool in ImageReady to position the content of the new frame. In this scenario, you want to make sure that the image size offers some room in the image window for you to move the content of each frame around. Follow these steps to convert a simple image to an animation:

1. Open the image file in ImageReady. A single frame, frame 1, appears by default in the Animation palette.
2. Click on frame 1 of animation in the Animation palette and then click the Duplicates Current Frame button (it has a document on it) at the bottom of the Animation palette. Frame 2 appears in the palette and is selected by default.

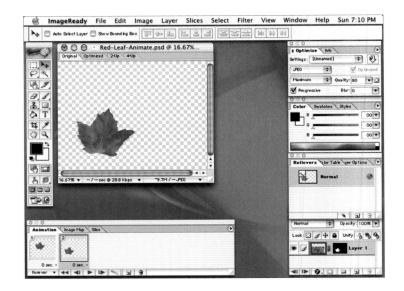

3. Click the Move tool in the ImageReady toolbox; then drag the content of frame 2 to a new position in the image window. Keep your eye on the individual frames in the Animation palette to get a sense of how to position the content of each frame.

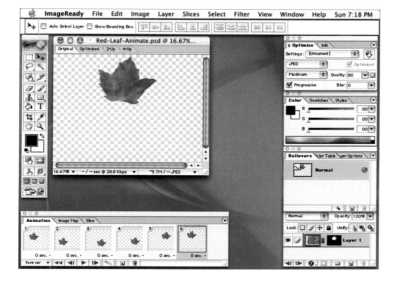

4. Repeat the process—duplicating the current frame and using the Move tool to position the content of the new frame—as many times as needed to create additional frames for the animation.

The paradox of creating animation is that more frames are required to sustain fluid motion. If you're creating animation for the Web, however, smaller files are better. In a nutshell, use as few frames as possible to create your Web animation. If you're working with larger image files (1,600×1,200 pixels or larger) ImageReady might move more slowly as the file grows bigger with more layers, masks, channels, and animation frames.

TWEENING

After you've created all the frames of the animation, use the Tween command to generate in-between frames. Tweening helps ensure that the animation will play back smoothly, because the small increment of movement between each frame added by the tween process will appear more natural to the eye than the larger differences between the frames you created.

Be sure to keep track of the amount of memory and disk space available on your computer as you work on your animation. (You may even need to close other applications like Photoshop to free up more memory for ImageReady.) Most of all, remember your audience. If this animation is for a Web page, will the person viewing your animation want to wait for a long or short period of time before he or she can actually view it?

The following steps show you how to add intermediate frames using the Tween command:

1. Click on the first frame in the Animation palette.
2. Click the Tweens Animation Frames button (it has a series of small frame boxes in a diagonal line) at the bottom of the Animation palette. The Tween dialog box opens.

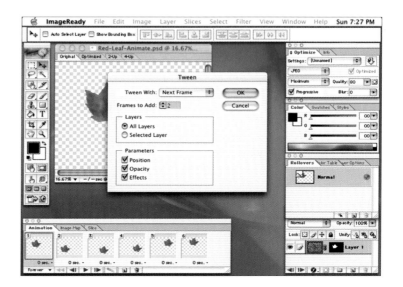

3. Make sure that Next Frame is selected as the Tween With choice and specify the number of Frames to Add. Click OK to generate the Tween frames.

4. Repeat the process for frames as needed in your animation. ImageReady renumbers the frames to reflect the number of frames inserted, so be sure to skip over to the appropriate frame rather than choosing one of the frames just generated by tweening.

When you select the last frame and display the Tween dialog box, be sure to choose First Frame as the Tween With choice.

Wait for ImageReady to render each tweened frame, which may take several moments.

VIEWING ANIMATION

The Animation palette contains a fully functional set of VCR control buttons. You can play, stop, pause, and step through an animation in the same way you control a videotape in a VCR. Choose the number of times you want the animation to loop from the pop-up menu in the lower-left corner of the Animation palette. Play the animation several times and take some quick notes if you see anything you want to change.

1. Click on the Play button in the Animation palette.
2. View the frames as they change in the image window.
3. Click on the Stop button to stop the animation playback.
4. Click on the Step Forward or Step Backward buttons to view the animation forward or backward manually, frame by frame.

To preview the animation at full-size in your Web browser, open the File menu, point to the Preview In choice, and then click your browser in the submenu that appears.

Animation playback might be slower if each image contains many layers, channels, or channel masks. Also, if the image is several megabytes in size, it might take ImageReady a little time to process each frame of animation.

ADDING ANIMATION EFFECTS

The previous sections showed you how to add frames to create an animation. You can manually add an effect to several frames of animation. You can also add effects using the Transform commands to distort the shape of the object at the beginning and end frames of an animation sequence.

In traditional animation, these distortions are called squash and stretch techniques. The squash motion flattens the image as it impacts a solid surface. The stretch motion pulls the object up or down as the image moves toward or away from the solid surface. This section provides brief examples of how you distort an animation in ImageReady.

SCALING AND DISTORTING IMAGES

It's best to use the Transform commands in Photoshop to distort the content of a frame in an animation. Working with the size and shape, in addition to the position of the content on each frame, enables you to make the animated content appear to grow or shrink, or to undulate or pulse. You perform the transform in Photoshop because doing so in ImageReady applies the transform to the specified layer in every frame, which may not be what you want. The following steps show you how to use the Transform commands to distort the shape of a frame's content. You start in ImageReady and flatten the frames into layers; then save and close the file. Next, you open the file in Photoshop and use the desired Edit, Transform submenu command to adjust the content of the desired layer.

This process doesn't work very well with masked content. I recommend that you apply the mask to each frame in ImageReady to discard unneeded layer content. To do so, choose a frame, Control/Ctrl+click the mask thumbnail in the Layers palette, and click **Apply Layer Mask**.

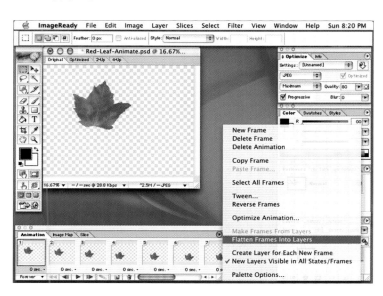

1. Click the Animation palette menu button; then click Flatten Frames Into Layers. ImageReady creates an image layer to represent each frame you previously created.
2. Save the file in ImageReady and close the file.
3. Start Photoshop and open the file.
3. Select the layer to distort by clicking it in the Layers palette. Also hide other Layers as needed to facilitate your work.
4. Use the selection tool or method of your choice to select the frame content in the image window. In this case, I chose Select, Load Selection, chose (Layer Name) Transparency as the Channel, and then clicked OK to select all non-transparent material on the layer.
5. Open the Edit menu, choose Transform, and choose the transformation to apply.

6. Drag a handle or specify the needed settings to apply the transformation. Here the layer content is being skewed. Click the Commit button or OK to finish the transformation.
7. Save the image in Photoshop and close it.
8. Reopen the image in ImageReady.

9. Make sure that the layer holding the distorted content is only displayed for the frame where it applies. In this example, Layer 6 holds the distorted content, which I want to appear in frame 6. So, I selected frame 6 and displayed Layer 6 there by clicking its eye icon box (clearing the eye icon beside other layers, as needed), and hid Layer 6 for all other frames.

 For some animation, such as making a character jump or walk, you can use the Transform commands to create a squash and squish effect across the frames of an animation. After you create the keyframes in Photoshop, save the image as a Photoshop file. Then create the in-between frames in ImageReady.

SAVING THE ANIMATION FOR THE WEB

The final phase of creating animation is to prepare it for playback, typically for the World Wide Web. The following section shows you how to prepare an animation as an Animated GIF file for the Web.

You can preview each frame of your animation using ImageReady's Web-savvy optimization tools and file formats. You may want to save two different versions of the same animated GIF to compare different optimization settings. The animated GIF is saved as a single file that can be embedded in an HTML file and posted to your Web site. If you're not sure which optimization settings to use, you can create multiple animated GIFs from the same source file, create a separate Web page for each animated GIF, and compare them.

The following steps show you how to optimize and save the animation as an animated GIF file.

1. Choose File, Save in ImageReady to save the final animation file in Photoshop (PSD) format. Taking this step enables you to reopen the file at any time to generate additional versions of the animated GIF.
2. Click the 2-Up or 4-Up tab in the image window to compare the original image to the settings you'll choose in the Optimize palette.
3. Select an Adaptive, Perceptual, or Selective palette from the Color Reduction Algorithm pop-up menu in the Optimize palette to ensure colors are consistent across frames. To reduce image size, increase the Lossy setting and decrease the Dither setting.

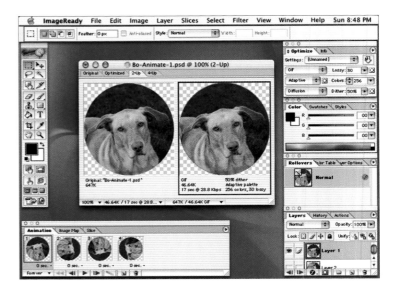

4. Review the quality of the GIF image compared to the original and note the file size and download time in the bottom of the right thumbnail in the image window.

5. Choose File, Save Optimized As. The Save Optimized As dialog box appears.

Save Optimized As

Save As: Bo-Animate-1.gif

Format: Images Only

Where: Documents

Settings: Custom

Slices: All Slices

Cancel   Save

6. Make sure that Images Only is the Format pop-up menu choice. Edit the file name in the Save As text box, leaving the .gif extension intact; then click Save to create the animated GIF. ImageReady creates a single GIF image containing the animation. You can view it in your Web browser or insert it into a Web page to preview the animation.

 Try to choose the shortest possible download time with the largest possible image size for your animation. If you think the person viewing the animation will have a broadband or T1 Internet connection, you can save larger image sizes. However, most people browsing the Internet have a 28.8 or 56k connection. If you want to download a large animation to your Web page, add a text message to let your Web visitors know that they should expect to wait a certain amount of time before they can view your animation.

 If your target audience is most concerned with file download time, create the smallest possible file, or break up the animation into smaller pieces, if possible. If your target audience wants to view animation containing better detail, keep the image at its full size and choose GIF with a 128-color palette.

 You can use other applications, such as Adobe AfterEffects, Macromedia Flash, Fireworks, or a Web-editing tool, to add more effects or elements to your GIF before sharing the final results on a Web page.

CHAPTER 15

COMBINING
IMAGES WITH TEXT

IN THIS CHAPTER, YOU LEARN HOW TO ENHANCE A PICTURE
WITH A FEW WORDS OF TEXT, OR CREATE A MONTAGE
CONTAINING TEXT AND IMAGES. PHOTOSHOP 7 ENABLES YOU TO
EDIT TEXT DIRECTLY ON ITS LAYER IN THE IMAGE WINDOW. YOU
THEN USE THE CHARACTER AND PARAGRAPH PALETTES TO
FORMAT AND VIEW TEXT SETTINGS.

ADDING TEXT TO IMAGES

Choose either the Horizontal Type tool or the Vertical Type tool to add text to any image file. After you choose the desired type tool, the options bar displays all the type tool options, such as font, font style, font size, anti-aliasing, alignment, and color. Select the desired text settings in the options bar. Click in the image window to position the insertion point and then type the text you want to add. Photoshop creates a separate layer to hold the text. The text itself is opaque, but the rest of the layer is transparent, so the text overlays the other image information. To finish adding the type layer, click the Commit Any Current Edits (check) button at the right end of the options bar.

FORMATTING TEXT

If you don't plan to create a design-oriented, multimedia masterpiece by adding text or line art to a photographic image, you might be perfectly happy with the font and formatting settings you initially select. If you change your mind, font size, styles, and other character and paragraph settings can be right at your fingertips. You also can edit the text itself on the type layer. The following steps show you how to format text and access the Character and Paragraph palettes:

1. Open the image that holds the text to reformat.
2. Select the layer that holds the text in the Layers palette.
3. Select the Horizontal Type or Vertical Type tool in the toolbox. This displays the options bar with the text settings.

4. Select the alternate font settings in the options bar at the top of the workspace. Photoshop immediately applies the changes and displays them in the type layer.

5. If you need to edit the text itself on the selected type layer, leave the Type tool selected. Drag over the text to change it, edit or type text as needed, and then click the Commit Any Current Edits button at the right end of the options bar.

6. Click the Toggle the Character and Paragraph Palettes button at the right end of the options bar. A window holding the Character and Paragraph palettes opens onscreen. These palettes offer text settings not available on the options bar, such as the ability to adjust letter spacing and line spacing, apply superscript and strikethrough, apply indention, and so on.

7. Adjust settings as needed on either palette. For example, here I've decreased line spacing and increased letter spacing slightly. New settings you select apply immediately to the text.

8. Click the Toggle the Character and Paragraph Palettes button at the right end of the options bar to close the palette window.

9. Finally, if you need to reposition the text on the layer, click the Move tool on the toolbox and drag the text to the desired position.

 The added text appears on its own type layer in the image file. If you want to animate the text, save it in a separate file. In ImageReady, create a frame showing the text, duplicate the frame, and use the Move tool to reposition the text for the next frame.

WARPING TEXT

The options bar for the type tools includes an amazing tool that can warp text in over a dozen ways: the Warp Text tool. When you select this tool, the Warp Text dialog box appears. Use the dialog box to customize each warp form by adjusting settings, or by typing percentage values for horizontal or vertical effects. The following steps show you how to warp text on a type layer:

1. Open the image file that holds the text to warp.
2. Click the layer that holds the text to warp in the Layers palette.
3. Select the Horizontal Type or Vertical Type tool in the toolbox. This displays the options bar with the text settings.
4. Click the Create Warped Text button near the right end of the options bar. The button has a T with an arc on it. The Warp Text dialog box opens.

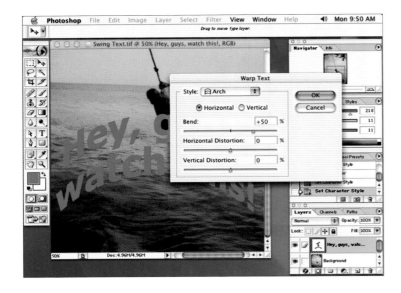

5. Open the Style pop-up menu and click on the desired style. The text in the image window previews the selected style, and the settings for customizing the warp become active in the Warp Text dialog box.

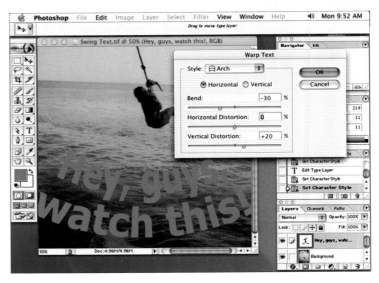

6. Adjust the Bend, Horizontal Distortion, and Vertical Distortion settings as needed to customize the warp effect. Move the Warp Text dialog box around as needed so you can view the impact of the selected settings in the image window.

7. Click on OK to apply the specified settings and finish warping the text.

Swing Text.tif @ 50% (Hey, guys, watch this!, RGB)

To create a drop-shadow effect for regular or warped text, copy the type layer by dragging it over the Create a New Layer button in the Layers palette. Hide the original type layer by clicking its eye icon. Select the layer copy; then choose the text tool. Click the Set the Text Color box on the options bar and select a new color in the Color Picker dialog box. Then use the Move tool to offset the copied layer text. Redisplay the original type layer.

RASTERIZING TEXT

By default, Photoshop creates the text on a type layer as vector objects. Each character remains resolution independent and can have its own font size, or style, independent of any character beside it. However, in order to apply certain effects to text, you must rasterize the text, or render the type layer contents into bitmap shapes (filled pixels), rather than vector shapes (defined by their outlines). After you've rasterized the text, however, you can no longer edit it with the type tools. But you can still use selection tools, such as the Magic Wand, to select text bitmaps. The following steps show you how to convert vector type into rasterized, or bitmap, type:

1. Open the image file that contains the type layer to rasterize.

2. Click the type layer in the Layers palette.
3. Choose Layer, Rasterize, Type. Photoshop immediately rasterizes the type, which you can see by reviewing the layer's thumbnail in the Layers palette.

FILTERING THE RASTERIZED TYPE LAYER

After you've rasterized the type layer, you can use the effects available via the Filter menu to jazz up the text.

1. Open the image file that contains the rasterized type layer.
2. Click the type layer in the Layers palette.
3. Open the Filter menu, select a filter category, and select the filter to apply.

4. If a dialog box of filter settings appears, choose the desired settings and click OK. Photoshop applies the filter to the rasterized text. The example here shows the Grain filter applied.

If you try to apply a filter to a type layer that has not been rasterized, Photoshop prompts you to rasterize the layer.

WORKING WITH MASKED TEXT AND TYPE LAYER BLENDING

Type layers interact with other layers just like normal layers. You can create a mask based on the text in the layer and apply that mask to another layer so that the layer's content fills the text. You also can apply different blend effects to a type layer to control how it interacts with the content of other layers.

APPLYING A TEXT MASK TO AN IMAGE OR ANOTHER LAYER

You can place an image inside some text to give the text a little more substance. To create this effect, first select the text; then use the selection to create a mask on another layer. The following steps show you how to create a layer mask based on text.

1. Open the image to alter in Photoshop. Typically, for this effect to work, you'll need three layers: the Background, a type layer, and another image layer copied from another image (or a fill, pattern, or gradient layer).

2. Click the type layer in the Layers palette to select that layer.
3. Choose Select, Load Selection. In the Load Selection dialog box that appears, make sure that the (Layer Name) Transparency choice is selected from the Channel pop-up menu and click OK. This selects the letters in the type layer.

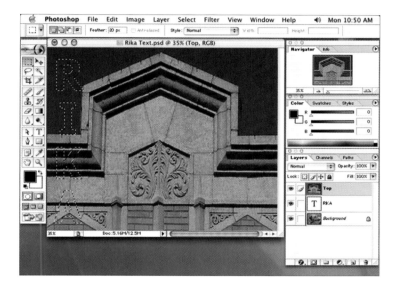

4. Click on the layer on which you want to create the mask in the Layers palette. This typically will be the second image layer (not the Background layer) you copied from another file, or the fill layer in the image. This image layer displays the layer content and shows the selection on the layer.

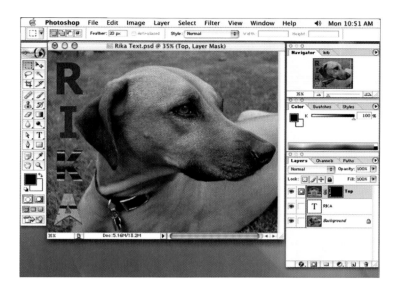

5. Click the Add Layer Mask button at the bottom of the Layers palette to create the text mask on the layer.

 If you still only see the text color after Step 5, it means that the type layer is above the image or fill layer you masked in the Layers palette. To fix the problem so that the image or fill appears, rather than the text color, drag the image or fill layer above the type layer in the Layers palette. You also can hide the type layer.

BLENDING A TYPE LAYER

As with any other layer, you can apply a layer blending style or a layer effect (such as a drop shadow or an inner glow) to any type layer in the image file. Use the following process to get started.

Change layer settings for the type layer itself or for a layer on which you've created a text-based mask.

1. Open an image file that holds the type layer to blend.
2. Click the type layer in the Layers palette to select that layer.
3. Click the menu button (with the right arrow) on the Layers palette; then click Blending Options in the menu that appears. The Layer Style dialog box opens.

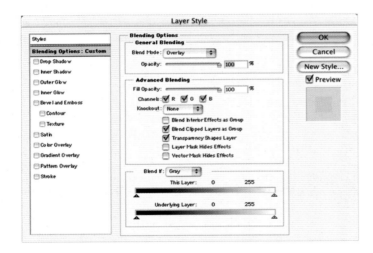

4. Choose a blending style from the Blend Mode pop-up menu at the top of the dialog box. Adjust other layer blending settings, such as Opacity, as needed.
5. To add a special layer effect style, click the desired style name (not just the check box for the style) in the Styles list at the left side of the dialog box. The settings for the selected style appear in the Layer Style dialog box.

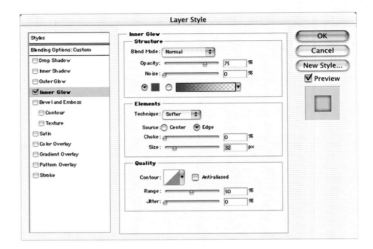

6. Adjust the settings for the specified style as desired and click OK. Photoshop applies the specified blending mode and effect(s) to the type layer in the image.

CHAPTER 16

AUTOMATING TASKS

A FEW DOZEN YEARS AGO WHEN COMPUTERS WERE BEGINNING TO TAKE ON THE FORM OF A DESKTOP MACHINE, A FEW WRITERS WROTE ABOUT A DAY WHEN COMPUTERS MIGHT TAKE OVER THE WORLD. TAKE THIS SAME PREMISE AND VIEW IT FROM ANOTHER PERSPECTIVE, AND YOU MIGHT THINK SOFTWARE WOULD BE EASY TO USE IF IT COULD RUN REPETITIVE TASKS ON ITS OWN, WITHOUT THE HELP OF SOMEONE TO SIT THERE AND CLICK THE MOUSE TO MAKE THE SOFTWARE GO.

THE ACTIONS PALETTE IN PHOTOSHOP ENABLES YOU TO RECORD AND PLAY BACK MOST TASKS IN PHOTOSHOP. THE COMMANDS ON THE FILE, AUTOMATE SUBMENU ENABLE YOU TO AUTOMATICALLY PERFORM COMPLEX TASKS SUCH AS CREATING A CONTACT (PROOF) SHEET OR APPLYING AN ACTION TO A BATCH OF FILES. THE FOLLOWING SECTIONS SHOW YOU HOW TO AUTOMATE YOUR OWN TASKS AND TAKE ADVANTAGE OF THE BUILT-IN AUTOMATION FEATURES IN PHOTOSHOP.

USING ONE OF PHOTOSHOP'S ACTIONS

Photoshop includes a default set of actions. Each action holds a pre-recorded set of steps that you can play back by running the action from the Actions palette. Like the other Photoshop palettes, the Actions palette has the same pop-up menu and toolbar. The palette organizes actions into folders called sets. You can load additional sets as needed. The following steps provide a brief tour of the Actions palette:

1. Display the Actions palette by clicking its tab or choosing Window, Actions.

2. To load another of the default action sets, click on the Actions palette menu button; then click one of the action set names near the bottom of the menu that appears.
3. View the list of actions in the newly-loaded set.
4. To expand or collapse a set in the Actions palette, click the triangle icon beside the action set folder.

5. To run an action, click it in the Actions palette and then click the Play Selection button at the bottom of the Actions palette. The Play selection button has a right arrow on it, just the like Play button on a VCR. In this example, I ran the Marble action from the Textures set. This action created a new layer with a marble fill texture, which I blended with the image Background layer content by changing the blending mode for the Marble layer to Soft Light.

 If the Actions palette is empty, choose Reset Actions from the Actions palette menu.

CREATING ACTIONS

You can record most tasks in Photoshop with the Actions palette. This enables you to create an action for any set of tasks you perform frequently, enabling you to use the action to reduce repetitive work or to be able to play back a favorite collection of settings without having to remember each individual one. The following steps show you how to use the Record button to record an action in the Actions palette:

1. Open an image file and perform whatever steps are needed before you begin recording the action. For example, you may want to load a particular selection and click a particular layer in the Layers palette.
2. Click the Create New Set (folder) button at the bottom of the Actions palette. In the New Set dialog box that opens, type a name for your new actions set and then click OK. The new set folder appears in the list in the Actions palette and is selected.
3. Click the Create New Action button (it has a sheet of paper on it) at the bottom of the Actions palette. The New Action dialog box opens.

4. Type a descriptive name for the action in the Name text box in the dialog box. Make sure your new set appears as the choice for the Set pop-up menu. Then click Record to start recording the action.
5. Perform the steps to save as the action. For example, I'll feather an area I selected in Step 1 and then use the selection to create a layer mask on the selected layer.

6. Click on the Stop Playing/Recording button (it has a box on it) at the bottom of the Actions palette to stop the recording. The new action appears in the Actions palette.

 Photoshop can't record everything you do as an action. Try to record small actions to verify that they can be automated in Photoshop. This is better than running through long combinations of tasks, only to find out that one or two of them cannot be recorded as an action.

BATCH PROCESSING WITH AN ACTION

You can apply an action to all the files stored in a single folder. This enables you to apply a consistent set of settings to all the files by using one command. All the files to alter must be in a separate folder. To preserve the changes, the process re-saves each of the files. You must specify what folder to save the files to. The following steps show you how to use the Batch command to apply an action to a folder of images:

1. Choose File, Automate, Batch. The Batch dialog box opens.

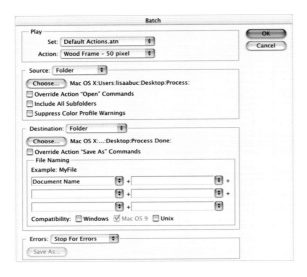

2. Click on the Set pop-up menu and choose the set that holds the action you want to apply. Click on the Action pop-up menu to choose the action to apply.
3. Click on the Source and Destination pop-up menus and choose Folder in each. Then use the Choose button to select the folder that holds the original images and the folder where you'd like to save the resulting images. Also use the choices in the File Naming section to specify how Photoshop should rename the processed images.
4. Click OK to run the action on the batch command. Photoshop processes each file in the selected folder and saves the processed file to the specified destination folder.

USING PHOTOSHOP'S AUTOMATED TASKS

You can fit an image to a particular size, change the color mode of a picture, generate a contact sheet, or create a Picture Package using commands on Photoshop's File, Automate submenu. The Fit Image choice enables you to resize the width and height of an image. You can use the Conditional Mode Change choice to change an image from RGB mode to Indexed color mode. The Contact Sheet II command can take a folder full of image files and create a thumbnail of each picture in a contact sheet, enabling you to view or print pages of pictures from Photoshop. If you want to view an image at one or two different sizes in the same image window, use the Picture Package feature to automatically resize and lay out the image in a new image window.

FITTING IMAGES

Most 2- and 3-megapixel cameras create large files ranging from 640×480 pixels to 1,600×1,200 or 2,000×1,500. Use the Fit Image command to let Photoshop resize your pictures to a much more practical size for your Web site.

 Resizing a large image to a smaller one works great if you're trying to add graphics to a Web site. However, if you have a 50×50-pixel image, resizing it to 640×480 will only enlarge the pixels, and the image might not be recognizable.

The following steps show you how to resize images using the Fit Image feature:

1. Open an image file that you want to resize.
2. Open the File menu, select Automate, and choose Fit Image. The Fit Image dialog box opens.

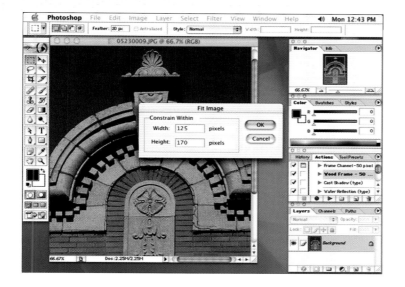

3. Enter new values in the Width and Height text boxes.

4. Click OK. Photoshop resizes the image within the selected image window. You can then save the file with its new dimensions, or select Edit, Undo Image Size to revert the image to its original size.

CHANGING IMAGE MODES

You can use the File, Automate, Conditional Mode Change command to switch the color mode of an image file. For example you can change an RGB Color file to another mode, such as grayscale or CMYK mode. The following steps show you how to change an image from RGB to Indexed Color mode using the Conditional Mode Change command:

1. Open the image file to change it to another color mode. The current color mode for the image appears in the title bar of the image window. For example, when you open an RGB color image, you should see (RGB) following the name of the image file at the top of the image window.

2. Open the File menu, select Automate, and select Conditional Mode Change. The Conditional Mode Change dialog box opens.

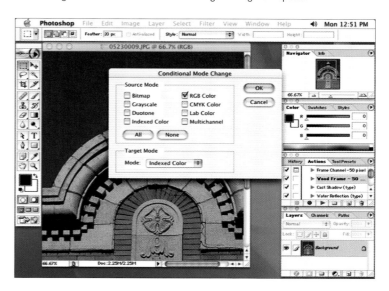

3. In most cases, the correct mode should be selected in the Source Mode section. To choose the new mode, open the Mode pop-up menu in the Target Mode area and then click the new mode to apply. For example, choose Indexed Color.

4. Click on OK. If the mode change requires you to specify additional settings for the transformation, a dialog box of settings appears. For example, when you're converting an image to Indexed Color, the Indexed Color dialog box appears.

5. Adjust settings for the color mode as needed and then click OK. Photoshop applies the new color mode to the current file.

 Most images produced from digital cameras use the RGB color mode. Unless you need to work with the image in CMYK or another image mode, I suggest retaining the RGB mode in Photoshop file until you are ready to optimize the file and save it for the Web.

CREATING A CONTACT SHEET

Let Photoshop put a folder of pictures onto a contact sheet. You can print a contact sheet to catalog all the digital pictures you take, create, or convert from a 35mm camera. Contact sheets help you compare and select images to work with. You can then preview the layout and adjust the settings for the contact sheet in the Contact Sheet II dialog box in Photoshop. The following steps show you how to create a contact sheet using the Contact Sheet II command:

1. Open the File menu, select Automate, and choose Contact Sheet II. The Contact Sheet II dialog box opens.

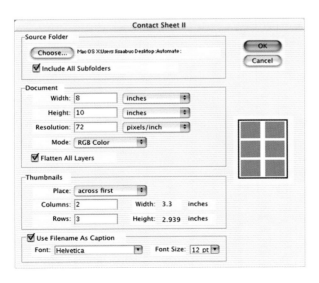

2. Click on Choose in the Source Folder area of the dialog box and choose the folder that holds the images you want to place on the contact sheet.

3. Adjust settings in the Document and Thumbnails areas of the dialog box. For example, you can choose the number of images on each contact sheet page by changing the Columns and Rows entries in the Thumbnails area.

4. To include the file name below each image, check the Use Filename as Caption check box and adjust the Font and Font Size settings as needed.

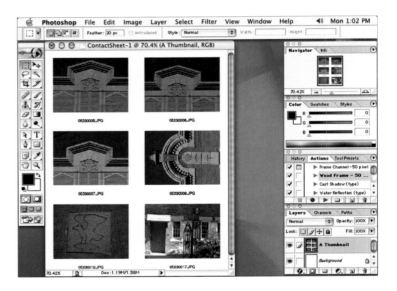

5. Click OK. Photoshop will automatically create a new image window for each contact sheet page until all images in the source folder have been processed. You can then view the contact sheet(s) in Photoshop.

 It may take a while to create a contact sheet. If you decide you want to stop the contact sheet process, press the Esc key.

 You can save each contact sheet image as a separate Photoshop file.

USING THE PICTURE PACKAGE FEATURE

Choose the Picture Package feature to create a page of photo prints of the specified image. Each picture package page can combine copies of the image file in a wide range of photo sizes, from four 4×5 or two 5×7 images on a page, or a combination of sizes, such as two 4×5 and four 2.5×3.5 images. Picture Package lays out the image copies to maximize the use of each page, enabling you to get the most for your money when you're printing on pricey photo paper. The following steps show you how to use the Picture Package feature:

1. Open the File menu, select Automate, and choose Picture Package. The Picture Package dialog box opens.

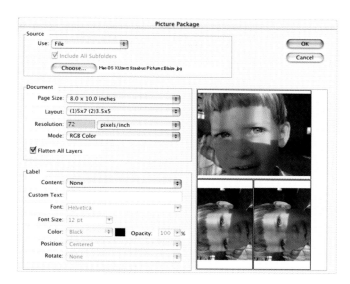

2. Use the Choose button in the Source area to select the file to prepare as a picture package and print.
3. In the Document area of the dialog box, open the Layout pop-up menu and choose the combination of sizes to print.
4. Click OK.
   Photoshop creates a new image to hold the picture package. It resizes and positions copies of the source picture to match the layout you specified. When it finishes, you can save and print the picture package, or discard it and try again.

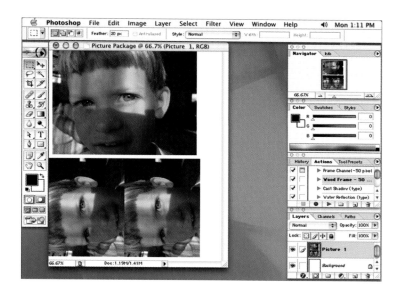

PART 4

PUBLISHING PICTURES

ONE OF THE ADVANTAGES OF TAKING PICTURES WITH A DIGITAL CAMERA OR WORKING WITH ANY DIGITAL PICTURE IS THAT YOU CAN SHARE THEM ON THE WEB WITH RELATIVE EASE. OF COURSE, IT HELPS TO HAVE YOUR OWN WEB SITE. HOWEVER, MANY WEB SITES, SUCH AS **SHUTTERFLY.COM** AND **OFOTO.COM**, WILL HOST YOUR WEB PHOTO ALBUMS FOR FREE. THE FOLLOWING SECTIONS SHOW YOU HOW TO OPTIMIZE YOUR PICTURES FOR THE WEB AND CREATE A WEB PHOTO ALBUM.

CHAPTER 17

OPTIMIZING IMAGES
FOR THE WEB

OPTIMIZING AN IMAGE FOR THE WEB WITH PHOTOSHOP OR
IMAGEREADY INVOLVES THE PROCESS OF REDUCING THE SIZE
OF THE IMAGE FILE WHILE RETAINING AS MUCH OF THE IMAGE'S
QUALITY AS POSSIBLE. THIS CHAPTER FOCUSES ON USING THE
OPTIMIZATION SETTINGS IN THE SAVE FOR WEB DIALOG BOX IN
PHOTOSHOP. HOWEVER, IMAGEREADY HAS MANY SIMILAR
FEATURES IN ITS OPTIMIZE PALETTE AND IMAGE WINDOW. AN
IMAGE WITH LARGE AREAS OF SOLID COLOR IS EASIER TO
OPTIMIZE THAN AN IMAGE CONTAINING A BROAD RANGE OF
COLORS AND LOTS OF SMALL, BRIGHT, OR ANIMATED
ELEMENTS. SINCE PHOTOS TEND TO FALL INTO THE LATTER
CATEGORY, YOU'LL PROBABLY BE OPTIMIZING AN IMAGE AS A
JPEG OR GIF 128 FILE FORMAT. THIS CHAPTER SHOWS YOU HOW
TO PREVIEW AN IMAGE, CREATE ROLLOVERS, USE THE SLICE
TOOL TO BREAK UP AN IMAGE IN PHOTOSHOP, OPTIMIZE
COLORS, AND WORK WITH TRANSPARENCIES TO CREATE WEB-
READY IMAGES.

ANALYZING WEB ELEMENTS

Previewing different file formats is the key to optimizing an image for a Web page. Of the file formats available for the Web, JPEG usually can create the smallest image because it uses file compression. However, the quality of the image can vary, depending on whether you choose to save the image as a low, medium, or high quality image.

A GIF image with 128 colors is another alternative for saving a Web image, especially if the image contains transparency settings. JPEG does not support transparency settings, so if an image needs to blend with a background image, you must save it as a GIF. Additional Web elements to consider when optimizing an image are download time and image quality.

CHANGING TO INDEXED COLOR MODE

After you've created the final RGB image, you can flatten the layers and channels by choosing another image mode, Indexed Color. This quickly gives you an idea of how your image will look on the Web. If you plan to share your picture on a Web page, smaller file sizes download faster than larger file sizes. You'll want to use the smallest possible image that preserves the best image quality.

The following steps show you how to change an image file from RGB mode to Indexed Color mode:

1. Open the image to convert in Photoshop. View the file size of the image by choosing Document Sizes from the drop-down menu in the lower left corner of the image window. In this example, the image file size is 900k. It is a 640×480 pixel image.
2. Choose Image, Mode, Indexed Color. The Indexed Color dialog box opens.

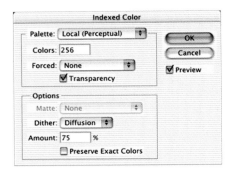

3. Choose either Local (Selective), Local (Perceptual), or Local (Adaptive) from the Palette pop-up menu to specify the method Photoshop uses to reduce the number of colors in the image. If you want to force the colors in the image to a Web, Primary, or Black-and-White palette, select the palette from the Forced pop-up menu. In this example, I've chosen None. Check the Transparency box if you want to preserve any transparency settings in the image.
4. Specify Options such as the Dither method and Amount of dithering.

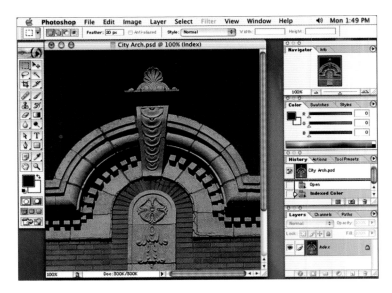

5. Click OK to apply the conversion. View the new file size in the lower left corner of the image window.

OPTIMIZING IMAGE SETTINGS

You can preview an optimized file in the Save for Web dialog box before actually saving the new file. Choose JPEG, GIF, or PNG file formats, which support different numbers of colors in their corresponding color palettes. Choose 2-Up or 4-Up modes to compare optimized files with the original picture. By using this process, you can identify exactly which settings produce the best-looking results for an image saved in JPEG or GIF format.

Some optimization settings, such as those in the Settings pop-up menu in the Save for Web dialog box in Adobe Photoshop, are tied to specific color palettes and default values. The following steps show you how to choose optimization settings and preview the changes in the Save for Web dialog box:

1. Open the image file to optimize in Photoshop.
2. Open the File menu and choose Save for Web. The Save for Web dialog box opens.
3. Choose Optimized File Format and Color Reduction Algorithm settings from the pop-up menus with those names in the Settings area at the right side of the dialog box. For example, choose GIF and Selective.

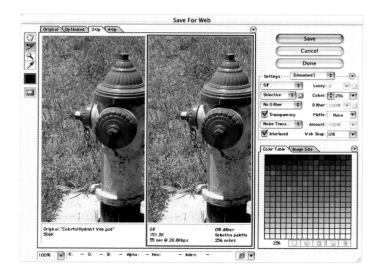

4. Click on the 2-Up tab to compare the new set of colors with the original image. Below the image preview, the left pane in the 2-Up tab shows the size of the original image file. The area below the image preview in the right pane lists the file size and download time that will result from the presently-selected settings.

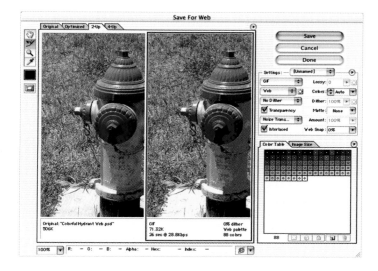

5. Now choose an alternate Color Reduction Algorithm setting, such as Web. After Photoshop generates the preview for the new settings, it appears in the right pane so you can review the new projected file size and download time.
6. Then click on the 4-Up tab in the Save for Web dialog box. This tab enables you to compare three different combinations of optimization settings to the original image in the upper-left pane.
7. Click on one of the lower panes and select new optimization settings in the Settings area at the right side of the dialog box.

 You can choose a preset collection of optimization settings by opening the Saved Sets of Optimization Settings pop-up menu (between Settings and the triangle menu button at the top of the Settings area) and then choosing the preset to apply to one of the preview panes.

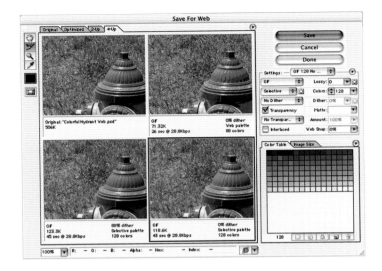

8. Choose optimization settings for the final pane. After Photoshop updates that pane, you can compare the three previews to the original image in the upper-left pane. The image with the best quality should look as close to the original picture as possible. When you identify the settings to use, click the appropriate preview pane, and then click the Save button to continue the save process, as described in the next chapter.

 You can resize a Web image directly from the Save for Web dialog box. Simply type the new (preferably smaller) dimensions of the image in the Image Size palette in the lower-right corner of the dialog box. In most cases, making an image smaller retains the image quality of the picture while shrinking the overall file size.

WORKING WITH ROLLOVERS

Rollovers are actions you can add to a linked graphic or linked text on a Web page. Clicking the link button or text takes the user to another Web page or another location on the same Web page. A rollover provides more dynamic behavior to the linked graphic or text. For example, you can swap the image of the unpressed button with a glowing button when the mouse is over the button graphic. Or when the button is pressed, you can show an image of a pressed button instead of an unpressed, glowing button. With text, you can change the color when the mouse pointer is over it or after the user has clicked it. The various appearances for each linked item are called rollover states. Create the original image (with the linked graphic or text) and then open the image in ImageReady to create the rollovers. ImageReady enables you to create each rollover state in the Rollover palette, storing each image state in the Layers palette.

Preview each rollover state in a browser window and then save the HTML and image files to your hard disk. ImageReady generates and saves the necessary JavaScript code for each rollover. Add the files with rollovers to a new or existing Web page, and then move the finished Web pages to your Web server.

CREATING A ROLLOVER

You can add several different rollover states to an image or create your own custom rollover state in ImageReady. Choose an image that includes a graphic or text you want to use as a hyperlink on a Web page. The following steps show you how to create a rollover with ImageReady:

1. Create the image file in Photoshop. For each rollover state you want to include, duplicate the layer that holds the rollover object or text. Adjust the formatting or appearance of the object or text to use as the rollover. For example, I created a type layer with some yellow text. I created two copies of the layer. I changed the text color to white on the first copy, to prepare for the state when the mouse pointer is over the text on the Web page. I changed the text color to purple on the second copy to prepare for the "after" state, indicating that the linked text has been clicked. Save and close the image file after you set it up.

2. Open the image file in ImageReady.

3. Display the Rollovers palette, if needed, by clicking its tab or choosing Window, Rollovers. Also move the palette so you can see the buttons at the bottom and resize the Layers palette so you can see the layers you want to work with. The open image represents the Normal state of the rollover object or text.

4. Click on the Creates Rollover State button (document icon) at the bottom of the Rollovers palette. The Over State rollover appears in the Rollovers palette.

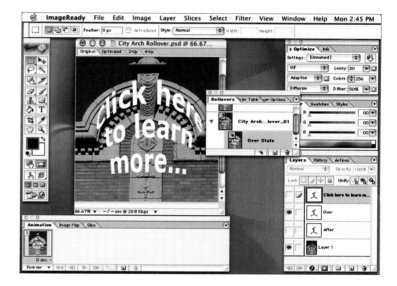

5. Make sure that the Over State choice is selected in the Rollovers palette and then use the Layers palette to hide the original text or object layer, as well as others for all other states except the state where the mouse pointer is over the graphic object or text. For example, if you look closely at the Rollovers palette in this example, you can see that the text is yellow for the default state and white for the new Over State entry in the palette.

6. Click on the Creates Rollover State button (document icon) at the bottom of the Rollovers palette. The Down State rollover appears in the Rollovers palette.

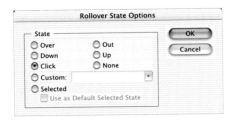

7. If you want to choose a rollover state other than the Down State, double-click the Down State entry in the Rollovers palette. This displays the Rollover State Options dialog box. This dialog box enables you to select the precise behavior you want to designate for the next rollover state. Click the option button for the state you want, such as Click, and then click OK to apply the state option.

8. Use the Layers palette to display the appropriate layers for the new state.

9. Create additional states as desired.

10. To preview your rollover states, click the Preview in Default Browser button on the toolbox. (It has an icon representing your Web browser on it.) For example, here's the click state for my example graphic.

11. Close the Web browser. Once the rollover states function the way you want them to, proceed to the next section to learn how to save the image with rollovers.

SAVING ROLLOVERS

When you've finished creating your rollover, save the image and HTML files to your hard drive. Use the Optimize palette to select optimization settings; then choose the File, Save Optimized As to save the image with the current optimization settings. When you finish the save, ImageReady generates a separate image file for each rollover state, as well as JavaScript code, which is then saved as an HTML file. The HTML code tells a browser how to create each rollover state using the rollover image files you created in ImageReady. The following steps show you how to save your rollover files to your hard disk:

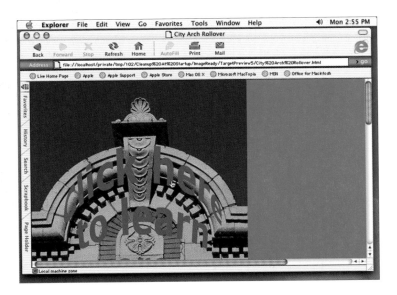

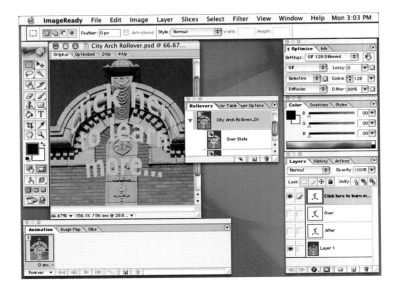

1. After creating the rollover states in ImageReady, as described in the last section, select the desired optimization from the Optimize palette. Preview and compare different file formats to the original. In this example, I chose GIF 128 Dithered.

 To see the image with the optimization settings applied, choose View, Show 2-Up.

2. Choose Save Optimized As from the File menu. The Save As Optimized dialog box appears.

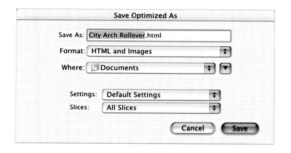

3. Type a name for the image files and select HTML and Images from the Format pop-up menu, if needed. Also specify the folder in which you'd like to save the HTML and supporting files.

4. Click on the Save button to finish the save.

 This process might seem a little confusing if you've never worked with Web pages before. In order to put information on a Web page, you must create an HTML file, which will eventually reside on a Web server. You will also need to upload each image file to the Web server. To update an existing Web page with the rollover, you have to add the HTML code file (which you named in the Save Optimized As dialog box) created by ImageReady to a Web page and then post the page and the images subfolder (also generated by the saving process) that holds a GIF image for each rollover state to your Web server. You can use an HTML editor application, such as Microsoft FrontPage or Bare Bones BBEdit software, to create or edit a Web page. Or, if you can code HTML without the help provided by such applications, you can work directly in Notepad or TextEdit.

SLICING UP AN IMAGE

You can use the Slice tool (K is the shortcut to select this tool in the toolbox) to break a big image into smaller pieces. Saving the sliced image generates HTML code to reassemble the slices so you can view the full image on a Web page. Photoshop and ImageReady can create two kinds of slices: user slices and layer slices. The following sections show you how to create user slices. To create a layer-based slice, click on a layer in the Layers palette. Then open the Layer menu and choose New Layer Based Slice. The image in that layer will be changed into a slice. In ImageReady you can link a slice to a URL, add rollover behaviors, and optimize the sliced image.

Slices enable you to break up a large image so that it will load faster in a browser window. You can create a single slice or slices on top of other slices. A secondary or tertiary slice (a slice below a slice) can also be called a sub slice. When you save an image file that contains slices, ImageReady saves each slice as a separate file. A sliced image can be made up of different image file formats. For example, one slice can be saved as a GIF, and the rest of the slices as JPEG files. Open the File menu and choose Save for Web to save your slices in Photoshop. Open the File menu and choose Save Optimized As to save your slices in ImageReady. Both applications can generate the HTML code to position each slice on a Web page. You can save the slice HTML code as a table or as a cascading style sheet. Add the HTML code from ImageReady or Photoshop to your own Web page and then upload the image files and HTML files to your Web server to add the sliced image to your Web site.

CREATING SLICES

Both Photoshop and ImageReady have a Slice tool in their toolboxes. You can create a sliced image in Photoshop or ImageReady. The tool works the same in both applications.

Select the Slice tool from the toolbox; then drag in the image window to create a slice. When you create a slice, you draw a single rectangle in the image window. Photoshop breaks the rest of the image up into corre-

sponding slices in the image window, assigning a unique number to each slice image.

Try to create a slice that breaks the image into equal sized parts. Alternatively, if there is one particular area of the picture that should load more quickly than the others or if you want to use the slice as a hyperlink and perhaps include rollover states, create a smaller slice around that area to set it apart. The following steps show you how to use the Slice tool in ImageReady:

1. Open the image to slice in ImageReady.
2. Click the Slice tool (K) in the toolbox. The mouse pointer changes to look like a knife blade.

3. Drag the tool in the window to create a square or rectangle around the area to designate as a slice. Photoshop creates additional automatic slices to surround the slice you created. The number of each slice appears in the upper-left corner of the rectangular slice. Each shaded slice area also contains a slice number.
4. To change the settings for a slice, make sure that the Slice tool is selected in the toolbox; then click the slice number.

5. Display the Slice palette by clicking its tab or choosing Window, Slice. Resize the window to see all its settings, if needed.

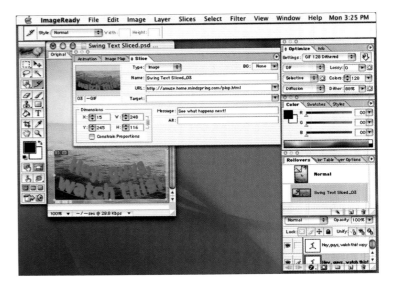

6. Enter the URL that the slice links to, such as **http://amuze.home. mindspring.com/plop.html**. Also enter a message that will appear in the browser status bar when the user moves the mouse pointer over the sliced image in the Message text box.
7. To preview your rollover states, click the Preview in Default Browser button on the toolbox. (It has an icon representing your Web browser on it.)
8. After testing the hyperlink, close the Web browser.
9. Use the File, Save Optimized as choice to save the final sliced document as described in the section called "Saving Rollovers." When you want to publish the sliced file to the Web, be sure to insert the .HTML file generated for the sliced image into your Web page, and be sure to copy all folders (for images) generated when you saved the sliced image to your Web server. Otherwise, the sliced image won't be able to display.

A slice affects all the layers, masks, and channels in an image. You can view additional information about a slice in ImageReady's Slice palette.

ImageReady has a dedicated Slice menu that you won't find in Photoshop. If you create a slice in ImageReady, you can duplicate, optimize, and choose from several menu commands to edit your image slices.

LOCKING SLICES

If you're working with several image layers or if you don't want any of the slices to be edited after you've chosen the optimization settings, choose Lock Slices from the View menu in Photoshop. When you lock slices, you will not be able to select or edit any slices in the image window. ImageReady does not have a lock slice feature, although it has a dedicated Slice palette and Slice menu. The following steps show you how to lock slices in the image window in Photoshop:

1. Open the sliced image file in Photoshop.

2. Select the Slice tool to see the slices in the image window. Each slice has a unique number in the upper-left corner. The slice you create appears as a highlighted slice in the image window.

3. Choose Lock Slices from the View menu. The slices in the image window remain unchanged. If you try to adjust a slice, Photoshop displays a dialog box telling you that the slices are locked.

4. Choose View, Lock Slices again to uncheck that command and unlock all slices.

PREVIEWING COLOR FOR MAC AND WINDOWS BROWSERS

Gamma settings correspond to the monitor used with your computer. Brightness and midtone values generated by a monitor are measured in gamma. Windows computers use a higher gamma value than Macintosh computers. High gamma values create darker images.

Gamma settings on Windows PCs tend to have more of a red tint than the Macintosh gamma settings. If you want the image to appear correct on both Macintosh and PC computers, you should save two copies, each with the gamma-specific settings. Then you have to add the HTML code that tells the Web page to show the correct picture to the client computer.

You should preview colors for the Mac and Web gammas before saving your images to the Web (described in more detail in the next chapter) before you save the final Web file, so that you can return to Photoshop and perform any needed color corrections.

SETTING MACINTOSH GAMMA

Before saving an image, choose the Standard Macintosh Color setting from the Save for Web drop-down menu to determine whether any of the colors will look differently on a Mac. If the Mac colors are different, choose the gamma settings that most accurately represent the colors in the image. You can also adjust the colors in the Color Table and then save a copy of the image to your hard disk. The following steps show you how to view an image with Macintosh gamma settings:

1. Open the image you want to preview in Photoshop.
2. Choose Save for Web from the File menu. The Save for Web dialog box opens.
3. Click the Optimized tab.

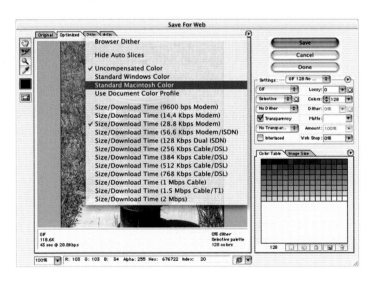

4. Click the menu button in the upper-right corner of the preview area, and then click Standard Macintosh Color in the menu that appears .

5. The colors in the image should change slightly. View the adjusted colors for the Macintosh. To adjust the Color Table, click on the Eyedropper tool and click on a color in the image. Its corresponding color becomes selected in the Color Table. Double-click a color to view or change it from the Color Picker window.
6. Click on Save to finish the saving process or click Done to return to Photoshop and correct the image.

VIEWING WINDOWS GAMMA

Alternatively, you can view or save the same image with Windows Gamma settings to preserve color settings for Windows browsers. If you do not want to save two separate images for each computer platform, try replacing differing colors with colors that are more compatible with both platforms. The following steps show you how to save an image with Windows gamma settings:

1. Open the image you want to preview in Photoshop.
2. Choose Save for Web from the File menu. The Save for Web dialog box opens.
3. Click the Optimized tab.

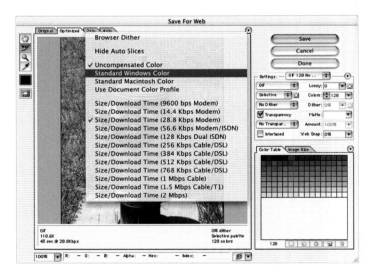

4. Click the menu button in the upper-right corner of the preview area and then click Standard Macintosh Color in the menu that appears.
5. Click on Save to finish the saving process or click Done to return to Photoshop and correct the image.

CHAPTER 18

SAVING IMAGES FOR THE WEB

IT'S EASY TO SCOFF AT WEB GRAPHICS THAT LOAD QUICKLY BUT ARE DIFFICULT TO RECOGNIZE, OR TO GET GRUMPY BECAUSE AN IMAGE TAKES FOREVER TO LOAD. A WEB PAGE LOOKS EVEN WORSE WHEN THE BROWSER TIMES OUT BECAUSE IT CAN'T LOAD ALL THE GRAPHICS. SURE, THE NETWORK AND THE WEB SERVER CONTRIBUTE TO MAKING WEB GRAPHICS LOAD PAINFULLY SLOWLY. BUT ALL THE NETWORK MECHANICS ASIDE, YOU NEED TO FIRST CREATE SMALL, GOOD-LOOKING GRAPHICS TO SPICE UP YOUR TEXT-BASED WEB SITE. PHOTOSHOP AND IMAGEREADY ENABLE YOU TO SAVE AN IMAGE FILE IN ITS NATIVE PHOTOSHOP FILE FORMAT OR ONE OF SEVERAL DIFFERENT, COMMONLY USED WEB GRAPHIC FILE FORMATS, SUCH AS JPEG AND GIF. THIS CHAPTER SHOWS YOU HOW TO SAVE SLICED IMAGES OR A GIF OR JPEG IMAGE.

SAVING FOR THE WEB

If you edit an image file, you can open the File menu and choose the Save command to save your changes to the original image. In most cases, you're probably going to save the file in the Photoshop (PSD) file format, so that you can preserve all the layers, channels, masks, paths, and effects you've added to the image. If you're saving the file for the Web, on the other hand, you need to choose one of the file formats that enable you to optimize and compress the image for the Web. These formats include:

✳ GIF—GIF is an acronym for Graphics Interchange Format. It is the most commonly used file format for Web graphics. The GIF file format employs LZW compression to minimize file size, which in turn enables a Web graphic to download faster to a browser window. GIF images can include transparent areas, which is why this format is frequently used for specialized graphics like page buttons. The GIF format does not support alpha channels.

✳ JPEG—JPEG is an acronym for the Joint Photographic Experts Group format. JPEG is another commonly used Web graphic file format. The JPEG file format enables you to specify compression settings, so you have greater control over the final file size and quality. This is why most true picture files on the Web use the JPEG format. Depending on the JPEG compression level chosen for the file, some image data might be selectively discarded to create the final, compressed file. JPEG does not support alpha channels but retains all color information.

✳ PNG—Portable Network Graphics is a patent-free Web graphics file format that combines the best of GIF and JPEG—you can preserve transparency and control compression. View and edit files in grayscale or RGB mode with a single alpha channel or files in indexed-color mode that do not contain alpha channels. Transparency can be preserved in the single alpha channel of a file, and the PNG file format supports up to 24-bit images.

✳ WBMP—This 1-bit color format optimizes images for wireless devices. Converting an image to this format converts it to simple black and white.

You shouldn't save the image into one of the Web formats until you've finished making all the changes you desire. If the image file contains layers, masks, rollover states, or animation, in particular, you need the original Photoshop file because the optimized JPEG, GIF, or other formats discard that information. Fortunately, the File, Save for

Web command that you use to save an image for the Web copies the original image to create the GIF or JPEG, leaving the Photoshop PSD file and the layer and other information it contains intact.

The following sections show you how to save a file a GIF, JPEG, and WBMP image in Photoshop.

SAVING A GIF IMAGE

When you save an image file as a GIF, you have the option of preserving the transparent areas of the image. This is vital if you want the Web background to show through transparent areas. The following steps show you how to use the Save for Web window in Photoshop to save an image file as a GIF image:

 Saving for the Web flattens the image, removing layer information, because the GIF and JPEG formats do not support layers.

1. Finalize the image that you want to save as a GIF for the Web. Notice that the text area within the leaf in this image is transparent.

2. Open the File menu and choose Save for Web. The Save for Web dialog box opens with its Optimized tab selected by default. Work on this tab to create your image. Note that many of the options in the Save for Web dialog box are not labeled. To see an option's name, move the mouse pointer over the option until a pop-up tip appears.

3. If needed, change the zoom in the image preview using the pop-up menu in the lower-left corner of the dialog box.

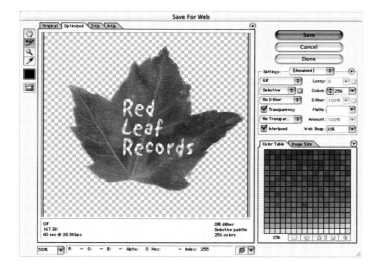

4. Make sure that GIF is selected as the top-left setting (Optimize File Format) in the Settings area of the dialog box. This ensures that the image will be saved as a GIF.

5. Check that the Transparency check box is checked if the image has transparent areas.

6. Adjust other settings as needed until the preview at the left looks as you want it to. For example, you can change the Color Reduction Algorithm, which is the choice directly below the GIF choice for Optimize File Format. This choice controls how Photoshop will combine colors in the image. (By default, you're probably reducing an image with millions of colors to one with only 256—or less.) You also can change the dithering method (the method used to blend pixels) for the image itself and the transparency; these are the settings directly above and below the Transparency check box.

7. Also check the Interlaced check box. This enables the image to download in stages, rather than all at once, reducing the amount of time the viewer may spend looking at a blank spot on your Web page.

8. Set other settings as needed, and review the file format, file size, and download time in the bottom-left corner.

9. If this is the image you want to share on your Web site, click on Save. The Save Optimized As dialog box appears.

10. Enter a name for the file in the Save As (File Name in Windows) text box. Remember that spaces are not allowed for graphics to be loaded on a Web page. If needed, also specify an alternate folder to hold the saved file.

11. Click Save. Photoshop creates the GIF image in the location you specified with the settings you specified.

Example GIF with Transparency

Red
Leaf
Records

12. Before you actually publish the GIF image to the Web, be sure you preview the Web page, including the image in your Web browser, to ensure the save worked correctly. In this case, it did. You can see the light yellow background through the transparent areas of the image, and even though the number of colors has been reduced in the image, it still "pops."

The Settings pop-up menu at the top of the Settings section in the Save For Web dialog box offers a number of presets for choosing the image format and colors. For example, if you choose GIF 128 Dithered from this menu, Photoshop will reduce the number of colors in the final GIF file to 128 rather than 256. You can use one of these presets to speed your work if you're converting numerous images. You also can save your custom settings by clicking on the menu (right arrow) button in the Settings area and choosing the Save Settings command.

Some semi-transparent layer styles and effects don't always save very well for the Web. For starters, decrease the resolution of the image to 144 or less before saving it as a GIF. You'll also need to experiment a bit with the elements in the original image, as well as the dithering choices in the Save for Web dialog box, to develop the best combination. For example, you may have better luck if you choose the PNG-24 choice from the Settings pop-up menu at the top of the Settings section in the Save for Web dialog box.

A halo effect can appear around an image containing transparent areas when it is placed against a background. If you create anti-aliased text or a gradient that contains a color that's marked as transparent in the image's color table, the colors in the image may appear incorrectly when the image is placed over the background color or background image of a Web page. You can map certain colors of the image to make those colors transparent, thus elimi-nating the halo. To do this, choose File, Save for Web, and choose the image optimization settings you prefer. Click the Eyedropper tool at the left side of the dialog box, click in the image preview to select the color you want to map as transparent, and then click the Maps Selected Colors to Transparent button (it has a checkerboard on it) at the bottom of the Color Table tab at the right side of the Save For Web dialog box. This maps the specified color to transparent, and should remove the halo.

You also can select a matte color (using the Matte setting in the Save for Web dialog box) to help the GIF blend with the Web page background. Just be sure to use the same color for the matte and page background.

SAVING A JPEG IMAGE

For larger or more detailed image files that you want to include on a Web page, consider saving to the JPEG format. You will be able to choose a specific JPEG compression level for the image. High-quality JPEG images lose little pixel information, yet are compressed versions of the original. If you select a lower level of compression, the JPEG encoding and compression algorithms remove certain pixels in order to make the file smaller. The following steps show you how to preview and save a JPEG image file for the Web:

1. Finalize the image that you want to save as a JPEG for the Web. In this example, the main layer in the image includes the Outer Glow layer style.
2. Open the File menu and choose Save for Web. The Save for Web dialog box opens, with its Optimized tab selected by default. Work on this tab to create your image.
3. If needed, change the zoom in the image preview using the pop-up menu in the lower-left corner of the dialog box.

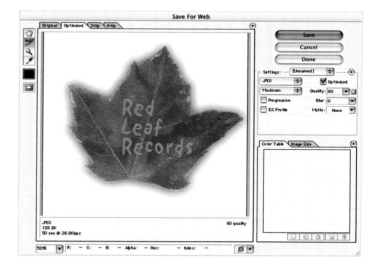

4. Select JPEG from the top left pop-up menu (Optimize File Format) in the Settings area of the dialog box. This ensures that the image will be saved as a JPEG and displays the settings for JPEGs in the dialog box.
5. Change the Compression Quality choice (which is directly below the Optimize File Format option) to specify how much of the image data to discard in order to compress the image.

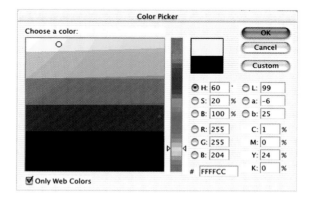

6. Adjust other settings as needed until the preview at the left looks as you want it to. For example, because JPEG images don't include transparency, you may want to add a matte color to help your image blend

into the Web page background, especially if the image doesn't use a rectangular shape like a traditional picture. To choose a matte, click on the Matte option in the Save for Web dialog box. The Color Picker dialog box opens. Click to check the Only Web colors check box in the lower left corner of the dialog box. Use the resulting color choices in the dialog box to specify a color that approximates the background color you'll use on your Web page and then click OK.

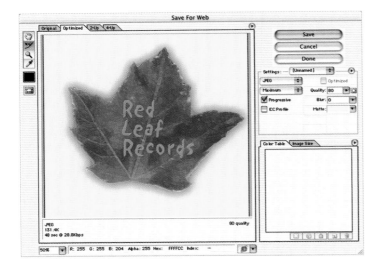

7. Also check the Progressive check box. Again, this enables the image to download in stages, rather than all at once, reducing the amount of time the viewer may spend looking at a blank spot on your Web page.
8. Set other settings as needed, and review the file format, file size, and download time in the bottom left corner.
9. If this is the image you want to share on your Web site, click on Save. The Save Optimized As dialog box appears.
10. Enter a name for the file in the Save As (File Name in Windows) text box. Remember that spaces are not allowed for graphics to be loaded on a Web page. If needed, also specify an alternate folder to hold the saved file.

11. Click Save. Photoshop creates the JPEG image in the location you specified with the settings you specified.

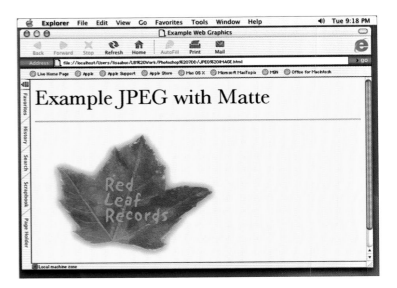

12. Before you actually publish the JPEG image to the Web, be sure you preview the Web page, including the image in your Web browser, to ensure the save worked correctly. In this case, it did. The Outer Glow layer style applied to the image content looks great, and the matte blends seamlessly with the background color.

 Although JPEG files can ultimately be smaller than GIF or PNG file formats, GIF128 files can store transparency layers as well as 128 colors and often produce a better Web image. Use the Magnify tool to take a closer look when comparing GIF to JPEG files for the Web.

 The process for saving a PNG file greatly resembles saving a GIF or JPEG, so I won't cover it again here, as that's a little-used format.

SAVING A WBMP IMAGE

The WBMP format optimizes images for small devices like handheld PCs and Web-enabled phones. While not many of these devices are Web-enabled today, this is a growing market, so you should be aware that Photoshop can save images for these platforms. Follow these steps to prepare a WBMP image:

1. Finalize the image that you want to save as a WBMP.
2. Open the File menu and choose Save for Web. The Save for Web dialog box opens with its Optimized tab selected by default. Work on this tab to create your image.
3. If needed, change the zoom in the image preview using the pop-up menu in the lower-left corner of the dialog box.
4. Select WBMP from the top-left pop-up menu (Optimize File Format) in the Settings area of the dialog box. This displays the settings for WBMPs in the dialog box.

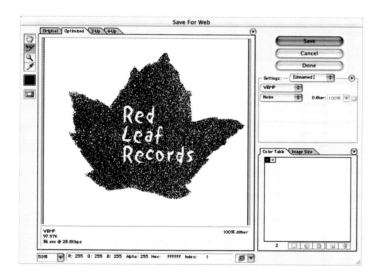

5. If you want an image with a bit more detail, change the Specify the Dither Algorithm choice (which is directly below the Optimize File Format option) to a choice other than No Dither. If the image appears as you want it to, click Save. The Save Optimized As dialog box appears.

6. Enter a name for the file in the Save As (File Name in Windows) text box. If needed, also specify an alternate folder to hold the saved file.
7. Click Save. Photoshop creates the WBMP image in the location you specified with the settings you specified.

SAVING A SLICED IMAGE FOR THE WEB

If you added slices to an image to create clickable "hot spots" leading to linked pages, as described in the last chapter, you may see slightly different options when you save the image for the Web. This is necessary because Photoshop must generate an HTML file as well as image files to save the slice settings. The following steps show you how to save an image with slices for the Web in Photoshop:

 Your final sliced image will look best in the Web browser at a lower resolution and 640x480 or 600x800.

1. Open the sliced image in Photoshop.

2. Choose File, Save for Web. The Save for Web dialog box opens.
3. Click the Save button immediately. The Save Optimized As dialog box appears. Click the Optimized tab, if needed.

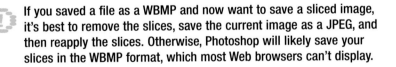

4. Enter a name for the main HTML and JPEG files to be generated for the sliced image in the Save As (File Name in Windows) text box. Be sure that HTML and Images is selected as the Format choice. This is necessary to ensure that Photoshop generates the needed image for each slice, so that your Web browser can reassemble the full image. If needed, also specify an alternate folder to hold the saved files.
5. Click Save. Photoshop creates the HTML file, as well as an "images" subfolder to hold the individual image data for each slice in the location you specified.
6. Preview the HTML file for the sliced image before posting it to the Web.

If you saved a file as a WBMP and now want to save a sliced image, it's best to remove the slices, save the current image as a JPEG, and then reapply the slices. Otherwise, Photoshop will likely save your slices in the WBMP format, which most Web browsers can't display.

COMPARING FORMATS WITH IMAGEREADY

You can open a Photoshop file in ImageReady to apply a broader range of optimization tools to your Web images. ImageReady supports the same Web file formats as Photoshop, plus a few more optimization settings. You can convert images or masks to rollover buttons or image maps in ImageReady, and then save the images as optimized for the Web instead of returning to Photoshop to run similar menu commands.

The image window in ImageReady has four document views, which you can access by clicking on its tab at the top of the image window: Original, Preview, 2-Up, and 4-Up. You can preview optimization settings in the Optimize palette on the 2-Up and 4-Up tabs by applying different settings to the preview thumbnails on the tab. The following steps show you how to use the 4-Up tab to preview images in ImageReady:

1. Open an image in ImageReady.
2. Click the 4-Up tab in the image window.

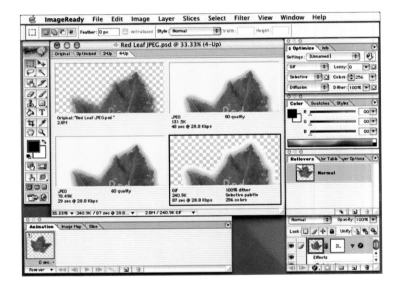

3. The upper-left thumbnail includes the original image settings, so don't change it. Instead, select each of the other three thumbnails and choose preview settings for the thumbnail in the Optimize palette.
4. When one of the thumbnails has the settings you want, click it and then click the Optimize tab in the image window and adjust settings further, if needed.
5. Open the File menu and choose Save Optimized As from the File menu. The Save Optimized As dialog box appears.
6. Adjust the file name and save location as needed; then click OK.

CHAPTER 19

PUTTING IMAGES ONLINE

THE IMMEDIACY OF DIGITAL IMAGING SPURS ITS GROWTH AS A HOBBY. MOMENTS AFTER YOU SNAP YOUR IMAGES, YOU CAN E-MAIL THEM TO FRIENDS OR POST THEM ON YOUR OWN WEB PHOTO GALLERY. IDEALLY, A WEB PHOTO ALBUM SHOULD DISPLAY A THUMBNAIL FOR EACH IMAGE. WHEN YOU CLICK THE THUMBNAIL, IT SHOULD OPEN A LARGER COPY OF THE IMAGE (TYPICALLY 640×480 OR LARGER) ON A SEPARATE WEB PAGE. IT MIGHT SOUND LIKE A LOT OF WORK TO COPY EACH IMAGE TWICE, RESIZE THE COPIES, AND THEN DEVELOP THE APPROPRIATE WEB PAGES. FORTUNATELY, WITH PHOTOSHOP YOU CAN USE THE BUILT-IN WEB PHOTO GALLERY FEATURE TO MOVE YOUR DIGITAL PICTURES TO THE WEB.

CREATING A WEB PHOTO GALLERY

The last item in the File, Automate submenu offers the Web Photo Gallery command. Using this command, you can have Photoshop create a Web Photo Gallery using all the images in a specified folder. You can then upload the resulting HTML files and images to a Web site. Then you and other Internet users can navigate the gallery images with a browser application. You can customize your photo gallery pages as you create them in the Web Photo Gallery dialog box. Or you can edit the HTML files generated by Photoshop using an HTML editing program. Although the Web Photo Gallery feature looks deceptively simple, it provides a wide range of flexibility, enabling you to choose from several styles, options, and image sizes. The following sections show you how to create a vertical frame and simple Web photo gallery.

GENERATING A WEB PHOTO GALLERY USING AUTOMATED TOOLS

You can start the process of creating a Web Photo Gallery with your image files by choosing the File, Automate, Web Photo Gallery command in Photoshop. The Web Photo Gallery dialog box that appears enables you to choose several different layout styles for your photo gallery. The Web Photo Gallery dialog box previews the selected layout.

The initial Web page for each Web Photo Gallery presents a thumbnail of each of your original images. If the user clicks on the thumbnail image from the initial page, another Web page containing some banner text and the full-size image appears.

When you use the Web Photo Gallery tool, you specify the folder that holds the images to prepare for the Web Photo Gallery, as well as specifying other options such as the style. When you continue, Photoshop resizes each image in the source folder and stores the resulting files in subfolders named Thumbnails and Images. Photoshop also generates the initial Web page, index.htm and, if applicable to the style, a ThumbnailFrame.htm file. Finally, Photoshop generates a separate .htm file for each image page and places those files in a new Pages subfolder that it creates. Then Photoshop opens your default browser and loads the frameset or index html file in a browser window so you can preview your Web photo gallery.

The following steps show you how to create a Web photo gallery in Photoshop:

 An alternative to creating your own Web Photo Album pages is to use a Web site, such as **http://www.ofoto.com, http://www.snapfish.com, http://www.shutterfly.com,** or **http://www.myfamily.com.** These Web sites offer a variety of photographic services ranging from converting traditional pictures to digital pictures, printing digital pictures to traditional photographic paper, and hosting your Web photo album.

1. Copy all of the images you want to include in your Web photo gallery to a separate folder on your hard disk. The folder should not contain any files that you do not want to include in the gallery.
2. Open the File menu, select Automate, and choose Web Photo Gallery. The Web Photo Gallery dialog box appears.
3. Open the Styles pop-up menu and choose the style to use for the Web photo gallery. A preview at the right shows what the initial gallery page will look like.
4. Enter a contact e-mail address in the Email text box and specify an alternate Extension for the Web page (HTML) files, if desired.

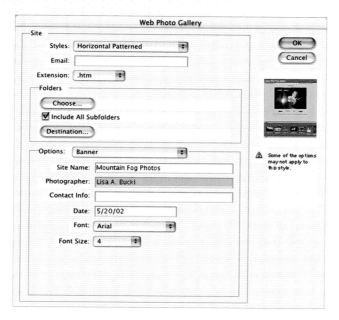

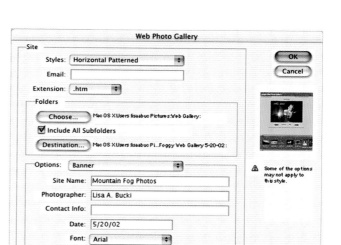

5. With Banner selected from the Options pop-menu, type a name for your gallery in the Site Name text box. Also enter the Photographer and Contact Info, if applicable. Choose a Font and Font size for the information.

6. Click on the Choose button to choose the folder containing image files that will be included in the photo gallery. In the Select Image Directory or Browse for Folder dialog box that appears, navigate to the folder holding your images, click on the folder, and then click the Choose/OK button to designate the specified folder as the source folder.

7. Back in the Web Photo Gallery or Browse for Folder dialog box, click on the Destination button to choose the folder to which the Web photo gallery files and subfolders for its images will be saved. (Use the New Folder or Create New Folder button to create a new folder in the Select a Destination or Browse for Folder dialog box.) Click on the folder to store the files generated by Photoshop. Then click Choose/OK to save your choice and return to the Web Photo Gallery dialog box.

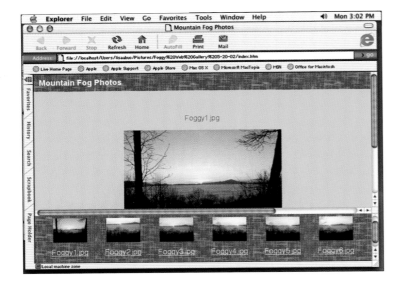

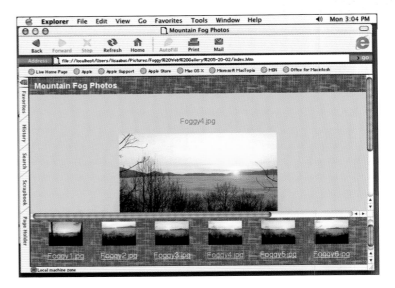

8. Click on OK. Photoshop may take a few minutes to process the images for the photo gallery and develop the HTML. When Photoshop finishes, your Web browser launches and displays the photo gallery.

9. To view one of the full-size images in the photo gallery, click on its thumbnail on the initial page.

10. Open the File or (Browser Name) menu in your Web browser; then choose the Quit or Exit command to finish viewing the photo gallery.

The destination folder for the Web photo gallery cannot be a subfolder of the source folder.

Make a backup of your source images before creating the Web photo gallery rather than moving them into a separate folder.

CUSTOMIZING SETTINGS

The Web Photo Gallery window contains many customizable settings. If you prefer to use a larger thumbnail image on the initial page, or if you want to use a larger size for each full-sized image, you can change a few settings in the Web Photo Gallery dialog box when you're creating the photo gallery. The following steps show you how to choose custom thumbnail and image sizes in the Web Photo Gallery window:

1. Open the File menu, select Automate, and choose Web Photo Gallery.
2. As in the prior set of steps, choose a gallery Style, enter Email and Extension information, specify Banner information, and choose the source and destination folders.
3. Choose Thumbnails from the Options pop-up menu. The options displayed in that section of the dialog box change.

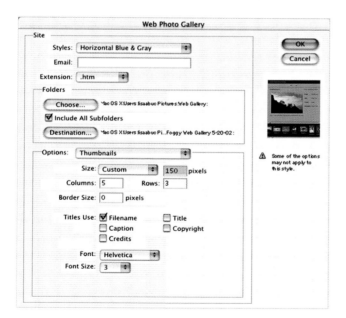

4. Click on the Size pop-up menu. Click an alternate thumbnail size from the menu or choose Custom. If you do the latter, type a number in the accompanying text box to create a custom thumbnail size for your photo gallery.
5. Open the Options pop-up menu again and choose Large Images. The sizing and quality options for the large images appear in that section of the dialog box.

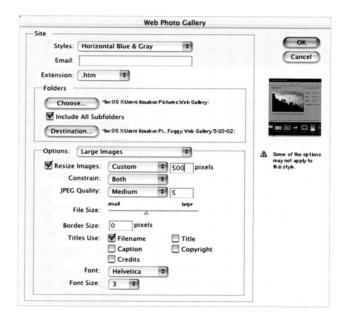

6. Open the Resize Images pop-up menu and choose an alternate image size, or choose Custom. If you do the latter, type a number in the accompanying text box to set the width of each large gallery image. Adjust the JPEG Quality and File Size settings as well, if desired.

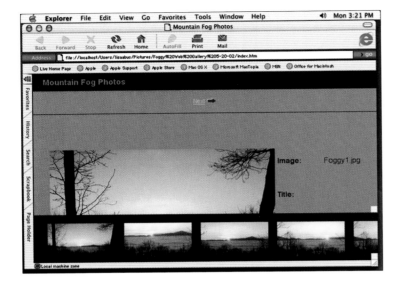

7. Click on OK. After Photoshop finishes creating your photo gallery with the adjusted sizes, you can view the results in a browser window and close the browser when you finish

PUTTING PHOTOS ON THE WEB

Although the biggest hurdle to creating a Web photo gallery can be generating HTML code that works, there are several additional steps you need to follow before you can access a Web site. You need to have login and password information to an Internet service provider's (ISP) Web servers, and you need to know which folder you can post your images to. Typically, your ISP gives you a subfolder that's a variation of your login name that you can use to house your Web pages. For example, if your login name is **figaro** and you have a **mindspring.com** account, your personal Web page might be **http://figaro.home.mind-spring.com**. To post your files there, you must use an FTP file transfer utility (as discussed later in this chapter) and connect to your ftp folder on the server; in this example,

the user would connect to **ftp.mindspring.com** and log in using his user name and password. Copying the index.htm file generated by Web Photo Gallery to the folder that appears would make that page the initial page for **http://figaro.home.mindspring.com**.

But copying the index.htm file is not enough. You must copy all the files, subfolders, and files in the subfolders generated by the Web Photo Gallery feature and place them in the destination folder you have specified.

If you are working on a company network, you might need to give your photo gallery files to a network administrator before they can be posted to the Internet. If you're not sure how to post Web pages to your Web server, contact your ISP, or refer to a book that's dedicated to configuring or working with a Web server (like Apache).

Before you upload your files and folders, you may want to make changes to your Web photo gallery. You can customize your HTML code using an HTML editor (a simple text editor, or more advanced Web page editing application) and view the results in a browser window. The following sections deconstruct editing and posting a Web photo gallery.

 When you're manually adjusting images for a Web page, try the Resize wizard. To start this wizard in Photoshop, choose Help, Resize Image. The wizard screens walk you through the process for resizing the current image for print or online viewing.

EMBEDDING IMAGES WITH HTML CODE

HTML code is made up of a series of tags. Each tag has a bracket on each side. For example the bold face text tag <B> is placed to the left of the text you want to format, and its closing tag </B> is placed to the right of the text. Every computer user can potentially edit HTML code. For simple Web pages, all you need is a text editor like TextEdit in Mac OS X or Notepad in Windows. For more complicated .htm files, you can use a dedicated HTML editor to make the changes. (You can find a number of affordable shareware HTML editors online.) Open your .htm file in the applicable program, make the necessary changes, and save and close the file. In order for a Web server to recognize a Web page, the Web page file name must end in .htm or .html. Just be sure to preserve the file name extension when you save.

You can add an image to a Web page by using the IMG src HTML tag.

When you embed an image, you use the IMG src HTML tag and then add the file name of the picture to the Web page. For example, you might use the following line of code to add the image file SCBeachUmbrella to a Web page:

```
<IMG src="thumbnails/SCBeachUmbrella.jpg" border="0"
alt=SCBeachUmbrella align="BOTTOM">
```

Let's dissect some of the above code. For starters, notice that the line of code uses angle brackets at the beginning and end. These brackets help your Web browser identify each tag and its attributes. *IMG src=* is the tag itself. The first attribute in quotation marks, *"thumbnails/SCBeachUmbrella.jpg"*, identifies the file to insert as well as the path to the folder holding it. The next bit, *border="0"*, indicates that the Web browser should not put a border around the image on the page. Even though you may be tempted to skip it, you should always include the *alt=* attribute and a description within quotation marks; that description will load to identify the content for users who are not viewing images in their browsers. Finally, the *align="BOTTOM"* attribute sets the alignment for the inserted image.

However, you don't need to create a Web page to learn more about how HTML code works. One way to find out how an image has been added to a Web page is to load a Web page containing an image. Then view its source code in the browser application. If the page is using HTML to display an image, you can view the HTML code to see which tags are used to make a picture appear on the Web

page. The following steps show you how to identify an embedded image in the Web photo gallery's HTML code, so that you can see how to add your own images manually to a Web page:

1. Visit a Web page that contains an image file. In this example, I chose a photo gallery posted on my Web site.
2. Choose View, Source if you're using Internet Explorer or View, Page Source if you're using Netscape. If the code for the image you want to view is within a frame on the Web page, Control+click (Mac) or right-click (Windows) the frame on the page and choose View Frame Source from the shortcut menu that appears.

3. A window opens containing the HTML code for the current Web page. Look for the image file name in the source code. For example, look for the image file name from the source folder you chose for the Web photo gallery. You can also look for the IMG src tag in the HTML code to see if you can find the image's file name used with this HTML tag. You may have to scroll to the right, as shown in this example.
4. Click the window close button when you've finished viewing the code.

IDENTIFYING TABLES AND FRAMES

Many Web pages use tables and frames to arrange related information on the Web page. Tables organize text and images in rows and columns, which are defined by unique HTML table tags. Frames divide a Web page into subpages. For example, you can load another Web page into a frame, even if it's on a totally different Web site than yours. Embedding an image into a table or frame is similar to embedding an image into any Web page. The following steps show you how to identify the HTML tags for tables and frames in your Web photo gallery HTML files. Then you can insert additional images into a table or frame, if desired.

1. Drag and drop the ThumbnailFrame.htm file generated by the Web Photo Gallery feature from a folder on your hard disk to the browser window. Wait for the page to load in the browser window.
2. Then open the browser View menu and choose Source.

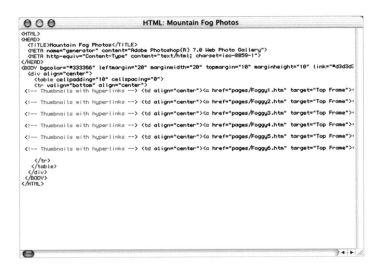

3. Look for the <table> tag to identify where the table begins in the HTML page. In this example, it's the ninth line from the top. The <tr> and </tr> tags identify the beginning and end of the actual table content. Each <td> and </td> pair identifies the contents of a single cell in the table.

4. Close the window with the source code.
5. Now drag the index.htm file generated by the Web Photo Gallery feature to the browser window. Its page loads in the browser.
6. Choose View, Source in the browser.

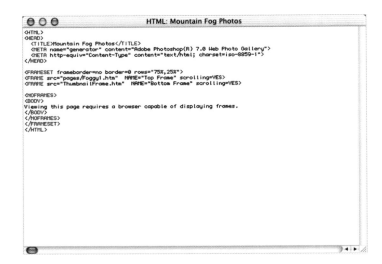

7. The FRAMESET tag defines the frame elements in the browser window. In this example, the frameset has a border size of 0 and two columns, the top one fills 75% percent of the page and the bottom one fills 25% of the page.
8. The FRAME tag is used to define each frame in the frameset. In this example, there are two frames, "Top Frame" and " Bottom Frame." The Top Frame opens the individual pages for the large images, in this case Foggy1.htm. The Bottom Frame opens the ThumbnailFrame.html file, which includes the small thumbnail images and links to the larger images.

CREATING A DROPLET
TO RESIZE IMAGES

If you want to create a more customized photo gallery, you could use a droplet to apply custom sizes to your images. A droplet is a small application that you can create in Photoshop. You can use a droplet to apply an action (which resembles a macro) to a folder full of image files. For example, if you create an action to resize all the images in a folder to 100×100 pixel size, you can save those resizing settings as a droplet. Then you can hand-tweak the HTML files generated by Web photo gallery to refer to the proper images. (Be sure to copy them to the Web server, as well, when the time comes.) The following steps show you how to create a droplet:

1. Open an example image, preferably a copy of one of the images you ultimately want to resize for the Web. You must have a "live" image open in order to record the action on which the droplet will be based.
2. Display the Actions palette. To do so, click on its tab or choose Window, Actions.
3. Click on the Create New Set icon at the bottom of the Actions palette to create a new actions folder. Type a name for the folder in the New Set dialog box that appears and click OK.
4. Click on the Create New Action button at the bottom of the Actions palette to add an action to the set. The New Action dialog box opens.

5. Type a name for the action in the dialog box and click on the Record button.

6. Perform the steps you want to record as the action. For this example, choose Image, Image Size. Adjust the Pixel Dimensions of the image to specify the desired size and then click OK.

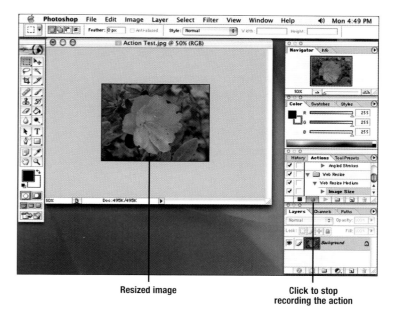

Resized image   Click to stop recording the action

7. Click on the Stop Playing/Recording button at the bottom of the Actions palette to stop recording the action.
8. Click on the new action in the Actions palette to select the action, if needed.
9. Choose File, Automate, Create Droplet. The Create Droplet dialog box opens.

10. Click the Choose button, specify a file name and location for the saved droplet in the Save dialog box that appears, and then click Save to return to the Create Droplet dialog box.

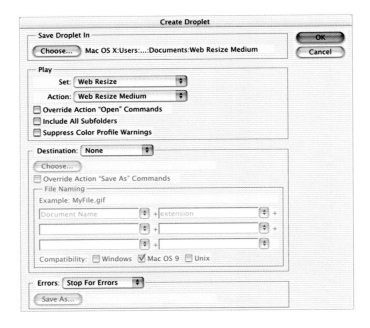

11. To create the droplet in the specified location, the desktop, click OK in the Create Droplet dialog box.

12. For easiest access, drag the droplet file from the folder where you created it onto the desktop.

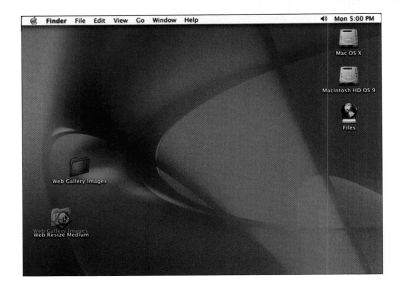

13. To test the droplet, create a new folder and place a few image files into it. Drop the folder on the droplet, open Photoshop, and repeat the action on all files in the folder. For example, here I've copied a folder of images for a Web gallery, and I'm dragging the folder over the droplet.

CUSTOMIZING YOUR WEB PHOTO GALLERY

What if you really like the automated Web Photo Gallery tool included with Photoshop, but it doesn't always have the capability to create the Web page you envisioned. Don't worry. With a little time and HTML code, you can customize the Web Photo Gallery with little changes that can make a big difference. The following sections show you how to adjust the frame size and add banner text to the vertical frame style photo gallery.

CHANGING FRAME SIZES

If you chose a horizontal or Vertical Frame style from the Styles pop-up menu in the Web Photo Gallery dialog box, Photoshop will create your Web photo gallery with two frames: left and right or top and bottom. You can adjust the frame sizes by editing the percentages for the FRAMESET tag in the index.html file generated by the Web Photo Gallery, as follows:

1. Open the index.htm file in an appropriate editor application. (Note that when the page contains frames, simple applications like TextEdit in Mac OS X or Notepad in Windows may not let you open the file; in such an instance, try a shareware HTML editor, such as WebDesign by Rage Software **www.ragesw.com**. You can find downloads at **www.apple.com/downloads/macosx/** or at **www.downloads.com**.

2. Choose File, Open.

3. Open the index. htm file from the folder where you specified that the Web Photo Gallery feature should save it.

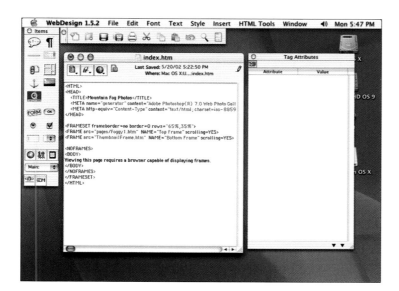

4. In the line with the FRAMESET tag, edit the default values, such as 75%,25% to the alternate values you prefer, such as 65%,35%.

5. Choose File, Save As and resave the file in Web Page (htm) format in its original location.

6. Close the file and the application you're using for editing.

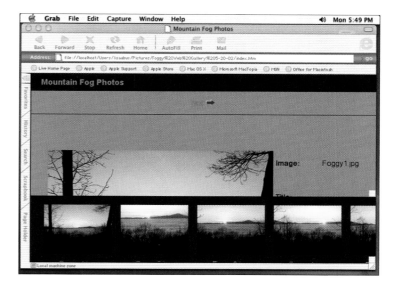

7. Drag the index.htm file to a browser window. The revised photo gallery Web page should load. You should see a wider left frame in the browser window.

 To learn more about creating Web pages, check out books like *Create Your First Mac Web Page In a Weekend*, *Create Your First Web Page In a Weekend 3rd Edition*, *Learn HTML In a Weekend*, *Microsoft FrontPage 2002 Fast & Easy*, all from Premier Press.

CUSTOMIZING PAGE BANNER TEXT

As you saw earlier, the Web Photo Gallery feature in Photoshop enables you to customize some banner settings. You can type a name, photographer, and date in the Web Photo Gallery window. Photoshop converts this text into HTML code and adds it to each page in the photo gallery. If you have a Web editor, you can add more detailed information to the banner section of each image's Web page, such as the copyright date for an image. Here's how:

1. Open your HTML editor application.

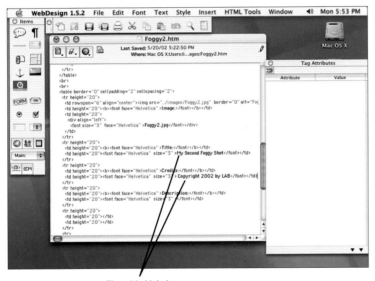

The added labels

2. Open one of the image page .htm files from the Pages subfolder. The file will have the same name as the image with htm as the file extension.

3. Add or modify the HTML code. For example, I added a title and copyright information.
4. Choose File, Save As and resave the file in Web Page (htm) format, in its original location.
6. Close the file and the application you're using for editing.

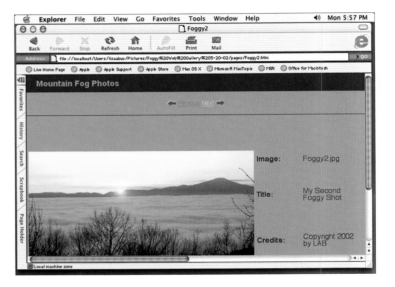

7. Drag the edited .htm file to a browser window. The revised photo gallery Web page should load and display the new information.

 You must follow the syntax of the HTML code. Adding extra spaces or commas could prevent your Web page from loading properly.

OTHER CUSTOMIZATIONS

Although Photoshop can create slices and perform some Web-related tasks, the bulk of the Web features, such as rollovers, and exporting HTML code are only available in ImageReady, as described in the last chapter. If you have enough memory to run both Photoshop and ImageReady on your computer, you can easily switch between the two applications by clicking on the Jump To button in the Toolbox. If you only want to access a particular action in ImageReady, you can record an action and save it as a droplet.

REVIEWING PHOTOS WITH A WEB BROWSER OR IMAGEREADY

Take the time to view all your Web pages in a real browser window before posting them to a Web site. Make sure that each image looks presentable and recognizable after being resized. If the pictures and Web pages look good enough to you, they're ready to share with the world. You can view an image in Internet Explorer, Netscape Navigator, or the browser application of your choice.

In addition, you can use a menu command in ImageReady to preview in-progress images using the latest version of Internet Explorer or Netscape Navigator. (Unfortunately, you can only preview images in browsers directly from ImageReady; Photoshop does not offer this feature.) Examining each image before you generate the final HTML files with the Web Photo Gallery feature in Photoshop can help you identify problem images or decide how you may need to optimize images for the Web.

 Click on the Jump to ImageReady button in the toolbox in Photoshop to switch to ImageReady. You can also press Command/Ctrl+Shift+M to switch between the two applications.

 Preview images with two or three browser applications. I recommend previewing with Internet Explorer, Netscape Navigator, and America Online's browser. Even though an image may look fine with one browser, it may look different with another.

The following steps show you how to use the File, Preview In command in ImageReady:

1. Start or switch to ImageReady and open the image you want to preview from the Images subfolder created by the Web Photo Gallery tool in Photoshop.

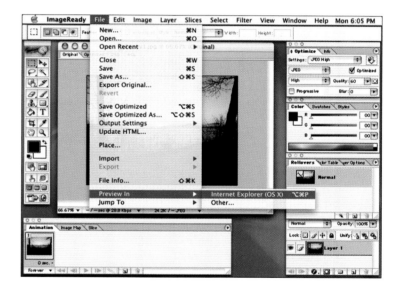

2. Open the File menu, choose Preview In, and select a browser from the submenu.

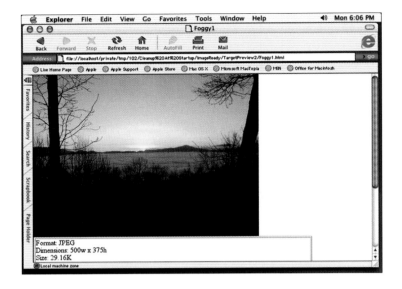

3. ImageReady switches to the browser application window and displays the selected image.

WORKING WITH FTP AND WEB SERVERS

When your photo gallery is complete and you've made all the required modifications, you can post it to your Web server. Most Web servers require that you use an FTP application to transfer files and folders to the appropriate folder. There are many File Transfer Protocol (FTP) utilities available for download on the Web. Whether you have a Mac or PC, one place to find reliable, virus-checked downloadable FTP applications is **http://www.download.com**. A popular shareware FTP utility for Mac OS X, called Fetch, is available at **www.apple.com/downloads/macosx/internet_utilities/fetch.html**. On the Windows side of things, you can try CuteFTP, available at **http://www.cuteftp.com/products/cuteftp/index.shtml**. The following steps show you how to use Fetch on a Mac to upload the files and subfolders generated by the Web Photo Gallery feature to your Web server.

1. Install Fetch on your Macintosh, or any FTP application to your PC.

2. Start the FTP application and log in to your folders on your ISP's Web server. Typically, to log in you must enter the following information:

Host: Typically includes the domain for your ISP, as in **ftp.mindspring.com**

User ID: This is your user name or e-mail address, as in **figaro@mindspring.com**

Password: This is your Internet account password.

3. After your system connects to the Internet, if needed, the FTP utility connects and logs into your home Web folder. This is the folder where you can copy all the files and folders generated by the Web Photo Gallery feature.

4. Open the folder that holds your photo gallery content on the desktop.

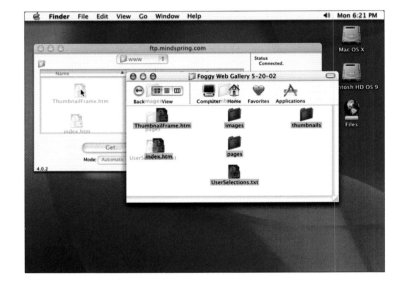

5. Select all the contents of the folder and drag them over the file list in the Fetch window.

Some Web servers require that you use a different name for your initial Web page, such as Home.htm. Consult your ISP as to the proper file name; then rename the index.htm file to use that name before you upload your files.

On a Macintosh, you can create an AppleScript script to automate posting a folder or file to a Web server. Pick an FTP application that supports AppleScript. Write the script and then test it with a sample folder on your hard drive.

6. Fetch begins "putting" the files and folders into the destination folder on the Web server. When it finishes, you can view the files in the Fetch window, as shown here.

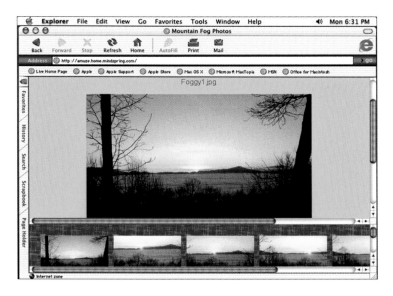

7. Start your Web browser, enter the URL to your home Web page (such as **figaro.home.mindspring.com**) in the Address text box, and see your Web photo gallery loads successfully in a browser window.

FORMATS

FILE FORMATS

FILE FORMATS SUPPORTED BY PHOTOSHOP

WHEN YOU OPEN THE FILE MENU AND CHOOSE SAVE AS IN PHOTOSHOP, YOU CAN SAVE YOUR IMAGE FILE IN ONE OF 18 DIFFERENT FILE FORMATS. OPEN THE FORMAT POP-UP MENU IN THE SAVE AS DIALOG BOX TO SELECT THE DESIRED FILE FORMAT. YOU CAN INSTALL PLUG-INS TO ADD SUPPORT FOR ADDITIONAL FILE FORMATS, TOO. DEPENDING ON THE FILE FORMAT YOU CHOOSE, A DIALOG BOX MAY APPEAR TO PROMPT YOU TO ENTER ADDITIONAL SETTINGS FOR THE SAVE; FOR EXAMPLE, WHEN YOU SAVE A JPEG IMAGE, YOU'RE PROMPTED TO SPECIFY SUCH SETTINGS AS THE IMAGE QUALITY.

AS MENTIONED BEFORE, USE THE PHOTOSHOP FILE FORMAT IF YOU WANT TO PRESERVE ANY LAYERS, MASKS, OR CHANNELS IN AN IMAGE FILE. YOU CAN SAVE, OPEN, AND EDIT A NATIVE PHOTOSHOP FILE IN PHOTOSHOP OR IMAGEREADY. THE FOLLOWING IS A LIST OF THE FILE FORMATS PHOTOSHOP CAN USE TO SAVE A FILE. EACH ITEM ON THE LIST CONTAINS A BRIEF DESCRIPTION OF THE FILE FORMAT.

* **BMP**—This is the standard Windows image format. Create a BMP file by saving an image using Internet Explorer 5.0 on a PC. Edit or view BMP files in RGB, indexed-color, grayscale, or bitmap color modes.

* **CompuServe GIF**—GIF is an acronym for Graphics Interchange Format. GIF (or CompuServe GIF format, as it was once more commonly known) is the most commonly used file format for Web graphics. The GIF file format employs LZW compression to minimize file size, which in turn enables a Web graphic to download faster to a browser window. Transparency in indexed-color images is preserved; however, alpha channels are not supported.

* **EPS**—EPS is an acronym for Encapsulated PostScript, a language file format created by Adobe. Photoshop converts EPS vector graphics into pixels when the file is opened. EPS files can also be saved as PDF (Portable Document Format) files. Use the Import command to open a PDF file in Photoshop. View or edit EPS or DCS files in CMYK, RGB, indexed-color, duotone, grayscale, and bitmap color modes. The EPS file format does not support alpha channels or clipping paths. However, DCS 2.0 formats support spot channels and single alpha channels. EPS TIFF and EPS PICT Preview formats can be opened but are not supported by Photoshop. EPS PICT Preview is available only on Mac computers.

* **JPEG**—JPEG is an acronym for the Joint Photographic Experts Group format, which is another commonly used Web graphics file format. View and edit files in RGB, CMYK, and grayscale color modes. The JPEG file format does not support alpha channels but retains all color information. Depending on the JPEG compression level chosen for the file, some image data might be selectively discarded to create the final compressed file.

* **PCX**—This is another common file format for Windows PC graphic images. View and edit files in RGB, indexed-color, grayscale, or bitmap color modes. The PCX file format does not support alpha channels.

* **PDF**—The Portable Document Format is commonly used to share files across applications and computer platforms. It is based on the PostScript imaging model (see the EPS file format for more information about PostScript files). View and edit PDF files in RGB, indexed-color, CMYK, grayscale, bitmap, or Lab color modes. Alpha channels are not supported. PDF files can only be saved in the Photoshop PDF file format; however, you can open Adobe Acrobat and generic PDF files with Photoshop.

* **PICT**—Most Macintosh graphics applications can view PICT files. View and edit PICT files in RGB, indexed-color, grayscale, single alpha channel, and bitmap file formats that do not contain alpha channels. A PICT file can be saved in 16- or 32-bit pixel resolution.

* **PICT Resources**—A PICT resource is a PICT file stored in the resource fork of a Mac OS file. The PICT resource format supports the same formats as a PICT file; however, you must import a PICT resource in Photoshop in order to open this particular file format.

* **Pixar**—This file format is specifically designed for exchanging files with Pixar computers that work with high-end graphics applications. View and edit these files in RGB mode or in grayscale mode with a single alpha channel.

* **PNG**—Portable Network Graphics is a patent-free Web graphics file format designed for displaying high-quality images on Web pages. View and edit files in grayscale or RGB mode with a single alpha channel or files in indexed-color mode that do not contain alpha channels. Transparency can be preserved in the single alpha channel of a file, and the PNG file format supports up to 24-bit images.

* **Raw**—Raw files consist of a stream of bytes that describe the color information in a file. A single pixel is described in a binary format, where 0 equals black and 255 equals white. This format can be used to transfer files between applications and computer platforms. View and edit files in CMYK, RGB, and grayscale files with alpha channels as well as multichannel, Lab, indexed-color, and duotone files without alpha channels.

* **Scitex CT, or Scitex Continuous Tone format**—This is used by Scitex computers for processing high-end images. Although alpha channels are not supported, you can view and edit CMYK, RGB, or grayscale files.

* **Targa, or TGA**—These files are used with the Truevision video board on MS-DOS applications. View and edit 32-bit RGB files with single alpha channels, indexed color, grayscale, or 16-bit and 24-bit RGB files that do not contain alpha channels.

* **TIFF**—The Tagged-Image File Format can be used in digital cameras to store large, raw image files. It is also a common file format that can support LZW compression and can be used to exchange files between applications or computer platforms. Most desktop scanners can create TIFF images that in turn can be read by most paint, image-editing, or page-layout applications. View and edit files in CMYK or RGB modes or in grayscale mode with alpha channels.

* **Amiga IFF**—Image files created by Amiga computer systems or with the Video Toaster can be saved as Amiga Interchange File Format files. This format does not support alpha channels, but it is compatible with many Windows PC applications such as Deluxe Paint by Electronic Arts. View and edit this format in RGB, indexed-color, grayscale, and bitmap color modes.

* **Photoshop DCS 1.0 and 2.0**—*See EPS.*

GLOSSARY

A

Adaptive Palette A custom palette derived from actual colors in an image.

Align Orientation of one or more objects. Open the Paragraph palette to align selected type to the left, right, or center of the image window.

Alpha Channel Mask Also known as a channel mask or mask. It uses 8 bits of grayscale information to define the masked area of an image.

Angle Bracket A character used with HTML to identify a tag: < and >.

Animation Two or more images or text objects that play back and forth to create the illusion of motion. Animate digital pictures in ImageReady.

Anti-alias The process of smoothing the edges of an object or text so that it blends with the background color.

AppleScript The name of Apple's built-in scripting technology for automating simple tasks such as copying or moving a file to the Trash.

Application Also known as an executable or a program. An application such as Photoshop or ImageReady embodies all the code and features that enable you to create image files on a computer.

Archive Also known as a backup. A folder, compressed file, disk, or CD-ROM containing a set of files and folders for a particular project, day, and so on.

ATM An acronym for Adobe Type Manager, it is Adobe's software for enabling operating systems and applications to work with Adobe's font technologies.

Automate The technique of making an iterative or redundant task automatic. Choose an Automate command from the File menu, or create one or a combination of actions from the Actions palette.

B

Background The original layer of a scanned image file or one from a digital camera. You cannot perform certain actions on the Background layer; in such cases, copy the Background layer and then hide it to make the desired changes.

Background Color The color of the background of the image window in the Photoshop workspace. It can also be the background color of a Web page.

Bit Depth Also known as the number of colors assigned to each pixel and visible on a computer screen. Most images created by digital cameras contain millions of colors per pixel. Images created for the Web usually contain anywhere from 256 to thousands of colors per pixel.

Bitmap Graphics A matrix of pixels that form an image. Digital pictures are created as bitmap graphics. Photoshop generates bitmap graphics. *See also vector graphics.*

BMP A standard bitmapped file format supported by Windows PCs.

Brightness The luminance of a color across pixels in an image.

Browser An application that can read Hypertext Markup Language (HTML) documents.

Button A user-interface element that can be used on a Web page to perform a specific action, such as a rollover to another Web page, or bring up a dialog box. If clicked, a button indicates a transition to a unique set of information on the same or a different Web page.

C

Canvas Actual workspace area of an image file. Non-canvas areas of an image window are marked with a gray color.

CCD An abbreviation for Charge Coupled Device. CCDs are used with most popular digital cameras. CCDs translate light into digital data, which is in turn stored as a file on the camera's storage media. CCDs are also used in scanner peripherals and video cameras.

CD-ROM An abbreviation for Compact Disc Read-Only Media. Can store up to 600MB of data. Most software is distributed on CD-ROM, as well as most music albums. DVD-ROM can store up to 14GB of data. They can also read CD-ROM discs.

CD-RW An abbreviation for Compact Disc Read/Write. If you take a lot of digital pictures, you can use a CD-RW drive to archive the images. CD-RW drives also let you write more than once to the disc. CD-R drives allow you to write only once to a recordable CD-R disc.

There are also DVD-RW and DVD RAM drives, which enable you to archive up to 10GB of data per disc.

Channel 8 bits of grayscale information, which can be used to define red, green, and blue channels of an image file in RGB mode, or a channel mask.

Channel Mixer A menu command in Photoshop. Mix a percentage of a channel with part of another channel of an image in RGB mode. This command is available in the Image, Adjust menus and the Layer, New Adjustment Layer menus.

Check Box A user-interface element that can be used on a Web page to indicate that a particular feature is on or off.

Clone Stamp Tool A tool located in the toolbox that enables you to copy part of a bitmap image and apply it elsewhere in the image window.

CMYK An acronym used to express Cyan, Magenta, Yellow, and Black color values. Each color component has a value between 0 and 255. Some applications and printers do not use the black channel of a CMYK image file.

Color Picker Color palette and color selection system that is available in Photoshop. Choose between Photoshop's color picker dialog box or the operating system's color picker dialog box (for example Apple's color picker in Mac OS).

Color Table A table or group of colors associated with a particular graphic file. The color table is located in the Save for Web dialog box in Photoshop. Add, lock, or snap a color to a Web palette in the Save for Web dialog box.

Commands A menu or dialog box choice that performs a task in Photoshop. The History palette displays a list of each command and procedure you've executed while working with the current image file.

Compositing The process of combining multiple image layers together. The resulting single image is called a composite image.

CompuServe GIF *See GIF*

Contrast The difference between light and dark pixel values in an image or object.

Convert Usually refers to changing the format of an image file from one file format to another.

Crop A tool that enables you to retain the subject of a photo, but remove unselected image areas. In Photoshop, you can crop an image, as well as an object or path.

D

Digital Camera A consumer electronic device, similar to a traditional analog camera, that can capture digital images and store them to a removable card. High-end digital cameras can capture images directly to a computer's hard disk.

Display To make a layer, frame, or graphic object visible in the image window. To display is a direct result of selecting something in the Photoshop or ImageReady toolbox, palettes, or image window.

Display Modes Display modes affect how a document appears on the computer screen. ImageReady can display an image in Original or Optimized modes.

Download To copy a file or archive from another computer on a network or from the Internet. For example, if you want to edit your Web pages, you can log in to your Web site and download a file to your computer using a network connection.

DPI An abbreviation for dots per inch, which defines printer resolution.

E

Edge Border of a selected graphic text object.

Edit To change, adjust, or reorganize text or image objects.

Editor An application or feature in an application that edits text or graphics.

Effect Also referred to as a filter. One or more ways to adjust the way an image appears in the image window. Some effects can be added as layer styles or as an adjustment layer. Each effect in a layer style can be turned on or off in the Layers palette. All effects are accessible from the Filter menu. Each effect installed with Photoshop is stored as a plug-in file in the Plug-Ins folder on your hard drive.

Embed An HTML tag used to add a sound or media file to a Web page. *See also IMG SRC.*

Eraser This tool erases pixels from an image. Photoshop has three different kinds of erasers: eraser, background eraser, and the magic eraser tools.

Export A command used to convert a native image file format to a non-native file format.

Eyedropper A tool that can capture a color from an image and move it to the foreground or background color in the toolbox.

F

File Format A generic term for describing the way a file is saved. GIF, PSD, JPEG, and PNG are all different types of graphic file formats.

Filter Photoshop includes image-editing filters that adjust contrast, brightness, and other types of filters to improve your images.

Font A character set of a specific typeface, type style, and type size. Some fonts are installed with the operating system on your computer.

Foreground The front-most layer of objects or images in an image window.

Foreground Color The upper-left color in the toolbox. If the Pen, Pencil, Paintbrush, or other drawing tool is selected, the foreground color is used with the selected tool.

Frames A feature of HTML that can be used to divide a Web page, enabling you to view and navigate more than one page in a browser window. ImageReady uses frames to create each frame of an animation.

FTP File Transfer Protocol. Available in some browsers. Can be used to upload or download files to the Web or network server that has an FTP server.

G

Gamma Also known as the gamma correction setting. Adjusts an image to avoid midtones from appearing too dark on a computer screen. Switch gamma settings to view your Windows graphics on a Mac or your Macintosh graphics on a Windows platform.

GIF Pronounced "jif," the Graphics Interchange Format is one of the two most common graphic file formats used on the Web. (You may see this file format listed as CompuServe GIF in the Format pop-up menu in the Save As dialog box in Photoshop.) The GIF format is most effective at compressing solid-color images and images with areas of repetitive color. In addition to supporting background transparency (which is great for animation), up to 256 colors can represent a GIF image. Best used with illustrations, text, and line art.

Gradient A progression of colors that gradually blend or fade into each other. Create a gradient within an object or across frames and layers.

Grayscale Represents a percentage of black where 0 is white and 100 is black and intermediate colors are shades of gray.

GUI An acronym for graphical user interface; pronounced "gooey." It represents all the buttons, windows, and menus you see if you're using Mac OS or Windows operating systems and any applications that support their correlating user interfaces.

Guides Visual interface element that indicates where a particular area begins and ends or enables you to position a selected object. In Photoshop, you can use slice guides, grid, or ruler guides to work with design elements.

H

Halo An off-colored ring of pixels that appears around borders of a graphic. Most noticeable around the edges of a mask or around the border of an image.

Hard Disk A hardware component commonly used in computers to store files and folders of data.

Healing Brush A new tool you can use to repair spots in images or blend away unwanted content. With this tool, you sample the area that holds the repair colors to use; then click and drag to apply the repair.

Hexadecimal A term to express red, green, and blue color values. Each component value is represented by a hexadecimal value, such as FF-FF-FF for white.

Highlight Color The color used as a visual interface to identify selected text or graphics.

History A command or action that has been performed on a Photoshop document. View a log of executed commands in the History palette.

HSB Hue, Saturation, and Brightness values. Hues range from 0 to 360 degrees. Saturation and brightness values range from 0 to 100%.

HTML An abbreviation for Hypertext Markup Language, which is the language used for most Web pages.

Hue/Saturation Hue is an adjustable range of colors from 0 to 360, or plus or minus 180. Saturation values encapsulate color intensity within a range of 0 to plus or minus 100.

I

Image A bitmapped matrix of pixels that represent a picture.

Image Map An image map is an image file broken up into slices. You can use the Slice tool to create an image map in Photoshop or ImageReady. Each slice is saved as a separate file on your hard drive.

Image Window The window containing the contents of an open image file in the Photoshop workspace.

IMG SRC HTML tag used to define the location of an image file on the Web server.

Import The command used to convert a non-Photoshop supported document into Photoshop.

Info Palette Displays the location, size, and colors of a particular object or document.

Integrate The process of combining two or more objects, components, or features.

Interpolation The process for calculating color when pixels are added or removed from an image during transformations. Bicubic interpolation creates the best results, but is usually the slowest method of interpolation.

ISP An abbreviation for Internet service provider. To access the Internet, a computer needs to have a connection to an Internet service provider. An ISP provides phone or network access to the Internet.

J

JavaScript A scripting language created by Netscape to add complex Web features to Web pages.

JPEG Created by the Joint Photographic Experts Group, JPEG is a popular graphic file format used on the Web. The JPEG file format preserves broad color ranges and subtleties in brightness and image tones and supports up to millions (24 bits) of colors. JPEG uses a lossy compression format that can remove some of the image data when a file is compressed. Best used with images and photographs. *See also PNG.*

K

Kerning Increases or decreases the spacing between specific pairs of letters. Used to improve the appearance of text.

Kilobyte Abbreviated KB; is equivalent to 1,024 bytes.

L

Lasso A selection tool that enables you to select a freeform set of pixels. Photoshop has three types of lasso tool: Lasso, Polygonal Lasso, and Magnetic Lasso.

Layer A particular plane in a document window that can create simple or complex graphics. Rearrange, add, remove, hide, and lock any layer in Photoshop.

Lossy compression An image file compression format that can be used to compress a JPEG image. Lossless JPEG compression preserves the original image without losing any image data. Lossy compression can lose image data when compressing a file. Photoshop lets you choose between 10 levels of JPEG compression.

M

Marquee Rectangular or ellipse tool that enables you to select an area of pixels in an image.

Mask A mask consists of two grouped objects. The mask itself is a sort of "cut-out" image that sits on top of the image being masked.

Megabyte Abbreviated MB. Equivalent to a million bytes, or more exactly 1,048,576 bytes.

Memory Also known as RAM. Refers to the amount of physical memory (in chips) installed on your computer. Virtual memory is the amount of memory or hard disk space allocated for use by the operating system and applications on a computer. Memory, in regards to an application like Photoshop, represents the amount of space required for an application to run its routines and functions.

Menu A user-interface element originating from the operating system and containing commands for an application.

O

Object Consists of one or more paths and points. Create and edit vector graphic objects with the Pen tool.

Onionskin View the contents of a previous or following frame in addition to the current frame with onionskinning turned on. Previous and following frames are slightly dimmed so that these images are easy to distinguish from the current image. This feature is only available in ImageReady.

Opacity The degree of transparency applied by a blending mode onto an object.

Optimize To reduce the size or image quality of a document in order to decrease the loading time for a Web page.

Optimize Window A tab in the ImageReady image window that enables you to see what an image will look like before you save or export it to your hard drive. Use this window to preview an image and compare it with other Web file formats to find the smallest, best-looking image for your Web page.

Options Bar Contains additional settings for tools in the toolbox. It is located at the top of the Photoshop workspace.

P

Paintbrush A drawing tool selectable from the toolbox in Photoshop. Can be used to define the masked or unmasked areas of a channel, layer, or quick mask.

Paint Bucket A fill tool selectable from the toolbox. Works with the color well to fill a selected object with a particular color.

Palette A floating window containing settings for Photoshop tools or objects for the current image. Each palette holds a particular type of information. You can hide and display palettes using the commands on the Window menu.

Patch A new tool that you can use to repair large imperfections in a scanned image, such as scratches. With this tool, you can select an area to use as the patch; then drag the patch over the area to repair.

Path Comprised of two or more points, a path object, also referred to as a vector graphic, can be one or more lines of an open or closed object. View paths in the Paths palette.

Pen A drawing tool located in the toolbox. Can be used to create vector graphics.

Pencil A drawing tool located in the toolbox. Draw with a single pixel of color in the image window.

Pixel An atomic element of color that can be grouped together to form a picture or an image.

Plug-In A special type of file that can be placed in a folder on your hard drive. If the plug-in preferences are configured correctly, all plug-ins will appear in the Filter menu.

PNG The Portable Network Graphic is a newer graphic file format growing in popularity on the Web. It effectively compresses solid-color images and preserves details. The PNG format might require a plug-in to be added to a browser, but can support up to 32 bits of color, in addition to transparency and alpha channels. It uses a lossless form of compression. It is best used for creating high-color graphics with complex live transparency, and general low-color graphics. *See also PSD, GIF, JPEG, and Lossy.*

Preferences Application and document-specific settings that you can customize to increase your productivity in Photoshop.

Preset A collection of saved settings for a particular tool in Photoshop. Rather than choosing all the settings individually, you can simply choose the preset.

Process A set of steps that, when followed, complete a task.

Processor The central processing unit of a computer. A faster processor will display graphics more quickly than a slower processor. Photoshop can take advantage of computers containing more than one processor.

PSD Photoshop's native file format. Preserve layers, layer sets, channels, and masks by saving them in a Photoshop file.

R

Radio Button A user-interface element found in applications and Web pages that has an on or off state.

RAM *See Memory.*

Resampling To use Photoshop to adjust an image in terms of its resolution (in pixels per inch by default) or size.

Resolution The number of horizontal and vertical pixels that make up a screen of information.

RGB Red, Green, and Blue values used to express a color. Each value can be within a range of 0 to 255.

Rollover A button or hotspot on a graphic that you set up to change in appearance depending on the mouse position (such as when the mouse is over it) or action performed by the user (such as when the button or hotspot has been clicked). You can specify several different appearances (called rollover states) for each rollover you create.

S

Save A command used to convert an image stored in memory into a file on the hard drive.

Scale A term used to indicate the size—larger or smaller—of an original object or image.

Scroll Bar A set of window controls consisting of directional arrows, a scroll button, and a horizontal or vertical bar that navigate an image window.

Size Usually refers to the file size of an image file. Pages created for the Web should be less than 1MB in size, if not closer to a few hundred KB.

Slice Create slices using the Slice tool. Each slice holds a particular portion of the image file. You slice an image for two different reasons: to break a large image into smaller images so that the image can load faster in a browser window, or to create a hotspot (hyperlinked area) in the image that the user can click to jump to another Web location.

Slice Guides Slice guides show you where Photoshop will split the image into separate files when the image is exported. Slice guides are created when you apply the Slice tool to an image window.

Submenu Also referred to as a hierarchical menu. A secondary menu containing a list of menu commands.

Swatches Palette Can be used to choose a foreground or background color, or to store or load a custom group of colors created with the Color Mixer.

T

Tag A building block of HTML, such as <HEAD>. Tags work with a browser to determine how HTML content appears on a Web page. Tags usually appear in twos. For example, the <HEAD> will eventually be followed by the </HEAD> tag.

Text Also referred to as Type. Alphabetic, non-alphabetic, and numeric characters that define the characters in a font. Use the Type tool to add text to an image window.

Transform A set of tools that enable you to scale, rotate, flip, distort, or skew all or part of an image in the image window.

U

Undo A menu command that enables you to reverse a previous command in the image window. Set the number of undo levels in the General Preferences dialog box. After you undo one operation, use the Step Backward command on the Edit menu to undo earlier actions. After you step backward, you can use the Step Forward command on the Edit menu to redo the last step you undid.

Update To make current. Photoshop automatically updates all windows whenever you change a value in one dialog box or palette.

Upload The process of copying a local file or folder to another computer.

URL An abbreviation for Uniform Resource Locator. Type a URL (such as **http://www.adobe.com**) into a browser window to go to a Web site or Web page on the Internet.

V

VCR Controls A set of buttons in the image window that enable you to navigate layers and interact with an image. ImageReady uses VCR control buttons to enable you to navigate image frames of an animation.

Vector Graphics Comprised of paths and points. They are used to create easily scalable drawings or graphic objects in Photoshop.

W

Web Also referred to as the World Wide Web. A group of computers running Web server software connected to an extended network around the world.

Web Client A computer connected to the Internet and configured with a browser and plug-ins to enable users to surf the Web.

Web Server A computer connected to the Internet and configured with server software to enable it to host one or more Web sites.

Wizard A type of application that provides a step-by-step method of configuring, installing, or converting files or programs on a computer. For example, choose Image Assistant from the Help menu to resize the image in the image window.

Z

Zoom Tool A tool that enables you to magnify the contents of the image window. Use with the Hand tool (H) to move the page while it is magnified. Press the Z key as a shortcut to select the zoom tool from the toolbox. Press the Command/Ctrl plus or minus keys to zoom into and out of an image in the image window.

INDEX

M